THE MAN WHO SEDUCED HOLLYWOOD

the Life and Loves of
GREG BAUTZER, TINSELTOWN'S
MOST POWERFUL LAWYER

B. JAMES GLADSTONE

CHICAGO
REVIEW
PRESS

An A Cappella Book

Published by Chicago Review Press, Incorporated
814 North Franklin Street
Chicago, Illinois 60610
ISBN 978-1-61374-579-3

Library of Congress Cataloging-in-Publication Data
Gladstone, B. James.
  The man who seduced Hollywood : the life and loves of Greg Bautzer,
tinseltown's most powerful lawyer / B. James Gladstone.
      pages cm
  Includes bibliographical references and index.
  ISBN 978-1-61374-579-3
  1. Bautzer, Greg (Gregson Edward) 2. Lawyers—United States—Biography.
I. Title.

  KF373.B3465G53 2013
  340.092—dc23
  [B]
                                        2013002773

Interior design: Jonathan Hahn

Printed in the United States of America
5 4 3 2 1

To my wife Selene, who made all my dreams come true

CONTENTS

FOREWORD

If anyone fits the definition of the word *legend*, it's Greg Bautzer. He was a legend with the ladies and a legend in the world of business. He was the only person I ever knew in Hollywood who was a star without being in a movie.

They don't make the likes of Greg Bautzer often. He pulled himself up by his bootstraps from life on the docks of San Pedro to become one of the most respected men in the entertainment industry. He was involved with the most beautiful women in the world and represented some of the biggest celebrities and tycoons. And, more important, he made people feel good.

I loved being around Greg; there was never a dull moment. He lived and loved life to the fullest and used all his assets—good looks, knowledge, and a gregarious personality—in love trysts and high-level decisions with the most powerful people of our times. He was the most charming person you could ever meet. As they say, he could "work a room," and then some.

He also had a hair-trigger temper that could result in some very interesting situations with people from all walks of life. When it came to barroom brawls, he knew how to handle himself. I know, because I was involved in some fights with him and I loved it!

Jim Gladstone has captured these qualities about Greg—and many more. So sit back and enjoy a wonderful book about one of the greatest characters Hollywood has ever known—my friend, Greg Bautzer.

ROBERT WAGNER

PROLOGUE

In 1969, Christmas came early for Greg Bautzer. By November, Las Vegas casino magnate Kirk Kerkorian had completed his hostile takeover of Metro-Goldwyn-Mayer, and everyone knew that Bautzer was the lawyer behind it. Masterminding the purchase of the legendary film studio was exactly the kind of thing that the debonair white-haired barrister had wanted to achieve in his career. Over a thirty-year span, he had advanced from humble beginnings as a trial lawyer to become counselor of the rich and famous. Now, with the MGM purchase under his belt, he was one of the most powerful men in Hollywood.

Three decades earlier, when Bautzer was dating MGM's Lana Turner, the studio had boasted "More Stars Than There Are in the Heavens." By the late 1960s the company was in such financial straits that it would have to auction off Judy Garland's ruby slippers from *The Wizard of Oz*. But a change in ownership of MGM was still front-page news. The MGM lion was among the most recognizable corporate logos in the world, and that's precisely why Kerkorian wanted it. And when a client wanted something, Bautzer got it for him.

Lawyers derive power from the clients they represent. The more wealthy, famous, or influential the client, the more powerful the lawyer. Bautzer had long represented Hollywood's elite movie stars and, most important, the richest man in the world—Howard Hughes.

Having the famous billionaire as a client inspired other corporate barons to seek his services, including Warner Bros. chief Jack Warner and Paramount Pictures owner Charles Bluhdorn. With MGM as a new full-time client, Bautzer would wield unprecedented influence over the entertainment industry. Albert S. Ruddy, two-time Oscar-winning producer of *The Godfather* and *Million Dollar Baby*, recalled Bautzer's preeminence at the time: "If you were going into the movie business, you went to Greg Bautzer. He was very close to Darryl Zanuck, Lew Wasserman—everybody. Greg Bautzer was *the man*."

The *New York Times* ran a full-page article profiling Bautzer and his role in the MGM takeover. The story was accompanied by a large photo of him laughing as he sat in an armchair. The *Times* credited Bautzer as the "architect" of the deal: "It was Mr. Bautzer who helped Mr. Kerkorian plot his strategy and plan his tender offers that resulted in the acquisition of forty percent of MGM's stock. It was he who negotiated with Edgar M. Bronfman—a fellow director of the Rheingold Corporation and for about a year the largest single MGM stockholder—during the in-fighting that ended in an unquestioned Kerkorian triumph. It was he who recommended James T. Aubrey Jr., former television executive and another client, for the presidency of the movie maker to replace the Bronfman appointee, Louis F. Polk Jr." The article went on to quote an industry insider reflecting on Bautzer's legal skills: "In the field of contracts and deal making, he has no peer."

In the same month that the *Times* story appeared, *Los Angeles* magazine published a four-page spread titled "Hello Greg? . . . This Is Howard Hughes." The magazine revealed that Bautzer was one of the few people in the world who could get the reclusive Hughes on the phone, and perhaps the only one who still met with him in person. Bautzer was quoted extensively as he explained his role in ushering in the new era of independent motion picture production, in which lawyers and financiers had more say than studio heads in what movies got made: "A director comes into my office with a story. He's got a star in mind and wants to do a picture. We control companies that can distribute the film he wants to make, so naturally we can put a package together better than anybody else. Distribution is the key. . . . So I fly to Germany and arrange financing. While I'm overseas, we set up an independent company in Paris to produce the film, and then we sell the U.S. distribution rights to another one of our clients." Normally, a lawyer would never say that he "controlled" his client companies; he would say that he *represented* them. But Bautzer was not like other lawyers—and his statement was close to the truth.

Both publications mentioned Bautzer's remarkable romances during the golden age of movies. For nearly two decades, gossip columnists had referred to him as "Hollywood Bachelor Number One." Now nearing sixty, he was embarrassed by his Don Juan fame. He thought such notoriety undignified for a man of his stature, calling it "a rinky dink sort of prominence, a kind of pseudo-prominence that I got just because I happened to have a dinner jacket and could open car doors for the ladies." But his tabloid-fodder relationships with stars including not just Lana Turner but also Joan Crawford, Dorothy Lamour, Ginger Rogers, Ava Gardner, Rita Hayworth, Merle Oberon, Jane Wyman, Ann Sothern, Greer Garson, Peggy Lee, and dozens of others could hardly be called "rinky dink."

Even in his senior years, Bautzer still had a flair. "Greg was so immaculately dressed, he looked like something out of *Gentlemen's Quarterly*," remembered another client, producer Andre Morgan. "You know, the French cuffs, perfectly starched, with the right cuff links. The pocket square matching the tie. The latest glasses, horn-rimmed, black, whatever. Appropriately suntanned with the best set of dentures you've ever seen in your life." Bernard Erpicum, sommelier at Patrick Terrail's exclusive West Hollywood eatery, Ma Maison, described the Bautzer wardrobe more succinctly: "Rudolph Valentino would have been jealous."

Like the potentate that he was, Bautzer held court in the best restaurants in Los Angeles. At Ma Maison, he was the center of attention.
Terrail's partner, chef Wolfgang Puck, remembered how they catered
to Bautzer's needs when he was there. "He was the most important
lawyer in Hollywood. You had to make absolutely certain his table
was ready when he arrived. You could keep other important people,
like Marvin Davis, waiting for a table and it would be no problem.
Not Bautzer." Seating was strategic at the restaurant. "There were two
rows of tables when you walked in," recalled Morgan. "Depending on
how powerful or popular you were, you sat in the first row or you sat
in the second row. Greg always had table one or table two."

The restaurant was filled with all the power brokers in the business. Everyone stopped by Bautzer's table to show their respect. Sommelier Erpicum, who went on to be maître d' at Puck's Spago restaurant, remarked on Bautzer's significance. "He was the most powerful
man in the room. People kept their eyes focused on him at all times.
When he stood up to summon the owner, everything stopped. The
place got quiet. It was like the entire restaurant shut down."

Bautzer also had an unchallenged reputation as the toughest lawyer in town. The most common thing said about Bautzer was that if
you were in a fight, he was the man you needed. He would do anything to further a client's cause. Albert S. Ruddy recalled, "The first
time I ever got into business with Greg, he cleaned up the problem
very quickly and the deal was done. We didn't have to go to court or
anything."

Like many successful lawyers and businessmen, Bautzer was
addicted to winning. He lived his life in competition from as early
as age fourteen, when he gained local fame for competing in national
oratory contests. It didn't matter whether he was arguing in court or
playing tennis or a card game, he had to come out on top. Talent-
agent-turned-producer Michael I. Levy, who represented the likes
of Elizabeth Taylor and Richard Burton, remembered how Bautzer

couldn't stand to lose even small amounts at cards. Levy was a client of Bautzer's, and the two had flown to San Francisco for a business meeting. The night before the meeting, they played gin rummy and Bautzer ordered room service, including a $1,500 bottle of wine. "He wound up losing $150 to me, and he was insane. He would buy a bottle of wine for $1,500, but losing $150 to me in gin pissed him off to no end."

A darker compulsion lurked below the surface. Bautzer was a confirmed alcoholic, and when he drank, his personality changed from Jekyll to Hyde. He would start the evening as the most gracious, mannered gentlemen in the room and end it as an enraged bull, challenging the nearest bystander to "step outside" for a fight. Bautzer's problem was likely both genetic and the result of a painful childhood; how much each of these factors contributed to his weakness for the bottle is hard to measure. Suffice it to say, alcoholism was the one adversary he could not overcome.

Amazingly, Bautzer's drunken public outbursts were tolerated, and his unbecoming behavior had little effect on his career or social standing. The reason people forgave Bautzer's sins was that his good qualities outweighed his bad ones. When he sobered up, he would return and apologize to the doormen, bartenders, and waiters, handing them wads of hundred-dollar bills. And he never allowed drinking to interfere with his performance as a lawyer. No matter how inebriated he had been the night before, he was always able to shine the next day at a court appearance or business meeting.

More significantly, people loved him for his code of friendship. He lived to do good deeds for other people, and he was fiercely loyal to clients and friends. Not only would he handle their legal problems; he handled their personal problems too. "Greg had a loyalty for clients and for friends rarely seen in the legal profession," said fellow USC alum Richard S. Harris. "If you couldn't afford to pay for legal services, he would give you his all, and then conveniently forget to send you a bill." Client Herbert Maass remembered Bautzer's kindnesses when he was going through a divorce or another tough time in his life. "I was usually very depressed. Then he would tell me about the beautiful girl he was having dinner with that night, and he'd insist that I join them. Or I would think about how he acted when I called him, as I did occasionally, and tell him I needed to borrow $5,000 or $10,000 for a few weeks. He never asked me what the problem was, or why I needed it. He would say, 'Give me five minutes to set it up, then call Bill Olsen at City National Bank and he'll tell you to come over and pick it up.'"

Bautzer could be called upon at any time, day or night, for a favor, and he would gladly run to the rescue. It is possible to view this in a cynical way—loyalty was simply good for business; it made people loyal to him and inspired business referrals. While this is true, it wasn't his primary motivation. Loyalty was the rule by which he lived his life and the quality he most admired in others. He would do virtually anything to help a friend or client in distress, and he stuck by them long after their careers cooled or the town turned against them in a scandal. He could forgive grievous flaws in others so long as they remained loyal. Everyone realized this, and they forgave his flaws in turn.

Bautzer never disclosed the secret of his success. Today's lawyers who got their start working for Bautzer late in his career saw only a well-dressed rainmaker moving in social circles they could scarcely imagine. They knew he was on a first-name basis with moguls, tycoons, and even the president, but they had no idea how he had achieved such status. The passage of time had covered his tracks.

This, then, is the story of Greg Bautzer, a celebrity lawyer who was himself a celebrity. More than just a brilliant trial attorney and negotiator, he was a well-connected problem solver who furthered his clients' interests through a network of relationships; a power broker in a way that no longer exists in today's legal profession, where one smart lawyer is virtually interchangeable with another; a self-made man who for fifty years used his legal brilliance and preternatural charm to dominate the courtrooms, boardrooms, and bedrooms of Hollywood. His career spanned the days of Zanuck, Goldwyn, Warner, and Mayer all the way to Eisner, Diller, and Katzenberg. He knew everyone and he knew their secrets. He knew what made them tick. He knew what made Hollywood tick.

I

WATERFRONT TO COURTROOM

1

DEBATE CHAMP

In 1898, San Pedro, California, was on the verge of major expansion. The town was only ten blocks long and four blocks wide, but beyond its waterfront, a mess of mud and shacks, was a harbor of untold potential. San Pedro Bay had been discovered in 1542 by the Portuguese explorer João Rodrigues Cabrilho, who promptly claimed it for his employers, the Spanish Empire. Three centuries later, the area was in private hands, and the US government wanted it for a port of entry. There was, however, a conflict: Collis Huntington, president of the Southern Pacific Railroad, wanted the Port of Los Angeles to be located in Santa Monica, where he could monopolize trade. Senator Stephen White thought Los Angeles deserved better and supported the San Pedro Bay location. A battle ensued in Congress, the Free Harbor Fight of 1896. When it was over, San Pedro was designated the site of the future port. In 1898, construction of a breakwater began, the first step toward the magnificent Port of Los Angeles. The town of three thousand people was suddenly significant—especially to a young man in Missouri.

Edward H. Bautzer was twenty-two and a payroll clerk. He had graduated at age seventeen from the University of Missouri, spent a year teaching school in Jefferson City on the Missouri River, and then joined the engineering department of the Missouri River Commission. He was a robust, ruggedly handsome, and thoughtful young man. He was also ambitious. Taking note of reports of San Pedro's expected growth, he headed west. When he arrived, he surveyed its businesses. The San Pedro distributorship of the *Los Angeles Times* was being operated at the corner of Sixth and Beacon Streets by a man named Sam Bennett. Edward and a business partner named McGee acquired it. This distributorship was a small version of a general store: in addition to newspapers and magazines, it sold tobacco and sundries. On occasion, Edward provided news stories to the *Times*.

The up-and-comer's interest in civic affairs had come from his father, Edward F. Bautzer. The senior Edward was born in Wiesbaden, Germany, in 1845. He married Nancy C. Benson on December 17, 1874, in Linn, Missouri. "Nannie," as she was called, was of Scotch-Irish ancestry and traced her American roots to before the Revolutionary War. The Bautzers had three children: Edward H., born in 1876; Cecile, born in 1878; and Paul, born in 1882. Edward Sr. supported his family by working in the local government of Osage County, Missouri, where he held the post of circuit clerk from 1879 to 1890. His duties primarily entailed copying official legal documents by hand. His penmanship was impeccable.

His son Edward H. prospered in San Pedro, becoming both politically and socially active. Within a year of his arrival, he was serving on a jury. He soon joined the Republican Party and became a member of the Elks Lodge. Within three years, he was being mentioned in the newspapers he sold. In August 1901, he and his brother, Paul, who had also come to San Pedro, were being described as "our popular young businessmen." The *Times* wrote that Nannie and Cecile Bautzer were visiting them.

The article did not say that mother and sister were there because father had abandoned them a year earlier. He had moved to Clayton, Missouri, and become publisher of the *St. Louis County Advocate*.

Edward Sr. was bombastic, critical, and contentious. Self-described as "a fighting editor," he even challenged a rival paper's owner to a duel over accusations that he had mishandled corporate finances. "I fought several duels while attending the University of Heidelberg and would not be a stranger on the field of honor," he told a reporter, but no duel occurred. Nannie and Cecile eventually returned to Missouri, and never saw Edward Sr. again. Paul stayed in San Pedro and became a bartender.

In 1902, Edward Jr.'s standing in San Pedro increased when President Theodore Roosevelt appointed him the city's postmaster. He was soon elected secretary of the District Republican Convention and campaigned for Roosevelt's second term. Edward furthered his political connections by becoming secretary of the San Pedro Chamber of Commerce and "Exalted Ruler" of San Pedro Elks Lodge No. 966. By 1905, he was representing his local government in a successful fight to keep the state from taking control of the harbor. He also lobbied Congress for a federal grant to dredge the harbor so bigger ships could enter. In 1907, his efforts were rewarded. The Los Angeles City Council created a Board of Harbor Commissioners, setting in motion the annexations that created the Port of Los Angeles.

Edward was an effective administrator. During his term as postmaster, postal revenue increased from $5,000 to $11,000 (approximately $300,000 in today's dollars). In 1909 he introduced improvements that included four mail carriers delivering mail twice a day, a new post office at Seventh and Beacon, and twenty-one mailboxes. Prior to this, people had to drop off and collect their mail in person at the post office. Perhaps concentrating too much on his career, the postmaster had yet to start a family.

By age thirty-three, though, he knew it was time to find a wife. Not surprisingly, his romantic prospect came from a civic connection. He was introduced to the young woman by a fellow Elk, a dentist named Verne A. Goodrich. In 1905, Goodrich and his wife, Martha, had been visited by her cousin, Blanche Buckhout, a twenty-one-year-old schoolteacher from Kalamazoo, Michigan. Two years later, the college-educated woman was living with the Goodriches and teaching school. Three years after moving in with the Goodriches, she was engaged to Edward.

The wedding ceremony took place on May 13, 1910, in the Los Angeles chambers of a justice of the peace named Ling. Only the Goodriches attended. There was no explanation for why the popular couple chose not to have a wedding party. The absence of family and friends from such an event was odd. Still, the wedding was covered in the *Los Angeles Times* with a well-placed photograph. Edward and Blanche appear perturbed with the photographer, but they make a handsome couple. Blanche is slim, with a heart-shaped face and dark, soulful eyes. Her brown hair is piled on top of her head under a wide-brimmed hat topped with a feather. She wears a light-colored jacket and skirt rather than a wedding dress. Edward wears a somewhat-wrinkled tan business suit, a celluloid collar, and a snap-brim hat.

"Did you stop to think that this is Friday the thirteenth?" a registrar asked the couple.

"We don't believe in hoodoos," replied Edward.

Despite their lack of superstition, bad luck did follow. Edward's father was facing difficulties. For three years he had been the editor of a newspaper called the *Squib*. In early 1910 he was fired and sank into depression. On May 27, exactly two weeks after his son's wedding, Edward Sr. took himself to Forest Park Highlands, an amusement park in St. Louis. At 8:40 PM he was sitting at a table near the bandstand, drinking a glass of beer. He suddenly slumped forward. The waiter who had served him thought he was drunk. Then Edward Sr. fell to the ground, an empty bottle of carbolic acid at his side. He had mixed the poison with his beer. He was taken to a hospital, but pronounced dead on arrival. An unsigned note was found in his coat pocket. "It's time to go," it said. "Will not some kind brother

Masons of mine bury me? It is night but let there be light." He was sixty-five.

Edward Sr. had been a stranger to his family for years, a man with a difficult personality at best. His penchant to challenge others to a fight was the only notable thing he passed on to his descendants. Few tears were shed over his passing.

Upon returning from their honeymoon traveling to Detroit, where Edward attended an Elks convention, the couple took residence at 478 Eighth Street, a small apartment building three blocks from the San Pedro waterfront. On April 3, 1911, eleven months after their wedding, Blanche gave birth to a son, Gregson Edward Bautzer.

Shortly before Greg's birth, the expectant father had resigned his position as postmaster and enrolled in the University of Southern California College of Law. In 1913, he was one of seventy-six people who applied for a license to practice law in California. The semiannual examination was given by the California District Court of Appeal on January 23, 1913. Sixty-six applicants passed. Edward was one of them.

At that time, there were almost no lawyers in San Pedro. Edward worked as deputy city prosecutor for two years before striking out on his own. His offices were located in the Bank of San Pedro building at 110 West Sixth Street, a block from the waterfront. The three-story structure, capped with an ornate clock tower, was the most impressive business edifice the town had to offer. He had space on the second floor along with a physician, a dentist, a realtor, and a tailor. The cases he handled were not lucrative. Two are preserved in the appellate record. In one, he represented a man seeking to avoid paying a commission to a real estate agent who had not negotiated the actual sale. He lost the case. In the other, he defended a truck owner against repossession. He won that one. Blanche, meanwhile, was teaching at the Fifth Street School.

Despite the seemingly ideal small-town existence, the Bautzers were dealing with a family problem: Edward's brother Paul was an uncontrollable alcoholic. To escape scrutiny, he sometimes traveled across the Mexican border for a binge. In the summer of 1914, Paul returned from one such trip in terrible shape. Blood poisoning from wood alcohol was the likely cause. Edward sent him home to Missouri for medical treatment, but he died a few days after arrival. His death certificate was succinct: "Alcoholism (years)." The examining doctor noted that various internal organs showed telltale signs of fatty degeneration. The deceased was thirty-two.

By 1921, Edward had lived in San Pedro for more than twenty years. He had seen its population grow from three thousand to thirty thousand. Though only forty-five, he was considered a founding father. Anyone of importance knew him on a first-name basis. He was a valued member of the community and was beginning to reap financial rewards. He and Blanche were building a house in the new suburb of Point Fermin. Greg was a popular boy and doing well in fifth grade. But everything was about to change.

On December 1, Edward was driving to watch some boxing matches in Point Fermin. He had just passed an electric trolley car on Pacific Avenue north of Twenty-Sixth Street when he came to a jog in the road. A car was parked in the narrowing lane. He crashed into it.

Edward's injuries were minor—cuts to his face and head and a broken finger that required simple surgery. He was expected to recover quickly. However, eighteen hours later, while sitting in bed, talking to his wife and friends, he was seized with chest pains. In a matter of minutes he was dead. An autopsy revealed a heart attack. The cause of death was listed as an occlusion of the left coronary artery. Although alcohol may have been involved in causing the motor vehicle accident, after hearing evidence about the circumstances, the coroner's inquest determined that the crash had been unavoidable. Edward H. Bautzer was posthumously absolved of blame, his death labeled a tragedy.

Funeral services were held at the R. S. Goodrich Funeral Parlor, which was owned by a relative of Blanche's. The chapel was filled beyond capacity, and its doors were kept open so mourners outside could hear Reverend Grice's eulogy. Newspapers wrote tributes to Edward, recounting his commitment to justice and his devotion to San Pedro. Some articles remarked that he had often taken unpopular cases because he believed it was the right thing to do, even though he made enemies along the way. He was credited with helping the town become the largest port on the West Coast.

Gregson Bautzer was ten when his father died. In the years to come, Greg would seldom talk about him, and the exact tenor of their relationship is unknown. Nevertheless, it is apparent that he inherited many of his father's attributes—intelligence, industry, generosity, civic-mindedness, and leadership ability. Both were blessed with magnetism and the ability to make friends. Even as a boy, Greg was able to enlist support for any endeavor he began. His enthusiasm and goodwill drew people to him. As he matured, townsfolk asked him what he wanted to do in life. "I want to be a lawyer," he would answer, "like my father." As the only son of a well-known and highly regarded man, Greg undoubtedly felt the need to take his father's place in society, to complete his unfinished work.

By the mid-1920s, Greg and his mother were living in an apartment on Pacific Avenue. The widow and her only child grew closer. According to Jack Huber, one of Greg's childhood friends, Greg would sometimes seek her attention jealously; to prevent her from leaving the apartment, he would nail her shoes to her bedroom floor. Blanche continued teaching, even becoming principal of the Harbor City School, but her income was limited, and Greg had to pitch in with after-school jobs. He sold newspapers, hauled garbage off yachts, and waited tables.

The clean-cut, conscientious youth was a model student at San Pedro High School, the picture of propriety, but his teenage years also revealed a contradictory personality. Late at night, after a long day of classes, work, and homework, the tall, precocious fourteen-year-old would surreptitiously slip down to the waterfront. There he would play pool with sailors and drink Prohibition liquor. He would sometimes get into fights.

About the same time, Greg began entering national oratorical contests. The *Los Angeles Times* called him "one of San Pedro's crack debaters." His speeches vanquished every local student's. Once after winning a contest, he was given the choice of a twenty-five-dollar award for himself or a bust of Abraham Lincoln for the school. He chose the bust, which earned him the nickname "Lincoln" on the football team, where he was second-string quarterback.

In 1926, Greg won second place and a $250 prize in the West Coast division of the National Oratorical Contest. His address on the US Constitution was published on the front page of the *Times*, and he performed it on the radio:

> We are living, friends, in a democracy that guarantees every citizen certain rights and privileges that are envied by the entire world. They have cost us nothing, and we forget the tremendous events that made them possible. . . . Are we progressing? Yes. But are we taking advantage of this right of government that is given us? Evidence proves that fifty percent of us are not, for in our last election only fifty percent of those having the franchise voted. . . .
>
> And so, let us raise our conception to the magnitude and the importance of the duties that devolve upon us. Let our understanding be as broad as the country in which we live, our aspirations as high as its certain destiny. Never did there devolve upon any generation of men higher trusts than now devolve upon us. If our government fulfills these trusts, it is because you and I make it possible. If it fails, it is because you and I do not accept our responsibility. But Americans, true American citizens, will shoulder their responsibility, realizing that our forefathers have done their part.

When he returned to the same competition in 1927, he gave the *Los Angeles Times* an optimistic assessment of his chances. Referring to the boy who had taken first place the previous year, he said, "Herbert Wenig took three shots at the contest before he landed. So far, I have only had two, and in the first I managed a second. I have made considerable improvement during the year, and shall at least start with every confidence of winning." Despite his confidence, he did not do quite as well the second time. In a field of forty thousand entrants on the West Coast, Greg placed third. The girl who came in first went on to become the national champion. Though he didn't win, his accomplishment was still praiseworthy.

Greg's oratorical successes were due to a regimen. He spent three hours a day writing and practicing. He also spent time in the school gymnasium, doing exercises to improve breath control. He was blessed with a resonant voice, and he cultivated it. He also had a commanding physical presence. He was six foot two in an era when most men were five eight. His conventionally handsome features were enhanced by wavy hair and large brown eyes, which made it difficult to look away from him. His eyes gave him the power to gain attention, to hold it, and to persuade.

Greg and his mother left San Pedro in 1927 when she became principal of the Fifty-Second Street School in Los Angeles. It was two miles south of the University of Southern California, which was three miles south of downtown. She and Greg lived in a rooming house on Arapahoe Street, north of the campus. With Greg continuing to attend school in San Pedro, the principal and the student took streetcars south every morning. In later life, Greg would tell people that his mother was one of the first women to be profiled in *Who's Who in American Education*. He carried her picture in his wallet, and decades after her death, he would take it out and show people. "Isn't she beautiful?" he would beam. "She was a teacher. Whatever scholastic record I had was entirely due to her."

In the fall of 1928, Greg entered USC on a scholarship. As in high school, he excelled and was very popular. He pledged Phi Kappa Psi fraternity, and based on his academic achievement, he became a member of the Skull and Dagger honor society. Before long, he was captain of the varsity debate team. Its topics included subjects that are still relevant today: "Resolved, that modern advertising is more harmful than beneficial to society"; "Resolved, that the United States should adopt socialized medicine"; "Resolved, that the power of the Presidency of the United States should be increased as a permanent measure."

In 1930, he was chosen as one of three university students to be on the All California Collegiate Debate Team; his two teammates were from Stanford and the University of California. The contests took them to other schools across the country and abroad, including Harvard, Columbia, Syracuse, Princeton, and Oxford. That same year, he won the international oratory contest held in Hawaii. His photograph taken aboard the returning steamship *Malolo* was published in newspapers across the country.

As an orator, Greg was known for his emphatic, dramatic style. During one debate, as he reached a point of rebuttal, a tremor shook the auditorium. His friend and fellow future lawyer Louis Blau turned to the student next to him and said, "Only Greg would think of an earthquake to accentuate the point he is making."

"He was a hotshot even then," recalled USC friend Richard S. Harris. "People were attracted to him for his ability as a debater. He was the star of the debating team, and the center of every discussion that took place in the fraternity house, in class, or when he was just out with the guys."

Greg also had an irreverent sense of humor. He once invited an eccentric professor to lunch at the fraternity house and urged him to play the piano. To everyone's amusement, they soon realized that the professor was terrible. Despite this, when the man had finished demolishing some standard, Greg would lead his fraternity brothers in a round of applause. The professor took bows, oblivious to his own ineptitude.

Not all of his collegiate exploits were so whimsical. While in England preparing for the debate with Oxford, he got into a fistfight with a professor. Greg was immediately sent home. He gave various excuses to cover his embarrassment, but the truth was that he had been drunk and attacked the teacher without provocation. It was an early manifestation of a problem that would follow him all his life. Many college students flirt with alcohol, but like his uncle Paul, Greg was flirting with alcoholism. His moods under the influence stood in stark contrast to his usually sunny personality. Something was bothering him, and it was not merely the idea of graduating from college during the Great Depression; Greg was also coping with tensions in his relationship with his mother, which clearly affected his psyche.

While Greg was living at USC, his mother was living in Lomita, a township slightly north of San Pedro. According to the 1930 US Census, Blanche had married Charles M. Smith, a real estate broker. The household census listed Greg as a stepson and included a boy named Charles B. Smith, age five. The boy was apparently from Smith's previous marriage. Charles M. Smith was listed as thirty-seven, but Blanche claimed she was forty-one, four years younger than her real age. There is no record of what happened to the marriage. Although Blanche would retain Smith's name until her death, they would not be living together at that time. Greg never discussed his mother's second marriage with anyone—not even those closest to him.

Blanche resumed her education. On June 4, 1932, she earned a master of arts in education from USC. On that same day, Greg graduated with a bachelor of arts degree. The *Los Angeles Times* ran an article noting how unusual it was for a mother and son to earn degrees from the same school on the same day.

Greg spent a year working and saving money and then returned to USC for law school. Greg's friends would remember his seemingly unshakable confidence. Law school classmate Virginia Trousdale claimed that Greg had at some point consulted a hypnotist who had him repeat the line, "I am the greatest. I am the best. Nothing is going to faze me." Her story may not be accurate, but one aspect rings true: Greg was supremely self-confident.

One benefit of attending USC at the time was that it provided access to the social set. During law school, Greg began seeing a young socialite named Marion Jahns. She was well educated, having attended the Marlborough School in Los Angeles, the Bennett School in Millbrook, New York, and the Finch School in Manhattan. Dating her gave Greg an entrée into Los Angeles society—a far cry from the waterfront of San Pedro. It also brought him closer to the glamour of Hollywood. On November 4, 1934, they were photographed watching a horseracing event at the exclusive Uplifters Club in Pacific Palisades. Also present were Hollywood celebrities, including movie star Robert Montgomery.

Greg Bautzer and Marion Jahns were wed in her parents' home on January 2, 1935, with only immediate family members present. Marriage did not appreciably change the life of either partner. Marion continued to grace society functions. Greg continued his studies, graduating with a law degree in 1936. Although the country's economy was poor, there were plenty of opportunities for a young lawyer with Bautzer's credentials. He could join a firm in Los Angeles. He could become an assistant district attorney. He could return to San Pedro and follow in his father's footsteps.

But Greg Bautzer was blessed with charm, armed with intelligence, and fueled by ambition. He had set his sights on a loftier goal. He just needed the means to achieve it.

2

"PRESTO! A CELEBRITY"

The first offer of work that Greg Bautzer received out of law school was less than tantalizing: a firm in Los Angeles was prepared to pay him eighty-five dollars a month for his services. Although these were not exactly starvation wages, he felt he deserved better. His upper-class wife had introduced him to high society, and a salary of $1,020 a year ($16,500 today) would not underwrite the lifestyle he wanted. It would not even pay the dues at the Uplifters Club. He thought he could do better on his own. And there was another consideration: Bautzer was enticed by the bright lights of show business.

Bautzer's interest in the entertainment industry came from witnessing the rise of the movie star and the establishment of Los Angeles as the moviemaking capitol of the world. In 1911, when Bautzer was born, the public did not consider movie actors to be celebrities. Movies were a cheap form of entertainment for the uneducated masses, viewed at tawdry storefront operations called nickelodeons (for the five-cent price of admission). Upper- and middle-class people looked down their noses at the new medium and those who worked in it. Movie actors were considered one rung on the ladder above prostitutes.

Even the idea of publicizing an actor's name as a means of encouraging ticket sales had been unheard of until 1910. Florence Lawrence, who previously was billed simply as "the Biograph Girl," because she worked for Biograph Studios, was the first movie actor identified by her own name on a movie poster. The shift came about when Lawrence left Biograph to work for a new company started by Carl Laemmle, who would go on to found Universal Studios. Laemmle could no longer bill her as "the Biograph Girl," so he decided to use her real name.

As Bautzer grew up, he saw the moviegoing experience evolve from a disreputable novelty into a middle-class obsession. Nickelodeons were replaced by luxurious movie palaces. Actors became famous and admired; Douglas Fairbanks, Mary Pickford, Buster Keaton, Lon Chaney, Clara Bow, Gloria Swanson, and Greta Garbo were all household names. Charlie Chaplin, who released his first feature masterpiece, *The Kid*, when Bautzer was nine years old, was the most recognizable person in the world.

Studio executives also realized that the public had an insatiable appetite for details of the private lives of stars. Movie actors' work seemed like play, and their exciting off-screen lives, whether real or fabricated, inspired fantasies of wealth, nonstop parties, and myriad sex partners. To the studios, gossip about their stars printed in newspapers and magazines was good for business—free advertising for their product.

Bautzer was enthralled by the movie-star lifestyle. The movie business was all around him, and it was booming. By the time Bautzer graduated from law school, the motion picture industry was America's sixth largest. The average movie studio owned film plants and theater chains, an exemplary model of a vertically integrated monopoly. There were five major companies: Metro-Goldwyn-Mayer, Paramount, Warner Bros., RKO, and the new Twentieth Century-Fox, which had risen from the bankrupt ruins of the Fox Film Corporation. The "major minors" were Columbia, United Artists, and Universal. The industry had weathered the Great Depression and emerged as the world's primary manufacturer of leisure-time product. Its 1935 revenues totaled more than $556 million.

In the fall of 1936, Bautzer rented an eighth-floor office in the Equitable Building at 6253 Hollywood Boulevard. For his law partner he chose G. Bentley Ryan, who had graduated from USC law school the year before. Their office comprised two rooms: a waiting area with a secretary's desk and, beyond that, the actual office with a desk, chairs, and a legal bookcase. To give clients the impression that there was an office for each partner, they put one of their nameplates on a closet door, switching them as necessary. If Bautzer had an appointment that day, his name went on the door to the real office and Ryan's went on the closet. That was the easy part. The hard part was getting clients.

"I evaluated myself very carefully," recalled Bautzer. "It sounds vain and egotistical for me to say it, but I knew I was good looking." Bautzer enjoyed sports and maintained a health regimen. Tanned and trim, he did as much for a tuxedo as it did for him. There was something else. "I had presence when I walked into a room," said Bautzer. It was true. He had an intangible star quality, the thing that makes people look twice. He also happened to be the best amateur dancer anyone had ever seen.

Bautzer was not angling for a screen test, but he wanted to crash Hollywood as badly as any aspiring actor. From his father, he had learned that a lawyer's social life is the key to making connections that lead to legal work. "I needed to become known," he said. "I needed to be recognized, and I needed to become prominent in the Hollywood community. You can't do all that without money, and I didn't have a nickel after splitting the first and last month's rent with Bentley." Nevertheless, he devised a plan based on dressing to impress potential clients. He thought that if he looked successful, it would bring in business.

"I decided to borrow $5,000," said Bautzer, "not knowing for a fact that I could ever pay it back, but knowing that if my theory was correct, I could pay it back very quickly." It is not known where the twenty-five-year-old found the money, but his wife's family was a likely source. "I used the money to buy the best wardrobe in town."

The Equitable Building stood at the corner of Hollywood and Vine, a hub of activity in the motion picture business. The building was full of attorneys, advertising agents, talent agents, brokers, illustrators, lawyers, and publicists. Everyone who was anyone ate lunch at the Brown Derby, located just across the street at 1628 North Vine. Executives from Paramount or RKO discussing a script at lunch began to notice the striking young man at the next table as he nodded courteously over his menu. "Greg had a flair for befriending people," recalled publicist Paul MacNamara. "Important people took a liking to him." It was only a matter of time before introductions were made. "Greg was ambitious and aggressive," recalled his future law partner Bernard Silbert. Bautzer wore a different suit each day and lavishly tipped the maître d'. "He always managed to be seated at the best table in the house," said Silbert. "It wasn't long before he knew everyone of importance who came to the restaurant."

The introductions led to work. Bautzer was at this point a trial lawyer. "I took any case that walked in the door," he recalled. This could be a criminal matter, personal injury, divorce, or anything else. When the volume of work picked up, Bautzer would invite Silbert, who graduated from USC one year after he did, to join him and Ryan in the now very cramped suite 803.

Bautzer's lunch appearances were soon augmented by nightclub entrances. On Hollywood Boulevard, in the Roosevelt Hotel, there was the Cinegrill, and on Vine, in the Hollywood Knickerbocker, there was the Lounge. On Sunset there was the Café La Maze, the Café Trocadero, and the Casanova. When Bautzer walked into a nightclub, resplendent in black and white, he was not with his wife. By early 1937, just two years after the wedding, the marriage was on its way to dissolution. The union of unformed personalities had not withstood the competing pressures of Pasadena and Hollywood. The gossip columns reported that Marion was vacationing without him in Hawaii "under the wing" of "Brit" Britton, purser of the luxury liner SS *Lurline*, and Greg was seen squiring a socialite named Roberta Swaffield Weber. "Friends say it's serious," noted one writer. It was not.

Bautzer had other things on his mind. On February 10, 1937, he got his first mention in the *Los Angeles Times* for a legal case. He was representing an actress named Margaret McKay in a divorce suit against a Chicago singer, Alan Rice.

On April 3 Bautzer celebrated his twenty-sixth birthday with a party for three hundred. It was, of course, as much a marketing event as a social occasion. Bautzer's efforts to attract clients continued to pay off. On April 8, less than a year out of law school, he had his first reported legal victory. He was representing theatrical agent Freeman Bernstein, who was known internationally as the King of Jade for his love of the stone. Bernstein had allegedly tried to bilk Germany's government out of $250,000 by passing off a boatload of pressed tin cans as a shipment of steel and nickel. New York wanted Bernstein extradited to stand trial. Bautzer fought extradition, pleading the case directly to the governor of California, Frank Merriam, by pledging that Bernstein would become a permanent California resident. Merriam granted Bautzer's plea and denied extradition. True to his word, Bernstein opened a jade shop in Beverly Hills.

In May, Bautzer won another kind of victory. The actress Isabel Jewell, memorable as the sad little blonde in *Lost Horizon*, went out with him. While there is no question he enjoyed dating the beautiful actress, it was also part of his far-flung plan to gain publicity for himself. "I met beautiful women whom I escorted to the best restaurants and nightclubs in town," he recalled. "And I introduced myself to the columnists who frequented these places." There were dozens of minor columnists in Hollywood. They were only too happy to print an item about an intriguing young attorney who danced with starlets by night. Before long, he had gained the attention of the gossip columnists who really wielded power. Louella Parsons wrote for the Hearst papers. Jimmie Fidler was syndicated in 187 newspapers. Both found Bautzer's dating life a worthwhile topic.

Years later, Bautzer would succinctly describe the success of his publicity campaign: "Presto! I was a celebrity." His legal career soon gained celebrity status also. In July, he found himself on the team of Hollywood's most celebrated lawyer.

Jerry Giesler was fifty, and fresh from a major triumph. In 1935, he had represented Busby Berkeley, the renowned director of numerous Warner Bros. musicals. While driving from a studio party, Berkeley had crashed into two oncoming cars on the Roosevelt Highway (now the Pacific Coast Highway). Three people had died, and Berkeley had been indicted on charges of manslaughter. It was obvious that Berkeley was drunk at the wheel, but Giesler was a miracle worker. Two trials resulted in hung juries. In the third trial, one year after his indictment, Berkeley was found not guilty.

Giesler had learned his craft from Earl Rogers, a turn-of-the-century Los Angeles lawyer famed for both his theatrics and his lack of scruples. "If you are guilty, hire Earl Rogers," ran the slogan. Rogers won more than 180 acquittals, but died of self-loathing alcoholism in a downtown flophouse. Giesler had no such compunctions; he was flagrantly ruthless. "Jerry Giesler was a hero to me," recalled Bautzer. "When I was in school I used to go to court just to watch him in action." Bautzer managed to meet Giesler and flatter him into friendship.

When Giesler was hired to defend a mysterious character by the name of John Montague, Bautzer took special interest. Montague was a golfer, and like many a Hollywood character before and since, he had come from nowhere and had no visible means of support. The stout fellow with the baby face and curly hair did, however, show a talent for golf. He made trick shots through barely opened windows. He introduced an oversized driver that could hit the ball three hundred yards down the fairway. He dressed well, drove fast cars, and became friends with celebrity golfers such as singer Bing Crosby. Montague was impressive, but he had a quirk: he was inexplicably shy of publicity. He stopped at the eighteenth hole rather than beat a course record. He refused to have his picture taken. It turned out that he was wanted by the police in Essex County, New York. Seven years earlier, under the name LaVerne Moore, he had allegedly robbed a restaurant and speakeasy. Now he was fighting extradition.

Bautzer got in touch with his idol and made an irresistible offer to work on the case. Bautzer knew the precedents for extradition and could write the briefs. He needed experience and he wanted the exposure. Payment for his work would be entirely within the master's discretion. Realizing the benefits of a hungry young apprentice, Giesler accepted.

The team secured affidavits as to Montague's character from celebrity golfing buddies including Crosby and actors Andy Devine and Oliver Hardy (Montague had lived in Hardy's home for a time), and submitted them to Governor Merriam. Giesler then took an unusual tack. Rather than deny the charges, he made a public plea for sympathy. "LaVerne Moore is legally dead!" he shouted to the press from the courthouse steps. "A new man has been created. He is John Montague. By your pen, Governor Merriam, you have the power of life and death. You can disinter the body of LaVerne Moore and send him back to face ruin and dishonor, or you can breathe life into this new man and christen the soul of John Montague." Giesler's legally irrelevant argument was followed by a brief presentation by Bautzer in which he summarized the purposes of punishment for the reporters present.

Despite his statements to the press, Giesler knew that the governor would not deny extradition in such a high-profile case and advised Montague to face the music. The accused man dropped his fight against extradition. On August 21, 1937, he was escorted by three officers to the Union Pacific Los Angeles Limited. He was tried in Elizabethtown, New York, where attorney James M. Noonan, who had been hired by Crosby, gained him an acquittal. Montague was carried from the courtroom on the shoulders of his supporters, but the judge was appalled by the verdict.

Bautzer continued his nocturnal publicity campaign. In October 1937, he was reported dating an eighteen-year-old actress named Mary Maguire. In November, he and the popular actress Claire Trevor were seen together so often that a *Los Angeles Times* columnist named them as a "new couple." Trevor was a cherub-faced blonde with sparkling brown eyes and a sly smile. She was also a bona fide leading lady at Twentieth Century-Fox. Her most recent work was in a loan-out to Samuel Goldwyn for William Wyler's *Dead End*, starring Humphrey Bogart. Her portrayal of a slum girl forced into prostitution would earn her an Academy Award nomination for Best Supporting Actress. Trevor was the most mature and sophisticated woman Bautzer had dated, yet the romance ended quickly. Trevor married another, and Bautzer moved on to the next beauty. Nightlife was his natural habitat, and he was making the most of it. Every week he had new friends.

In January 1938, a headline-making case landed in Bautzer's lap. A well-educated screenwriter from New York named Emanuel "Buddy" Adler was arrested and charged with grand theft for issuing bad checks. When he claimed it was all a misunderstanding, the press labeled him a "playboy" and questioned his character. Bautzer stepped in. "The investigation which authorities are conducting will itself entirely absolve Mr. Adler of these charges," said Bautzer. He was right; the charges were dropped and Adler became a lifelong friend. In years to come, the friendship would be mutually beneficial. Adler would go on to become a distinguished producer, winning the Oscar in 1953 for *From Here to Eternity*. With Bautzer's help, he would also one day become president of Twentieth Century-Fox.

Bautzer's career was on the right track. He was getting publicity and meeting important people, and business was coming his way. Soon his efforts would bear fruit in more ways than he could have possibly imagined.

II

MASTER PLAN

3

THE SWEATER GIRL

In early 1938, Greg Bautzer was living in an attractive one-story stucco house at 8134 West Fourth Street, in a quiet neighborhood on the edge of West Hollywood. His mother, Blanche, had been ill for a time and was living with him. At the office, he was working with Bentley Ryan and Bernard Silbert on a series of low-profile divorce cases. Unlike today, divorce in the first half of the twentieth century could not be attained merely because one spouse wanted to get out of the marriage. It could only be granted if the court determined the fault of one of the parties in ruining the marriage. Bautzer would have to show that the opposing spouse had committed adultery, disappeared, or done something that could be described as cruelty, whether physical or mental. Often the allegations were fabricated so that a couple who no longer got along could separate. California Judge Stanley Mosk described the courtroom tableau: "Every day, in every superior court in the state, the same melancholy charade was played: the 'innocent' spouse, generally the wife, would take the stand and, to the accompanying cacophony of sobbing and nose-blowing, testify under the deft guidance of an attorney to the spousal conduct that she deemed 'cruel.'" Until California's "no-fault" divorce law of 1970, this was the procedure for ending a marriage.

As he helped unhappy spouses dissolve their marital bonds, Bautzer continued to fortify his own social connections. He made sure to join organizations that would provide new career opportunities. He was secretary of the Young Men's Political Association and would eventually become president of the Hollywood Aerie of the Fraternal Order of Eagles.

But it was Bautzer's dating life that was about to take his career to a level he could hardly have thought possible. He started seeing a young ingénue named Lana Turner. She wasn't a star yet, but she was on her way. She would soon be called "lushly lustrous," with "a figure worthy of a bathing suit ad." One columnist would write, "She always looks like someone just told her to take a deep breath."*

On Sunday, February 13, 1938, the *Los Angeles Times* column "Beau Peep Whispers" whispered that Bautzer had attended an equestrian exhibition at the Riviera Country Club in Pacific Palisades "with a new titian-haired beauty decorating his arm." This was his first reported date with Turner. She was sixteen going on seventeen. He was twenty-six. She was mature for her age, spending her evenings at nightclubs with a group of young stars that included Mickey Rooney, Ann Rutherford, and Bonita Granville. It is likely that Turner caught Bautzer's eye at the Café Vendome or the Café Trocadero. He certainly caught her eye.

"He was tall and husky," recalled Turner in her autobiography, "with soulful dark eyes, a tanned complexion, and a flashing smile that showed a lot of white teeth. He was so smooth, so self-assured, that all the other boys I knew seemed like children." The soulfulness that distinguished Bautzer's eyes was the result of unusually heavy lower lashes (a trait that he inherited from his mother). The expression in those eyes came from his native intensity. The effect was hypnotic.

---

*Turner was once onstage with the multitalented Dorothy Lamour and Mickey Rooney. "I can't sing or dance," she plaintively sighed into the microphone. "There's nothing I can do." "Just stand, there, sister," shouted a man in the audience. "Just stand there."

He wasted no time in captivating Turner. He escorted her to the nightspots he knew so well, impressing her with his contacts and savoir faire. "We went dancing at the most glamorous places," Turner wrote later. "I'd always wanted to be older and know what life was all about. I was seventeen, romantic, and a virgin. When we went dancing, he would rub his body up against mine. It would thrill me, make me shiver, those first flushes and tingles, and the wondering, when, oh, when would it happen?"

Bautzer timed his sexual campaign to exact the maximum suspense. "I was scared," recalled Turner. "And Greg never rushed me, never tried to hustle me into bed." He may have been waiting for her birthday, thinking that she would turn eighteen in February. The truth was that she was turning seventeen. "Greg didn't take me to a hotel but to his own home," wrote Turner. "His mother lived with him, but he thought she was out for the evening. She wasn't, but we didn't find out until later, when we heard her moving around in her bedroom." If this was not awkward enough, there was the problem of inexperience. "Greg was loving and patient with me," said Turner, "even though I had no idea how to move or what to do. . . . But I loved being close to Greg and holding him, and the feeling that now, at last, I was giving myself to him."

While one door was opening for Bautzer, another was closing. On February 13, 1938, Blanche Bautzer Smith died. She was fifty-four. Services were conducted at Little Church of the Flowers at the Glendale Forest Lawn Mortuary, and there was a memorial tribute at the Fifty-Second Street School, where she had been principal since 1927. The Parent-Teacher Association planted an evergreen sapling in her memory. "My only regret is that she never got to see me try my first case," said Bautzer. At nearly twenty-seven, he had lost the last connection to his life in San Pedro.

No one could replace his mother, but his budding relationship with Lana Turner would do what no other had done. It would elevate him to the level of the Hollywood elite. This was fitting, given that Turner's background was even more of a rags-to-riches story than his.

She was born Julia Jean Turner on February 8, 1921, in Wallace, Idaho, to John Turner, an Alabama miner, and Mildred Cowan, the daughter of an Arkansas mining engineer. John Turner deserted Julia and her mother after the little girl inadvertently tipped off police that he was manufacturing bootleg liquor in the basement. Mildred became a beautician in San Francisco. John gambled, but occasionally visited his daughter, who was now called Judy by her parents. In 1930, after winning a bankroll in a floating crap game, John was robbed and murdered. In 1936, Mildred moved to Los Angeles and enrolled Judy at Hollywood High School.

One day, Judy Turner cut a typing class and walked across Sunset Boulevard to the Top Hat Café, which was located at 6750 Sunset, near the corner of McCadden Place. She was sipping a Coca-Cola at the soda fountain when an older man approached her. He had the eyes of a Bassett hound, a waxed, pencil-thin mustache, and wavy, Brilliantined hair parted slightly off-center. He wore a very expensive suit. He was William R. "Billy" Wilkerson, an executive who walked to the Top Hat from his nearby office every day to buy a Coke.

"Would you like to be in the movies?" Wilkerson asked the teenager.

Turner was dubious until she learned that Wilkerson was the publisher of the *Hollywood Reporter*, a trade paper that kept the motion picture industry informed of projects, trends, revenue, and gossip. If that wasn't sufficiently impressive, he was also owner of the Café Vendome and the Café Trocadero. In short order, Wilkerson made good on his introduction. He connected Judy with Zeppo Marx, the youngest Marx Brother, who had left Groucho, Harpo, and Chico after five films to join the fifth brother, Gummo, at his talent agency. Zeppo in turn connected Judy with director Mervyn LeRoy, who cast her as a provocative small-town girl in the aptly titled *They Won't Forget*.

It was a risky proposition. "She was so nervous her hands were shaking," wrote LeRoy. "She was so shy she could hardly look me in the face. Yet there was something so endearing about her that I knew she was the right girl. She had tremendous appeal, which I knew the audience would feel." LeRoy changed Judy's name to Lana, carefully coached her, and had her wear a form-fitting sweater. Wilkerson personally reviewed Turner's debut in his paper. "This young lady has vivid beauty, personality and charm," he proudly announced. Turner needed no help to connect with the audience. She began to receive fan mail addressed simply to "the girl in the sweater."

LeRoy switched studios from Warner Bros. to MGM. On February 20, 1938, LeRoy had Turner sign with him at MGM. She was known on the lot as his protégée, which kept lecherous executives away.

It did not keep Bautzer away. By mid-March, he and Turner were going out constantly, prompting comments in gossip columns. They were seen at the Racquet Club in Palm Springs, at an Assistance League benefit at the Roller Bowl, and mostly at La Conga, his new favorite nightspot where he could show off his rumba dancing skills. They broke up briefly in May, when Bautzer dated French actress Simone Simon, but were soon back together on a steady basis. In short order, they were engaged to be married.

Turner began to look forward to their evenings in bed. "I did feel passion for him," she wrote, "and eventually I did achieve orgasm, but what I really wanted was to have Greg hold me, keep me safe in his arms." MGM chief Louis B. Mayer took note of Turner's nighttime activities and demanded a meeting with her mother to try to put a stop to it. Mayer shocked Mrs. Turner when he pointed to his crotch and said that this was all the young woman cared about. Mother took daughter by the hand and stormed out.

Despite his crudeness, Mayer's concern was understandable. He needed to protect a valuable asset. The studio had big plans for

Turner. Nevertheless, Mayer had to admit that Bautzer was a suitable escort, and he made no further attempt to break them up. Instead, the MGM publicity department made sure that the golden couple was invited to every movie premiere. In September, they attended the opening of *The Private Lives of Elizabeth and Essex*. The roster of attendees also included Charlie Chaplin, Dorothy Lamour, Tyrone Power, Joan Crawford, Darryl F. Zanuck, David O. Selznick, Samuel Goldwyn, Harry Cohn, and Mayer himself. Gregson Bautzer was the only non–movie star mentioned in the papers. The October premiere of *Babes in Arms* saw them on the red carpet with Clark Gable, Carole Lombard, Cary Grant, and Alfred Hitchcock. At the December premiere of *The Hunchback of Notre Dame*, they were photographed with the likes of Jack Benny, Gene Autry, Mickey Rooney, Walt Disney, Orson Welles, and Lucille Ball. For an unknown young lawyer to have his name listed in print with these celebrities was an achievement. For Bautzer, it was merely part of his plan. He had grabbed a comet's tail.

"Lana Turner gets fresh flowers from Greg Bautzer daily," Hedda Hopper wrote in the *L.A. Times*. The actress-turned-gossip-columnist was giving veteran Hearst columnist Louella Parsons a run for her money. Bautzer was, of course, feeding Hopper items. (Gossip columnists required tips for their favors, and Bautzer was happy to oblige.) He had begun to use expensive gifts to gain favor, as if lavishness could buy either influence or romance.

In early 1939, one of his gestures went wrong. Turner and Bautzer had made a pact that if one ever grew tired of the other, he or she would send a dozen red roses. Bautzer had to go to Chicago on business. Before he left town, to remind Turner that he was thinking of her, he ordered a dozen white roses to be delivered. When Turner opened the florist's box she saw a dozen red roses. She went into hysterics. She cried for days. Meanwhile, unaware of his fiancée's distress, Bautzer was getting long-distance coverage of his business trip from the *Times*. On February 13, Read Kendall wrote in his column, "Greg Bautzer, Lana Turner's best boyfriend, is no weakling with his mitts. At a recent confab over a lawsuit in Chicago, the lie was hurled at Greg. He ups and punches the opposing counsel on the jaw and that was the end of any such quips."

When Bautzer returned to Los Angeles, he phoned Turner with his usual salutation, "My beloved sweetheart, my darling." Turner was baffled. She thought the engagement was over. When she asked him why he had sent red roses, he said that he had not. He had ordered white roses. The florist made a mistake. The affair resumed—though he hesitated to set a date for a wedding.

"I didn't sleep with him very often," wrote Turner. "I was busier than ever at Metro with larger parts." Bautzer was accommodating. If Turner had an early call at the studio the next morning, he didn't pressure her for sex. As she later learned, he could afford to be accommodating. "I was too young and inexperienced to realize that Greg was getting his action on the side," Turner recalled. "He'd enjoyed a reputation as a playboy. He was so attractive and desirable that a lot of women threw themselves at him."

While the middle-class population at large seemed puritanical and prudish in the first half of the twentieth century, the motion picture community was, in the words of celebrity biographer Charles Highan, a "sexual merry-go-round." Multiple partners were a way of life under the warm California sun. Divorce and serial marriages were the norm, not the exception. Although Turner would herself go on to have numerous tabloid-fodder romances, at this young age she imagined love as something permanent and exclusive.

Turner began to suspect Bautzer's infidelity, but she never dreamed he was romancing an even bigger star than her. One day, Turner received an unsolicited telephone call from the glamorous and powerful actress Joan Crawford. Turner was baffled when Crawford invited her to a tête-à-tête at her Brentwood home. "Well, dear," began Crawford, "when you're young you see things a certain way, but that's not always how they are. As you get older you realize that life can be very complex." At thirty-three, Crawford was quite a bit older. She was also in the midst of a career slump and divorcing her second husband, actor Franchot Tone.

"Joan, what are you trying to tell me?"

"Well, darling, I feel it's only right to tell you that Greg doesn't love you any more, that he hasn't for a long time."

Turner was stunned into silence.

"Lana, I couldn't let you go on, hoping, believing. Because, you see, Greg wouldn't tell you. It's me he truly loves. But he hasn't figured out how to get rid of you."

"Get rid of me?" Turner asked indignantly. "Trash is something you get rid of. Or disease you get rid of. I'm not something you get rid of." Turner made a hasty exit and pulled herself together.

When she questioned Bautzer, he denied a sexual relationship with Crawford. Turner wanted to believe him, but seeds of doubt had been planted. She began to wonder where he was when he wasn't with her. She became suspicious, almost obsessed. Music that reminded her of Bautzer, once a sweet sensation, became bitter. "Deep Purple" was a popular song to which she and Bautzer often danced. She began to avoid it.

Turner's third MGM film, *Dancing Co-ed*, was released in September 1939. It was her breakthrough. "Lana Turner is a full-fledged star," reported Hedda Hopper. *Dancing Co-ed* also featured a man who would have a profound effect on her life—Artie Shaw. The virtuoso clarinetist was a recording star, famous for "Begin the Beguine," but he was not popular with his colleagues. His own band members thought him an intellectual snob, and film folk found him arrogant. He made no secret of his disdain for Hollywood. "The film business reeks to high heaven," he said. MGM publicists could not prevent Turner from complaining about him to journalist Irving Wallace. "That Shaw is the most egotistical thing!" exclaimed Turner. "He hogged the camera and spent more time with the hairdresser and the makeup man than any actor on the lot!" Five months later, Shaw visited the set of Turner's next picture, *Two Girls on Broadway*. He was unusually pleasant, so she gave him her phone number. He asked her to dinner, but she suggested lunch. Dinner was reserved for Bautzer, but she never knew if work would keep him late at the office. She sometimes went home alone. In Hedda Hopper's opinion, this was not the worst thing. "If Lana Turner would forget about nightclubbing and get down to hard work," wrote Hopper, "that girl could be a big star within a year. Talk about 'oomph.' She oozes it."

In February 1940, Bautzer had invited Turner and her mother, Mildred, to dinner to celebrate her mother's birthday. At six-thirty, he phoned to cancel. He said he had a stomachache. Turner was incensed. When the phone rang again a few minutes later, she expected to hear him apologize. Instead, she heard Shaw's voice. He suggested dinner. Turner was so angry with Bautzer that she agreed, removing her engagement ring on the way out.

After dinner, Turner and Shaw parked at the beach. He talked of marriage, a home, children, all the things she wanted from Bautzer. She confided that her strongest desire was to be married and have children. She didn't care if she never made another picture. And although she didn't say it, she wanted to punish Bautzer.

"Suppose I were to call up right now and charter a plane?" asked Shaw. "Would you come with me?"

"Yes, I would."

"Swell," said Shaw. "Let's go."

In a few hours, they were in Las Vegas, standing before a justice of the peace who was wearing a bathrobe and pajamas. "Got married in Las Vegas," she telegraphed her mother. "Call you later. Love, Lana." Her mother assumed that Lana had married Bautzer, then on second thought decided to try his phone number. He answered. Bautzer was as shocked as she was. He promised to find out what had happened. After pulling a few strings, he did. He called Mildred back within an hour. Yes, it was true. She was married to Artie Shaw. "I've lost her," Bautzer said in a quavering voice.

The marriage was troubled from the start. Turner discovered that Shaw was involved with more women than Bautzer. He had been married twice. Judy Garland had assumed that she would be the third Mrs. Shaw. Betty Grable had recently been impregnated by him. He was secretive, snide, and condescending. He wanted Turner to improve her mind by reading Nietzsche and Schopenhauer but refused to explain the more abstruse passages. When she protested, he became abusive. He was jealous of her work. "MGM means more to you than I do," he yelled at her. At home he expected her to dress plainly and not wear makeup. Turner had never learned to cook, yet he demanded that she prepare meals for him and his friends after she had been working at the studio all day. When she made spaghetti, he rudely sniffed it. "What is this crap?" he snarled, and tossed it on the floor. He was no better in public, humiliating her in front of friends and strangers alike. On top of it all, he was a lousy sexual partner. "I had to fight hard to keep Greg out of my thoughts," wrote Turner. "I began to feel as if I'd betrayed him."

Shaw took Turner to Ciro's nightclub, which had opened in January and therefore held no memories of Bautzer. She saw Bautzer sitting at an adjoining table with actress Dorothy Lamour. Jimmie Fidler reported that there was "great tension" in the air. Bautzer had been hurt by Turner's elopement. Turner was desperately unhappy. Shaw was endlessly mean.

By June, Turner saw that she could never meet Shaw's neurotic demands. His tantrums were pushing her toward a nervous breakdown. She began crying, shaking uncontrollably, and finally screaming. Shaw called a doctor. Turner was sedated and admitted to a hospital under an assumed name. When she came to, she called

Mildred and escaped the hospital. Yet she went back to Shaw. One morning, as he charged out of the house, he ordered her to get his shoes shined. That did it. She had finally had enough. She called Bautzer.

"Get your things together," he said. "I'll have you out of there today." Bautzer brought Turner to meet Shaw at a restaurant and initiate a divorce. Shaw was predictably petty. He insisted on keeping an expensive grand piano that had been a gift from Turner's mother. When Turner told him she was pregnant, Shaw first questioned the paternity and then left her to deal with it on her own. Nineteen, newly single, her career hanging in the balance, Turner submitted to an illegal—and painful—abortion.

After her divorce from Shaw, Turner and Bautzer were often seen in public together. Though Turner claimed they never rekindled their romance, photos taken shortly after World War II show them holding hands under the table at club Mocambo and gazing longingly into each other's eyes on the Stork Club dance floor on a trip together to New York. For the rest of her life, Turner would rely on Bautzer for help and guidance, whether legal or otherwise. At a tribute in the 1970s, Turner was asked why she had married seven times. "Let me put it this way," she said. "With one bitterly painful exception, when I fell in love, I married." The exception was Greg Bautzer.

4

TWO GODFATHERS

From the very beginning, the motion picture business has been a magnet for ambitious young people seeking fame and fortune. Shortly after Bautzer started his legal career, a writer named Budd Schulberg published an exposé about the business titled *What Makes Sammy Run*. Schulberg knew his subject well. His father ran Paramount Pictures. His book was a character study of the type of personality that succeeded in Hollywood. The main character, Sammy Glick, is so ruthlessly ambitious that he will stop at virtually nothing to reach his goal of becoming a successful producer. He steals screenplay ideas from others and backstabs those who help him along the way. Bautzer wasn't trying to be a producer, and he would rather cut off his right arm than double-cross a friend, but he possessed the same driving ambition as Glick. He was willing to do almost anything to succeed.

Bautzer's romance with Lana Turner had gained him attention. He was seen as a new personality and perhaps a competent attorney. Celebrity had gotten him in the door, but it was not enough to keep him there. He knew that the path to success required friends in high places. As an inexperienced young lawyer, he needed mentors to teach him how to handle difficult lawsuits and unfamiliar business transactions. Most of all, he needed information from insiders that could give him an edge over other lawyers. He had one prospect: William R. Wilkerson, the *Hollywood Reporter* publisher who had discovered Turner. Billy, as he was known, maintained an interest in the actress, and he promoted her career in his paper at every opportunity. He did not ask favors in return; instead, his interest seemed almost filial. And when Turner became engaged to Bautzer, Wilkerson practically adopted him as well.

Wilkerson was a multitalented individual. Almost immediately after arriving in Hollywood, the man with the waxed mustache had become an overnight sensation as both a pioneering publisher and an inspired restaurateur. Wilkerson started the *Hollywood Reporter* in 1930, and within two years it was neck-and-neck with industry leaders such as the *Motion Picture Herald* and *Harrison's Reports*. He made enemies of studio executives by exposing corrupt studio practices, then threatened not to write good things about their pictures unless they purchased copious amounts of advertising. Studio heads who at first tried to blackball the outspoken Wilkerson were soon buying large ads in his paper and hoping that his weekly "Trade Views" column would treat them kindly. He created a new slang vocabulary for the paper—studios were referred to as "the plant," and directors signed on to "megaphone" a picture. Wilkerson could also make careers; his raves about young Clark Gable contributed to the actor's meteoric rise to fame.

Wilkerson was a force in Hollywood. "Billy Wilkerson couldn't topple heads of studios," said Bautzer, "but he could cause them a hell of a lot of trouble. At one time he was having a controversy with Harry Cohn, head of Columbia Pictures, so Billy published the names of Columbia's principal shareholders. At the top of the list was one Joan Perry, Cohn's lady friend. You could hear Cohn screaming all the way from Gower to Highland. But Cohn came to terms."

Wilkerson had spent time in Europe and thought Hollywood nightclubs like the Café Montmartre were pedestrian. He decided to upgrade Hollywood's cuisine. In 1933, he opened the Café Vendome at 6666 Sunset Boulevard. In 1934, he opened the Café Trocadero at 8610 Sunset Boulevard. It became the keystone of the Sunset Strip—and made $1.7 million in one year. "Billy brought Paris to Hollywood when stars were eating sandwiches and drinking Coca-Cola," said producer Joe Pasternak, a patron of the "Troc."

Curiously, Coca-Cola was one of Wilkerson's guilty pleasures. He drank twenty bottles a day (and smoked three packs of cigarettes). He was married and divorced numerous times, but not because of philandering. "Billy's real mistress is his work," said ex-wife Edith Gwynn Wilkerson. It was not. His real mistress was Lady Luck.

Wilkerson was born in Nashville, Tennessee. When he was seven his father won the bottling rights for Coca-Cola in thirteen Southern states at a poker game. Regrettably, father swapped them for a movie theater. As a teenager, Wilkerson considered becoming a priest. His father was horrified and convinced him to attend college in Maryland and then Jefferson Medical College in Philadelphia. Unfortunately, he had to drop out when his father's unexpected death revealed huge gambling debts.

Wilkerson went to work managing a friend's theater in Philadelphia. Soon, he found a more lucrative profession tending a speakeasy in Manhattan at the corner of Fifty-Second Street and Park Avenue. The initiation fee for customers was $1,500. The swanky saloon catered to both a high-class clientele and low-class gangsters. Whether by luck or an inside tip, when the police raided the place Wilkerson was out of town.

Seeking a more legal profession, he turned to publishing and resurrected a faltering theatrical trade paper. One day in 1929, after cashing out his share of the publication and borrowing some more money, he walked into the New York Stock Exchange, expecting to double the $45,000 he had in his pocket. That was October 24, the day the stock market bubble burst. Forty-five minutes later, he walked out of the Exchange with empty pockets and decided to move to Los Angeles.

This scene would be repeated many times, in card parlors and casinos, on gambling ships, and at racetracks. He was addicted to gambling. When he gambled with the public's taste, Wilkerson won; every restaurant he opened was a success. When he gambled with money, his taste and objectivity melted into the smoke over the felt-topped table. He lost, and lost badly—an average of $150,000 a year. His salary could not cover his bets, so he began to stake the magazine's payroll. After he went through that, he bet the prepaid advertising receipts. To pay that back, he sold more prepaid advertising, importuning sponsors like Howard Hughes to cover his losses.

Bautzer saw none of this turmoil when he first met Wilkerson in 1938 at the Troc. The attorney was engaged to Turner at the time, and Billy was quite happy to meet Lana's fiancé. He had noticed Bautzer's incredible wardrobe as he glided beautiful girls across the dance floors of his nightclubs. He had also seen the young man's name in the gossip columns. Wilkerson knew Bautzer was hustling for speedy success, and he admired him for it. He would note Bautzer's charm every time he joined the couple for a drink in one of the mint-green-and-cocoa-striped booths at LaRue.* As soon as the topic of card games came up, they were off and running. Bautzer loved gambling as much as Wilkerson. Both of Bautzer's parents had been skilled card players, and bridge, gin rummy, and poker were as much a part of Bautzer's portfolio as the fox-trot, waltz, and rumba.

Hollywood card games were the stuff of legend. In the mid-1930s Irving Thalberg, MGM production chief, had hosted a weekly game in his Santa Monica beachfront mansion. Regulars included

---

*According to Wilkerson's son, Willie, Bautzer became Wilkerson's lawyer at this time after pitching his services during an elevator ride and offering to work for free for six months. Bautzer successfully cleared Wilkerson of multiple pending charges for moving violations and remained his lawyer for life.

comic actor Chico Marx and studio heads David O. Selznick, Joseph Schenck, Darryl F. Zanuck, and Sam Goldwyn. The stakes were perilously high. "You don't gamble unless you stand to win something. Or lose something," said Thalberg. "If I can win $40,000 or $50,000 and buy a house at the beach and have Schenck pay for it, then I enjoy it. But if I go up there and bet only $400 or $500, I don't care whether I win or lose. You see, it's got to count. It's got to get to where you get hurt. You're either going to win something or get hurt. Really hurt."

By the late 1930s, Thalberg had died and the card game had moved on. Twentieth Century-Fox chairman Joe Schenck was now hosting the card parties, and Billy Wilkerson was included. Bautzer thought that if he could get into the game, he could meet and impress important men who could help propel his career. All he needed was an introduction. Wilkerson was happy to oblige, but there was one problem.

Incredible as it sounds, the brash young lawyer was suing Schenck. Bautzer was representing Nicky Arnstein, the former husband of Broadway's Fanny Brice, in a lawsuit against Twentieth Century-Fox. Arnstein had seen himself portrayed in a new film without his permission and had hired Bautzer to sue its makers. *Rose of Washington Square* told the story of a Tin Pan Alley songstress (Alice Faye) and her abusive, thieving husband (Tyrone Power). Film critics noted both the similarity of *Rose*'s main character to Brice and the unpleasantness of the character's husband. Arnstein had served two prison terms—first in Sing Sing for wiretapping in 1915 and then in Leavenworth in 1924 for conspiracy to traffic in stolen bonds. One of the film's featured songs was "My Man," a torch song that had been Fanny Brice's signature number.

The film premiered on May 3, 1939, and three weeks later, Bautzer filed a complaint under Arnstein's real name, Jules Arndt Stein. The complaint named as defendants the studio; stars Faye and Power; director Gregory Ratoff; writers Nunnally Johnson, John Larkin, and

Jerry Horwin; and executives Darryl Zanuck and Joseph Schenck. The lawsuit asserted that a character in the film was based on Arnstein and that it used elements from his life. He was asking $150,000 for violation of his privacy, $150,000 for libel, and $100,000 for use of material from his life without his authorization. In addition, he was seeking an injunction to prevent future showings of the film and an accounting to recover profits.

"I have tried industriously to live down my mistakes," Arnstein told the *L.A. Times*. "Now this moving picture comes along. My friends, most of whom know all about me, have been literally knocked off their feet. It's obviously about my life. And what's worse, it depicts a lot of things I never did." Arnstein cited scenes that showed the ne'er-do-well lead character selling furniture from a friend's home, stealing a necklace, and jumping bail—things he had not done.

In naming Schenck as a defendant, Bautzer was taking on a formidable adversary. Schenck was one of the most powerful men in Hollywood. Technically, the only legitimate reason to name a company executive in a suit against that company is if the executive acted outside the course and scope of his or her employment or failed to maintain a separation between personal and corporate business. Otherwise, naming an executive is simply a tactic to make that person so uncomfortable that he or she will agree to a settlement. But Schenck had been running cutthroat businesses before Bautzer was born. It would take more than putting his name on a lawsuit to make him uncomfortable.

Joseph Schenck was born in Rybinsk, Russia, in 1876. He and his brother Nicholas came to America in 1893 and slept on the floor of an older brother's pharmacy in the Bowery until they could get a foothold in the new country. Years of odd jobs enabled them to buy the pharmacy, then a dance hall, and eventually Palisades Amusement Park in New Jersey. After Joe and Nick leased space in the park to pioneering silent film exhibitor Marcus Loew, he recognized their business ability and enticed them into working with him owning and managing movie theaters.

Both brothers were brilliant businessmen, but their personalities were radically different. Nick was cold, tough, and inscrutable. Joe was easygoing and made deals by finding common ground. Nick was content to manage money. Joe wanted to manage filmmaking.

As the holdings of Loew's grew from 12 theaters to 112, Nick grew rich. Joe booked films, which gave him the opportunity to meet movie stars. He decided to leave Loew's Inc. and strike out on his own. In 1916, he married the actress Norma Talmadge. He had been producing films for comedians Roscoe "Fatty" Arbuckle and Buster Keaton, so he started a film company with Norma, making her and her sister Constance into major stars. In 1923, he moved their company to California. A year later, he became president of United Artists, the powerhouse company formed five years earlier by Mary Pickford, Douglas Fairbanks, D. W. Griffith, and Charlie Chaplin. These megastars had decided to create the independent operation because they felt they deserved more money than any studio was willing to pay, and they wanted to make their movies without the interference of tightfisted studio bosses. That they would pick Joe Schenck to run their company is testimony to how well-liked and trusted he was by artists. While his brother Nick ruled by intimidation, Joe found ways to make friends and compromise.*

Despite his easygoing demeanor, after eight years as head of United Artists, Joe tired of dealing with the egotistical Chaplin, so he left the company. Meanwhile, producer Darryl F. Zanuck, who had shined at Warner Bros.—he created the wildly profitable Rin Tin Tin wonder-dog series, among many other hits—had tired of Jack

---

*When Marcus Loew died in 1927, Nick Schenck replaced him as head of Loew's Inc., which owned MGM. Many people considered Louis B. Mayer the most powerful man in Hollywood, but it was his boss, Nick Schenck, who had the real power.

Warner's broken promises. He left Warner Bros. and joined Schenck. They formed a small production company, Twentieth Century Pictures. It made profitable movies on the United Artists lot but needed more room. In 1935, it merged with foundering Fox Film to form Twentieth Century-Fox, a super studio that was soon making super profits.

Short, bald, and stout, Joe Schenck could buy and sell Gregson Bautzer ten times over. Yet for some reason, Schenck was intrigued by the young lawyer. Perhaps it was his audacity. Wilkerson prevailed upon Schenck to meet Bautzer to discuss settlement. The meeting took place in mid-May 1939 at Schenck's house. Legend has it that a card game was starting when Bautzer arrived, and Schenck was one player short. He asked Bautzer to sit in and play for a while before discussing settlement. It didn't take long for Bautzer to impress Schenck. After the card game, Schenck told Bautzer what he would pay to settle the lawsuit. They shook hands and made the deal.

On June 6, the *L.A. Times* reported that "attorneys Gregson Bautzer and G. Bentley Ryan, representing Nicky Arnstein, moved for a dismissal yesterday of the action by their client for $250,000 [*sic*] against the film concern. The motion was granted." The settlement was undisclosed but estimated to be $20,000. Arnstein was pleased. Schenck was pleased. Bautzer had made a new friend. "When Joe Schenck put his arm around me and said 'This is a pretty good fellow,' I was off to a good start," said Bautzer.

As Bautzer had hoped, Schenck invited him to the weekly card parties at his Holmby Hills estate. Bautzer did not have the money to gamble that Wilkerson did. Luckily, the game did not call for bets until three cards had been dealt. If Bautzer did not have a strong hand, he could fold at the outset. This strategy kept him in the game for a time, but it was eventually discovered. The house changed the rules and he was forced to bet up front. Still, he played close to the vest and managed to keep his losses down.

Schenck's card parties had another element that suited Bautzer's interests. Beyond the smoky light of the card table, up-and-coming actresses beautified the room, hoping to advance their careers. These nubile and willing young ladies were supplied by an individual named Pasquale "Pat" Di Cicco, who was nominally a talent agent, a career that didn't have much sway in the studio era. At the time, an actor would sign a long-term contract with a particular studio; the commitment could last as long as seven years, and the actor had no say in the roles he or she was assigned. A performer who refused to play a part was suspended, and the time spent idle was added to the length of his or her contract. As Bautzer would one day admit, in those days "all an agent could demand was a new dressing room or limousine service to and from the studio."

Dark-haired and handsome, Di Cicco was a constant figure at Schenck's card table, and he would become one of Bautzer's good friends. Di Cicco was also in the employ of Howard Hughes, although no one is certain what he did for Hughes, other than introduce him to girls. Some have suggested that Di Cicco had ties to underworld figures, including fronting for Lucky Luciano, but that has never been proven.* Like Di Cicco, Bautzer also introduced young actresses to Schenck. According to actor Tony Curtis, Bautzer 's most noteworthy introduction would come in the late 1940s when he presented Marilyn Monroe to the mogul. Monroe became Schenck's mistress and lived at his house. Schenck in turn gave her a contract at Twentieth Century-Fox, starting one of the most iconic acting careers in history.

Bautzer credited Schenck for advancing his career. Schenck was a masterful negotiator. He knew everyone of importance in the industry, and on both coasts. There was no favor he could not call in. He helped Bautzer with referrals and with advice, becoming exactly the

---

*Di Cicco's cousin, Albert R. "Cubby" Broccoli, was also one of Bautzer's good friends. Broccoli would go on to produce the highly successful James Bond motion picture franchise.

type of mentor Bautzer had hoped for. Wilkerson, too, took Bautzer under his wing. The young man who had no immediate relatives suddenly had a new family—or at least two godfathers.

Of course, no amount of favors or inside information would make Bautzer's career a success if he weren't a talented lawyer. In 1940, he and Bentley Ryan proved that despite their youth, they were capable of taking cases all the way to verdict, and to the court of appeals if necessary, when they sued Warner Bros. and its police chief, Blaney Matthews, on behalf of two union organizers. Their complaint stated that Matthews and his security guards had falsely arrested union officials Ralph Pekham and Herbert Sorrel for participating in a 1937 studio strike that ended in violence, with at least one studio employee badly beaten and property destroyed. Matthews kept the two union officials locked up for days without charging them.

The trial started in January 1940. In April, before the case went to the jury, Judge Walter S. Gates granted the studio's motion that the complaint against it be dismissed. The judge decided that the unlawful arrests were not within the course and scope of Matthews's employment and thus weren't authorized by the studio. He instructed the jury not to issue a monetary damage award against Warner Bros. After hearing Bautzer's closing argument, the jury ignored the judge's instructions. The runaway jury returned a verdict against both Blaney Matthews and Warner Bros., ordering the studio to pay Pekham $7,500 and Sorrell $5,500.

Judge Gates was incensed. He set aside the verdict against the studio, holding that the jury had no right to disregard his directions. He also nullified the verdict against Blaney Matthews, personally ordering that the plaintiffs would get nothing. Bautzer appealed. In December, the Court of Appeal reversed the judge's ruling, proclaiming that the jury and not the judge should decide whether the plaintiffs had presented sufficient evidence to hold Warner Bros. responsible. The award to the plaintiffs was reestablished. The California Court of

Appeal published their decision, making it a precedent to be followed in the future.

It is apparent that Judge Gates was biased in favor of the defendants. Why he granted Warner Bros.' motion is something of a mystery. Perhaps he was swayed by the amount of violence that had taken place during the strike and thought that, in comparison, holding Sorrel and Pekham in jail for a few days without being charged was not worth complaining about. Then again, something more nefarious may have taken place. Gates had been previously indicted in a scandal over judges appointing receivers in exchange for bribes. (Receivers are court-appointed business managers who collect debts for insolvent companies). Although Gates was acquitted, such judicial misdeeds were not unheard-of in prewar Los Angeles.

Only four years into his career, Bautzer was proving that he was a lawyer to take seriously. By successfully appealing Judge Gates's orders, Bautzer showed that he was more than a handsome young man who took starlets to nightclubs. He was a professional at the beginning of a distinguished career.

5

THE SARONG GIRL

Nineteen forty was a nervous year for Americans and a brutal year for Europeans. Hitler was beginning a war against Great Britain. Americans, still recovering from the atrocities of the First World War, were not eager to join the fray. The mood in Los Angeles was jittery, but Greg Bautzer seemed impervious to it. After his mother's death, he moved with law partner Bentley Ryan and boyhood friend Jack Huber to a house at 2092 Mound Street. He busied himself with divorce cases by day and dancing by night. He had momentarily forsaken La Conga and the Trocadero and was patronizing the Victor Hugo, a Beverly Hills nightclub that had been going strong since 1934, a remarkable feat in fickle Los Angeles. He was spotted there in late February dancing with the brainy, raven-haired Gail Patrick, who was married to Bob Cobb, the founder of the Brown Derby and inventor of the Cobb salad. Cobb was also there, making it a threesome, but he was about to become an ex-husband. Hollywood was sometimes described as high school with divorce.

Bautzer was also seen at the Victor Hugo with British actress Wendy Barrie and later with Patti Brilhante. Gliding across the dance floor with a beauty did not mean that he was smitten with her. Dorothy Lamour, a Paramount Pictures star, knew him from various clubs. "Bautzer was a real Beau Brummell and an incorrigible flirt," wrote Lamour. "I remember seeing him dancing with Lana Turner and smiling at me over her shoulder, but, knowing of his reputation, I didn't give his come-on a second thought."

Lamour's name was on everyone's lips in April 1940. *The Road to Singapore*, the first pairing of Bob Hope and Bing Crosby and her first film with them, was a held-over hit, and she was opening two more films simultaneously, *Johnny Apollo* and *Typhoon*. She had made her first splash in Paramount's 1936 South Sea adventure *Jungle Princess*, but her image as an island siren was crystallized in John Ford's 1937 epic *The Hurricane*, made on loan-out to Samuel Goldwyn. Lamour had worked nonstop since *The Hurricane*, often wearing nothing more than a sarong.

Paramount decided that Lamour's next film would be *Aloma of the South Seas*. When Lamour complained about having to wear yet another sarong, Jimmie Fidler took her to task. "You've won many fans," he wrote in his syndicated column, "not because you're a great actress or even a great singer but because you're simply terrific in those South Seas scanties."

Dorothy Lamour was born Mary Leta Slaton in New Orleans in 1914. Her dark, exotic looks came from a background that included Creole, Spanish, and Irish ancestry. Her stage name was a variation of the family surname Lambour. The onetime Miss New Orleans was discovered in Chicago by bandleader Herbie Kay, who made her a vocalist in his band and then married her. She was appearing on NBC radio when the band eventually played Hollywood. She decided to give acting a try. Most studios thought her too unusual-looking. Luckily, Paramount needed a female Tarzan. In 1940, Lamour, like so many others in Hollywood, was newly divorced.

Plainspoken and direct, Lamour was perhaps the most down-to-earth actress in the business. Hearst columnist Louella Parsons complimented Lamour's humble nature in a feature profile: "Dottie, as she is known to her friends, doesn't put on an act when she is asked to let her dinner get cold and pose for some cameraman, and she does it without a complaint. She naturally likes to make people happy and she has never learned to high hat anyone, whether it's the doorman at Ciro's, the girl in the powder room at the Scheherazade or the waiter at the Brown Derby."

Lamour had an unusual encounter with Bautzer, which could have been taken as an omen. On April 4, Bautzer had an accident that was eerily reminiscent of the one that had led to his father's death. He was driving to Palm Springs on Old Highway 99, near Crystal Springs, when he crashed into another car. He was apparently the only one injured. Coincidentally, Lamour happened to be driving by shortly after the accident and saw Bautzer on the side of the road, though she didn't stop. He was hospitalized with a broken leg and put in a cast and on crutches. Later that same month, Lamour and her agent Wynn Rocamora were at Ciro's, the new club on Sunset with splashy yet tasteful décor that Billy Wilkerson had opened earlier that year. "Greg Bautzer stopped by the table," Lamour recalled. "The huge plaster cast on his leg didn't stop him from asking me to dance. Greg was a very determined gentleman. We not only danced; we did a rumba." Plaster notwithstanding, a romance ensued.

It was interrupted by another hospital visit, as Bautzer suffered an attack of appendicitis. Lamour, meanwhile, had braces put on her teeth, and on April 18 she and her mother left for Hawaii. While there, she graced the premiere of *Typhoon* and made sure she was quoted—"Where would I be without my sarong?" Being hospitalized caused Bautzer to miss a number of events, including Lamour's departure and a speaking engagement at the annual banquet of the Newsboys' Club on Spring Street (Bautzer had delivered newspapers as a boy). He didn't miss everything, though. He was visited in the hospital by Margaret Roach, eighteen-year-old daughter of producer Hal Roach. A gossip column said that she was mistaken for Lana Turner by the hospital staff.

When Lamour got back to Los Angeles, she resumed her relationship with Bautzer. In June, they drove south for the gala opening of the Del Mar Hotel near San Diego; they returned to the hotel the following month, and Bautzer puckishly played Lamour's gramophone recordings in front of some vacationing Knights of Columbus. She was embarrassed by the scene he was causing and tried to ignore it. They continued dating for more than a year, adding glitter to the gossip columns with their red carpet appearances and public demonstrations of affection. In October, Lamour was flying east to visit a former boyfriend and booster named Bob Stein. Bautzer saw her off. Their farewell embraces were so prolonged (and pronounced) that the airline had to resort to the public address system: "Will Miss Lamour please board the aircraft!"

While dating Lamour, Bautzer started to land the type of clients for which he had been striving. In August 1940, he represented movie star Paulette Goddard against her own father. At that time, an affluent child was expected to care for an aging parent, and Joseph R. Levee had filed a suit seeking $150 a week for living expenses. Goddard was not concerned with others' expectations; she was already paying Levee $75 per week, more than enough for an estranged relative. Goddard needed Bautzer to extricate her with a minimum of damage to her good name.

For a lawyer with only three years of legal experience, this case was a jackpot. It was certain to be heavily covered in the press. It was also a delicate matter that, if handled well, could inspire other celebrities to seek his services. Bautzer must have exuded great ability in order to gain Goddard's confidence that he was right for the case. There was no shortage of prominent lawyers with much more experience who should have been a logical choice ahead of him.

Goddard was born Pauline Marion Goddard Levy (or Levee) in 1910 in Queens, New York. After an apprenticeship with Hal Roach and Samuel Goldwyn, she attracted the attention of Charlie Chaplin, the most famous and powerful filmmaker in the world. He made her his leading lady in the 1936 film *Modern Times* and then let her sign with David O. Selznick, who groomed her for stardom, which only came after she left Selznick and signed with Paramount. *The Cat and the Canary* (1939) made her a star, but she was not the only star to emerge from this comedy-thriller. "*The Cat and the Canary* was the turning point for my movie career," wrote Bob Hope. They teamed up again for the spring 1940 hit *The Ghost Breakers*, a glossy, scary, funny vehicle tailored to both of them. When Bautzer met Goddard, she was flush with success, but there was still mystery about her private life. It was rumored that she was married to Chaplin. They neither confirmed nor denied the reports, but her father's lawsuit required her to reveal that they were, in fact, husband and wife.

That Charlie Chaplin, the most famous man on the planet, would put his wife's career in the hands of such a young lawyer is hard to believe. In all likelihood, Joe Schenck recommended Bautzer. Schenck had run United Artists for Chaplin, and Chaplin trusted his judgment.

Bautzer began by enlisting sympathy for Goddard. The answer to the complaint, which he filed with the court, painted a grim picture of her father, detailing the hardships his neglect had supposedly caused her as a child. Levee had defaulted on court-ordered payments of ten dollars per week after divorcing her mother. According to Bautzer, his failure to pay alimony forced Goddard to leave school at age fourteen and work as a fashion model in order to support both herself and her mother. In response to her father's claim that Goddard had great wealth, Bautzer denied that she received $7,000 per week for film work. He maintained that her financial situation was uncertain, because of the six-month option in her contract.

The papers that Bautzer filed in court were almost fictional. Her father's failure to pay alimony had nothing to do with her leaving school. Goddard was not fourteen at the time of her parents' divorce; she was sixteen. Furthermore, she had worked as a department store model from the age of thirteen—three years before the divorce. A few years after becoming a model, she appeared in the Ziegfeld Follies, gaining fame as the "Girl on the Crescent Moon." At age sixteen she married a wealthy man named Edgar James. At age twenty she divorced him. She and her mother bilked rich men on steamships. And to claim that she had an uncertain financial situation was preposterous; Charlie Chaplin was the wealthiest entertainer in the world.

Notwithstanding all the press, or perhaps because of it, the lawsuit was quietly settled. But the public now knew that she and Chaplin were married.

On September 17, 1940, Bautzer acquired another movie-star client. He and Bentley Ryan filed divorce papers on behalf of Carole Landis, a striking twenty-one-year-old blonde. The former bit player had just been elevated to lead by Hal Roach with the caveman epic *One Million B.C.* Despite her tender years, Landis's love life had already made headlines. In 1934, she married Irving Wheeler. Because she was fifteen, the marriage was annulled. Then she married him again, presumably to do it properly. In 1938, Wheeler suspected his wife was having an affair with director Busby Berkeley and sued the hapless dance auteur for stealing Landis's affections. Landis convinced the court that there were no affections, stolen or otherwise, then divorced Wheeler. In 1940, Landis eloped with a new love, the once-divorced Willis Hunt Jr., a playboy described as a "young yachtsman and dealer of yachts." Two months later, she hired Bautzer to handle her divorce from Hunt, claiming that he had treated her in a cruel and inhuman manner, embarrassing her with unprovoked physical and mental abuse. In early November, the divorcing couple glared at each other across the foyer of La Conga. He was leaving with sexy actress Martha O'Driscoll. She was arriving with the handsome and influential Cedric Gibbons, head of MGM's art department.

On November 12, Superior Court judge Ingall W. Bull heard the Landis/Hunt divorce case. Obtaining the divorce and a favorable settlement for Landis was a foregone conclusion. For Bautzer, it was all fun. He and Landis gave a theatrical performance for a packed courtroom that included members of the press. Bautzer called his pretty client to the witness stand and led her through a well-prepared script. She wiped tears from doe-like eyes as she testified that she and Hunt frequently argued over her acting career. Before they married, he had been in favor of it, but he had since become violently opposed to it and developed an "ugly and surly" demeanor. He finally told her that he did not love her. She quoted him as saying: "I no longer care to have you as my wife." It was just like a scene from a movie. When it was over, she and Bautzer might as well have taken a bow. Husband Hunt never even bothered to testify in his own defense; he knew he could not compete with his adorable wife's emotional scene. He also knew that if he so much as uttered a word against her, Bautzer would have made him look like a heel on cross-examination. Before the judge could issue a ruling, an out-of-court property settlement was reached.

Landis later dated both Bautzer and Bentley Ryan. Bautzer would ultimately represent her in three divorce cases, a record for him. Sadly, she went on to commit suicide at age twenty-nine over a doomed love affair with married actor Rex Harrison. Hollywood blamed him for her death, and he did not receive any good roles for over ten years.

With the Goddard and Landis cases under his belt, more celebrities turned to him for legal services. In February 1941, Bautzer handled another high-profile divorce case—this one with some unusual twists. He and Ryan represented Marguerite Roach, the wife of comedy producer Hal Roach. Bautzer had been to many premieres and social events with the Roaches and knew them quite well. Roach was an industry pioneer from the silent era, renowned for teaming comic legends Stan Laurel and Oliver Hardy, and for creating the *Our Gang* (a.k.a. *Little Rascals*) comedy shorts with child actors. Daughter Margaret Roach had visited Bautzer while he was in the hospital and had a crush on him. Marguerite was claiming that her husband had subjected her to mental cruelty.

In a surprise move, shortly after filing for divorce, Marguerite decided to drop her action in favor of a separation agreement. Her religious convictions would not allow a divorce, so she was willing to live apart from her husband. The couple agreed on a property settlement. Marguerite would receive a half interest in the Hal Roach Studios and title to their Beverly Hills home at 610 North Beverly Drive. Roach agreed to pay her one-third of his income, with a guaranteed minimum of $1,250 per month. Marguerite was given custody of nineteen-year-old Margaret. Their son, Hal Jr., was twenty-one and did not need a guardian.

But the truly shocking turn was still to come. On March 17, a few weeks after the property settlement was signed, Marguerite Roach suddenly died at age forty-five. Her estate, said to exceed $200,000, was left entirely to her two children. The family home was left to Margaret. Bautzer was named a trustee of Margaret's inheritance, along with Hal Jr. and the Bank of America. At age thirty, Bautzer found himself managing the estate of a deceased client and minding her nineteen-year-old daughter. This was very mature work for a lawyer with less than five years of experience.

A month later, Hal Roach surprised Bautzer by asking him to draw up a petition to appoint him his daughter's legal guardian. The legal brief stated that the guardianship was necessary to take proper care of Margaret's property, which now included a quarter of Roach's studio and the Beverly Hills home. That Roach would choose young Bautzer over his own divorce lawyer shows that he liked Bautzer— and, of course, there was another consideration: Bautzer was one of

Margaret's trustees, with a one-third vote in the management of her property until she turned twenty-one. Nevertheless, Bautzer assumed and discharged these added responsibilities without incident.

By May 1941, Bautzer had decided that he deserved a break from his growing legal practice. He and Dorothy Lamour embarked for Hawaii for a monthlong vacation. Bautzer was late to the dock. Waiting for him to board the Matson liner *Lurline*, Lamour burst into tears, fearing that he would miss the boat. He arrived just in time to run up the gangplank before it was taken away. An alert press photographer snapped a shot of the couple just before the ship sailed; they look stylish but unhappy that their picture is being taken during a private moment. He is wearing a tropical-weight suit and peering over his shoulder. She is wearing a light-colored dress with a large white corsage and a peaked turban.

Their luck did not improve in Honolulu. Bautzer and Lamour were in a restaurant when people at an adjoining table made unflattering remarks about Lamour. Bautzer jumped to his feet, removed his dinner jacket, and said, "You want to make something of it?" The offending party backed down. Shortly afterward, Lamour made unkind remarks about the inhabitants of Honolulu. An argument ensued. The press picked it up. An editorial on the front page of the *Honolulu Advertiser* urged the couple to go back to where they came from. They took the hint and ended their trip early. This was the first time the press had reported Bautzer's tendency to get into public fights. It would not be the last.

Back in Hollywood, Lamour and Bautzer continued dating. "Greg and I had lots of fun, some serious moments, too, and, of course, lots of intrigue," wrote Lamour. "We would break up for a couple of days, make up again, then break up a couple of weeks later." At one point, he presented her with his mother's diamond solitaire. But their engagement was soon overshadowed by world events. "I had just taken a company out of receivership," recalled Bautzer. "I could see myself president of that company—a millionaire for sure in three years. Boy, I had the world by the tail. Then they bombed Pearl Harbor."

The Japanese attack on December 7, 1941, pulled the United States into World War II. Three days later, Lamour was waiting for Bautzer to pick her up. It was her twenty-seventh birthday. He had sent her a corsage of white orchids. She had just finished pinning it to her dress when the lights went out. It was an air raid. It angered her— the interruption, the inconvenience, the senselessness of war. She had friends in Hawaii and was upset by the Japanese bombing. It was then that she decided to use her name to sell war bonds.

This gave Lamour an excuse to end the engagement. She told Bautzer she needed to devote herself to the war cause. They could not go on seeing one another. "I knew that Greg was not a one-woman man, but that I was definitely a one-man woman," wrote Lamour in her autobiography. Romantic questions that would have been important a year earlier, even a month earlier, suddenly lost their gravity when compared with the urgent need to mobilize.

Unknown to Lamour, Bautzer had already performed covert war services for his country. Services that would remain a secret his entire life.

III

WAR

6

THE SPY WHO
LOVED HIM

By the time World War II started, Greg Bautzer was known around the globe as "Hollywood Bachelor Number One." His picture had been in the papers as often as a movie star's. Unbeknownst to him, his country was about to enlist his playboy talents for a matter of national security. Billy Wilkerson approached him one day in early 1940 and asked his help with a very unusual project. Billy was an informant for the FBI and friendly with bureau director J. Edgar Hoover. Wilkerson told Bautzer that the FBI needed information about a German actress named Hilda Kruger who had recently come to town, allegedly seeking acting work. Billy asked Bautzer to see if he could get a date with her and find out what she was up to.

Bautzer couldn't resist performing favors. He knew that every good deed helped cement his relationships. Moreover, obtaining personal information about beautiful women was Bautzer's specialty. He would be only too happy to do this small task for Wilkerson and his country. He didn't imagine there could be any danger involved.

Kruger was a well-endowed blonde with a dozen supporting-role credits in German movies. To advance her career under the Nazi regime, she left her non-Aryan husband and offered her favors to Joseph Goebbels, Hitler's minister of propaganda. As one US consul described it, "She was one of a bevy of gals that were called upon occasionally to furnish a little 'joy thru strength' to the Hitler-Goebbels combinations by night frolicking a la Nero." An FBI report goes so far as to say that Hitler himself was known to fawn over her in public and pinch her thigh in the presence of others. In 1938, she attracted the attention of US oil tycoon J. Paul Getty, who was visiting Germany. They met at a party thrown by Nazi leaders at the Reich Chancellery. Getty was a Nazi sympathizer who may have suggested and even underwritten Kruger's spy career. While Hollywood would seem an unlikely target for espionage, Los Angeles was a major industrial city with many war material factories. Plenty of residents had classified information that could be useful to the Germans should the United States join the British in the war. Upon her arrival in the States, the FBI labeled Kruger a security threat.

According to an FBI memorandum of June 29, 1940, Bautzer wasted no time in making contact with Kruger and retrieving important information for Wilkerson:

William R. (Billie) [sic] Wilkerson advised that Hilda Kruger was in Los Angeles, Beverly Hills, and Hollywood, California, for a period of about four months, during which time she represented herself as endeavoring to get into motion pictures, but so far as Mr. Wilkerson knows, she never even has registered with any booking agencies. Kruger told Gregson Bautzer that she was a special friend of Dr. Paul Joseph Goebbels and Adolf Hitler. She associated with Donald Flam of New York City and James McKinley Bryant of New York City, and is a friend of Regina Crewe, motion picture columnist of the "New York American". She attended a dance at Ciro's Café [sic] with Fritz Wiedermann, German Consul at San Francisco, on May 18, 1940, and left the next day for New York City.

Additional details in the report provide further insight: "Mr. Wilkerson stated that Miss Kruger was or attempted to be quite mysterious in her actions and talk, that she appeared to have a lot of money and a good wardrobe of striking clothes, and that she was on every occasion announcing and declaring that she had come to Hollywood for the purpose of going into motion pictures."

How Bautzer came to obtain information on Kruger becomes clear in Wilkerson's final report about her to the FBI:

> Mr. Wilkerson stated that while Miss Kruger was in Los Angeles, she associated quite a great deal with Gregson Bautzer, young attorney of the firm of Bautzer and Ryan with offices in the Taft Building [sic], Hollywood, California. He stated that during a portion of the time that Miss Kruger was in Hollywood, California, and while she was associating with Bautzer, that Bautzer had a broken leg which was caused by an automobile accident, and that Miss Kruger visited him at his apartment on many occasions, both day and night. Mr. Wilkerson requested that in case Bautzer is interviewed about this matter that he be not informed of the source of this information.

Wilkerson's request that the FBI not mention his name to Bautzer suggests that Bautzer was simply sharing details of his personal life with a friend, with no knowledge that Wilkerson was passing along the information to the government. This was not the case, however. Bautzer knew full well that the information he was providing about Kruger was for the benefit of the FBI, as evidenced by the fact that he kept their relationship a secret from the press. It was unusual for Bautzer to date a woman without having it noted in gossip columns. In the period before and after his accident, he was reported as dating at least three other women. He was proud of them and he courted publicity. Although Bautzer was a playboy, he was also a gentleman, and he never discussed what went on with girlfriends behind closed doors. It was out of character for him to relate pillow talk to Wilkerson.

Bautzer kept his covert mission a secret until near the end of his life. In the 1980s, Bautzer met author Charles Higham for lunch and discussed the Kruger affair. Higham had written the controversial biography *Errol Flynn: The Untold Story*, in which he revealed the famous actor's Nazi involvement. Higham came across Bautzer's name many times in researching the book and regretted that he had not interviewed him. Higham had seen the FBI papers that identified Bautzer as the man who provided the agency with information on Kruger, and he wanted to know more. They met for lunch at the Bistro Gardens, and Bautzer confirmed that he had been asked by Wilkerson to find out what he could about Kruger for the FBI. He decided the best way was to seduce her. To Higham's delight, Bautzer also told him that he admired the Flynn book and said he was interested in acquiring the motion picture rights for MGM. The lunch ended on a cordial note, and Higham had great hopes for a motion picture deal. However, the following day Bautzer contacted Higham's lawyer and said that MGM was not interested in the book rights, and threatened to sue Higham if he mentioned the Kruger affair to anyone. Higham was shocked and thought that Bautzer had been influenced by a third party. Perhaps Bautzer feared reprisals from the FBI for disclosing his participation in such undercover work. More likely, he simply wanted to avoid a salacious story appearing in print about him.

After her fling with Bautzer, Kruger departed Hollywood for Mexico and began socializing with government officials. J. Paul Getty used his influence to get her a visa, telling the Mexican consul that she was an American citizen. Getty soon traveled to visit her in Mexico. Her activities were sufficiently suspicious to arouse the interest of J. Edgar Hoover. He wrote a personal letter to Adolf Berle Jr., assistant secretary of state, relating the information that Bautzer had provided. Kruger left luggage behind at the Beverly-Wilshire Hotel, which the

FBI searched. They found no evidence that she was a spy—other than the humorous presence of a book titled *Mata Hari, Courtesan and Spy* with pertinent passages underlined. She seemed to be using it as an espionage textbook.

In Mexico, Kruger became the lover of Mario Ramón Beteta, undersecretary of finance. He paid for her luxury apartment in the fashionable Colonia Roma district of Mexico City and unwittingly introduced her to other government officials, whom she then proceeded to seduce. She resumed her film career in Mexico, securing more prominent roles than she had in Germany. Kruger was later involved with Beteta's boss, General Juan Almazán, the major presidential contender, and Miguel Alemán Valdés, then secretary of state and the eventual president of Mexico. Perhaps because of these alliances, Kruger escaped arrest when several other prominent Nazis were taken into custody at the FBI's request. J. Edgar Hoover was certainly surprised that she was not arrested and made note of it in another personal letter to Berle, which he also sent to the assistant chief of staff of the War Department and the director of Naval Intelligence.

While it has not been conclusively proven that Kruger was in fact a Nazi spy, all the circumstantial evidence indicates that she was. Not only have multiple sources confirmed that she was one of Hitler's favorite party girls in Berlin, but in New York she was also frequently in the company of other well-known German operatives. In Los Angeles, the filmmaking community concluded she was a spy when she showed up at a party with the German consul Fritz Weidemann. The FBI interviewed many Germans working in the movie business about Kruger, including Marlene Dietrich, who said that she did not know her but had heard things about her. Hungarian-born producer Joe Pasternak told the FBI that he was certain she was a spy, and he offered to host a party so that agents could trap her. Unfortunately, Kruger fled to Mexico before the party could be arranged. In Mexico City, her romances with government officials attracted attention in the press, and she was labeled a spy in print. There can hardly be any other plausible reason for her multiple sexual relationships with Mexican politicians. It is difficult to imagine that she was simply some kind of governmental groupie.

The most damning fact is that no one could ever account for where she got all the money she spent on her wardrobe and other luxuries. Even friends who tried to defend her reputation confessed that they were befuddled by her unaccountable wealth. As one FBI analyst concluded, if she wasn't being paid to be a spy, then she must have been one of the highest-priced prostitutes in history. The only missing piece of evidence necessary to complete the picture is an actual document showing the information that she passed on to the Nazi government. To this day, that has never been found.

While Kruger proclaimed her innocence, she never lifted a finger to try to clear her name. She even used her wartime notoriety to start another career as a scholar and author. Kruger first wrote a book about La Malinche, the legendary Aztec woman who slept with Hernán Cortés and reinvented herself. Her second book, titled *Eliza Lynch or Tragic Destiny*, was about a French mistress to a Paraguayan dictator. It was reviewed by *Time* magazine in 1946. The critic devoted more words to her activities as a suspected spy than to her writing.

Bautzer made the first report that inspired FBI director Hoover to dedicate manpower to following Kruger in both the United States and Mexico. If it weren't for the information he passed on to Wilkerson about her association with Hitler and Goebbels, she might never have received such attention. The Kruger case also provides proof of Bautzer's catnip effect on women. Seducing at will is the stuff of fiction, but for him it was reality. Throughout history, as far back as Samson and Delilah, female spies seduced men for information. By seducing the seducer, Bautzer turned the formula on its head.

7

LIEUTENANT
COMMANDER, USN

When the United States entered World War II, Bautzer and his law partner Bentley Ryan desired officers' commissions. They promoted their slightly younger associate Bernard Silbert to full-fledged partner, put his name on the firm letterhead, and left for Washington, DC. On February 2, 1942, Bautzer filed an application for appointment as a lieutenant (junior grade) in the Navy Reserve. Later in life, he would say that he chose the navy because he wanted to avoid being drafted into the infantry. As personal references he listed W. R. Wilkerson, publisher; law school friend Thomas H. Kuchel, who at that time was a California state senator; John J. "Jack" Huber, businessman with the Yawman & Erbe office furniture company; and Mrs. J. C. Huber, Jack's mother. For all his Hollywood razzle-dazzle, Bautzer maintained friendships with people such as Kuchel and the Hubers all his life. He listed his grandmother, Mrs. N. C. Bautzer of 2331 Albion Place, St. Louis, Missouri, as next of kin.

The navy required three letters of recommendation. Bautzer's first was from Brien McMahon of the Washington law firm of McMahon, Dean, and Gallagher, who said he had known Bautzer a year. The second was from Anthony Muto, Washington supervisor of the newsreel company Movietone News. He said that Bautzer was "well and favorably known in the executive circles of the motion picture industry." The third was written by a navy lieutenant commander named H. Spitzel, who had known Bautzer for ten years and wrote that he would be a valuable addition to the military forces.

In his application Bautzer admitted to arrests for "traffic violations," which was likely a euphemism for drunk driving. This admission caused no problem, but Bautzer soon found that military bureaucracy, even in wartime, and even with high-ranking endorsements, was difficult to navigate.

The application process was begun by navy commander H. G. Sickel of the Priorities Committee of the Army and Navy Munitions Board. He wrote to the chief of the Bureau of Navigation (later the Bureau of Naval Personnel) that Bautzer was particularly well qualified for duty in the Compliance and Planning Unit. He requested that Bautzer's case be processed in the most expeditious manner possible. The competition for noncombat officer jobs was fierce. Bautzer must have used considerable charm to impress Commander Sickel.

Sickel's recommendation was endorsed by George Pettengill, commandant of the Washington Navy Yard, who interviewed Bautzer on February 3 for an opening on the Army and Navy Munitions Board (Priorities Committee). Bautzer was also interviewed by Ross T. McIntire, chief of the Bureau of Medicine and Surgery, and Randall Jacobs, chief of the Bureau of Navigation. As it turned out, the Munitions Board had no use for Bautzer's services, but the Bureau of Navigation did. Bautzer was enrolled in the Navy Reserve and ordered to duty in the Enlisted Personnel Division. On February 14, he received his commission as lieutenant (junior grade) and was assigned to the Volunteer Reserve for Special Services. It turned out to be a desk job.

During his first months in Washington, Bautzer became interested in blimps (formally known as "lighter-than-air" craft) through a budding friendship with Vice Admiral Charles E. Rosendahl, who had been flying "rigid-frame" airships (dirigibles) since 1924. Rosendahl became a hero in 1925 when he flew the *Shenandoah* to safety after it broke up in midair. Since then, he had commanded numerous airships and participated in German flights including the first transatlantic crossing of the *Graf Zeppelin*. In 1936, he was put in command of the airfield at Lakehurst, New Jersey, and he was present on the ground when the *Hindenburg* exploded there in 1937. He witnessed the tragedy and testified at the official inquest. In September 1942, he went to sea, commanding the cruiser USS *Minneapolis*. It was torpedoed in the Battle of Tassafaronga, losing eighty feet of its bow, but he managed to save the ship and received the Navy Cross for heroism.

Bautzer shared Rosendahl's enthusiasm for blimps. The navy was building an airship fleet, and Bautzer wanted to serve in it. He wrote a request for transfer to the lighter-than-air (LTA) division, detailing everything he could imagine that might help his case. The document made many extravagant assertions. Bautzer said that he was president of his law school class. He professed familiarity with Pacific Coast hydrography and topography. He claimed to have taken correspondence courses in navigation, gunnery, seamanship, and naval regulations and customs. He also claimed that he had served on a Merchant Marine vessel called the SS *Calaw II*. There was no such ship—but he had, of course, worked in the field of *Ca*lifornia *law*. Finally, he proclaimed an extensive acquaintanceship with blimp technology, citing the titles of numerous books and journals. This far-fetched application was endorsed by Captain C. F. Russell, director of enlisted personnel, even though he noted that Bautzer had no actual naval training.

Bautzer passed his physical at Anacostia Naval Air Station, but before his application for assignment to the LTA division could be considered, the navy realized he wasn't technically qualified to be an officer. In August 1942, Bautzer was detached from active duty and ordered home. A memo dated September 26 informed him that he lacked sufficient training for active duty.

He could, however, request a hearing to challenge his dismissal— welcome news to someone who had been persuading judges and juries. On October 5, Bautzer appeared before Captain G. V. Stewart, USN (retired), to plead his case. Whatever Bautzer said, it worked. Stewart recommended that Bautzer be retained. Five days later, Randall Jacks, chief of naval personnel, wrote a note for Bautzer's file: "This officer will be sent to sea." But the next document to enter Bautzer's file was a page torn from a desk calendar with the notation "Asst. Chief has indicated that assignment to lighter than air will be OK—MD." Admiral Rosendahl had probably pulled some strings. Bautzer was saved from duty at sea and admitted to the LTA program.

The United States was the only country to use airships in World War II. Rigid-frame dirigibles were too expensive and dangerous, so the government ordered a fleet of 168 nonrigid blimps from Goodyear Corporation. The helium-filled K-2 blimp was 253 feet long and 60 feet in diameter. Powered by two 425-horsepower engines, its top speed was 50 miles per hour. The K-2 was used for search and rescue, photographic reconnaissance, scouting, minesweeping, and anti-submarine patrols. Blimps also escorted ships. A blimp crew could spot a German U-boat and radio its position to a ship on the surface. This was vital; in the first six months of 1942, U-boats had sunk 454 merchant ships. By 1943, thanks in part to blimp reconnaissance, the number had dropped to 65. Unlike airplanes, blimps could hover, and, if necessary, drop a depth charge and sink a U-boat. Blimps could also rescue survivors of sinking vessels and planes.

In October 1942, Bautzer reported to Lakehurst, New Jersey, for active duty. A physical examination revealed that he had ten missing teeth, including three of his front teeth, which had been replaced with a bridge.* His height measured 73 inches; weight, 176 lbs.; chest, 37

---

*According to a law school buddy, Judge Robert Gardner, Bautzer lost his front teeth in a fight on the beach behind the Rendezvous Ballroom on Balboa Island. Fights behind the Rendezvous were very common at the time, Gardner recalled, and fun to watch. The judge also said the false teeth were a big improvement on Bautzer's natural teeth.

inches; waist, 32 inches. Prior surgeries included a tonsillectomy and his recent appendectomy. He was certified physically fit for duty.

Even though Bautzer was away from Hollywood, his legal services were still in demand. In October 1942, Ensign Dan Cavalier, who was on duty with Bautzer at Lakehurst, answered a telephone ringing late at night. "Is Bautzer there?" asked an unidentified male caller. Cavalier handed the phone to Bautzer.

"Greg listened for a while," recalled Cavalier. "Then he told the guy that he couldn't drop everything and go back to Los Angeles. He was an officer in the navy now and they wouldn't give him enough time off to handle the case. The guy kept insisting, and Greg kept trying to tell him no. This went on for quite a while. Finally, Greg had had enough and said it was simply impossible. He was sorry, but he couldn't take the case."

Bautzer hung up. "That was Errol Flynn," Cavalier recalled Bautzer telling him. "He was just charged with statutory rape, and he wants me to handle the case."

The situation was serious. Flynn, an Australian born in Tasmania, had been naturalized in August and wanted to serve for the United States, but was classified 4-F. He had become a star playing strenuous physical scenes in films like *The Sea Hawk* but had numerous health problems. On October 15, he was questioned by a grand jury, under accusations of having had sex with an underage girl at the Bel Air home of British bobsled champion Fred McEvoy on September 27. After hearing witnesses, the grand jury declined to indict Flynn. One day later, District Attorney John F. Dockweiler chided the grand jury for ignoring evidence and filed a complaint.

"I was absolutely flabbergasted," recalled Cavalier. "The following day, it was in all the papers. I couldn't believe it was *the* Errol Flynn. I knew Greg was a Hollywood playboy, but I didn't know he was such a powerful lawyer. I got the impression that Flynn was a steady client. Greg was actually a bit annoyed that Flynn would think he could drop everything and come back to Los Angeles."

Flynn was arraigned on October 22, and he engaged Jerry Giesler's services. When another underage girl came forward, claiming that Flynn had also had sex with her on his yacht the previous year, the prosecutor combined the charges against him into one complaint. The case went to trial in January. Giesler let the defendants (who looked older than teenagers) give their accounts. The girl on the yacht claimed to have seen the moon through a porthole in Flynn's stateroom just before they had sex. The district attorney put an astronomer on the witness stand to back up the girl's story about the moon. Giesler, however, demonstrated that she could not have seen the moon through the porthole, because it was only visible from the other side of the ship. Flynn was acquitted in February. Giesler got the credit. But the fact that a major star would seek Bautzer before Giesler in a high-profile case said a great deal about the young attorney's standing at that time.

Bautzer was promoted to full lieutenant on January 5, 1943. His training took him to the Richmond Naval Air Station in Florida to pilot new blimps back to Lakehurst. The bridge of the K-2 blimp was about the size of a bus. There was a crew of ten. The commander sat in front on the port side, the elevator man to his right. Radio and radar operators sat behind them. The crew also included a bombardier and a mechanic. The average mission lasted twelve hours, so there was a fold-down bunk and a hot plate for heating food.

On August 1, 1943, Bautzer was assigned to command Blimp Squadron 15, which was based in Glynn County, Georgia, at Glynco Naval Air Station. "Greg seemed to be a loner," wrote Ensign John Fahey, years later. "He was in his thirties, older than the base commander and other senior officers, but junior to them in rank. Most of us were junior officers in our early twenties. Senior officers did little flying, and although Bautzer was not a senior officer, he didn't do much flying either. Most of the time he was happy to spend his time sunning himself on the patio of the bachelor officer's quarters." Fahey worked in the communications office in the airship hangar. One day he answered the phone and a woman asked for Bautzer. When she identified herself as Paulette Goddard, Fahey couldn't believe he was speaking with a movie star. "Bautzer was in a different world," recalled Fahey.

Later in August, Bautzer's aunt Cecile wrote to tell him that his grandmother had died in St. Louis. Cecile Bautzer Smith had written to the navy for his address; she was his only living relative, and he had not answered her recent correspondence. About the same time, Bautzer requested that he be reassigned from active flight duty to performing only executive work in headquarters. His stated reason for requesting the change was to gain experience in construction and maintenance, but he more likely wanted to get away from young crews. He was authoritative and sophisticated, and found no common ground with youths from the provinces. Bautzer's new duties in Squadron 15 consisted mainly of designing training programs for blimp crews, something he would do for the rest of the war.

As a headquarters staff officer, Bautzer was privy to one of the more colorful events that occurred at Glynco. On August 28, blimp pilot Jack P. Hely IV was in command of the K-34 that was escorting the merchant marine ship *Albert Gallatin* off the coast of Georgia, not far from Savannah. He suddenly saw that the onboard magnetic anomaly detector (MAD) was registering the presence of a submarine. Hely spotted the periscope of a U-boat, and then saw two torpedoes streaking toward the *Albert Gallatin*. Hely ordered his crew to drop two sets of depth charges. The torpedoes missed the ship and the depth charges missed the submarine. Hely maneuvered the blimp in search of the U-boat and got another MAD contact. He dropped more depth charges. There was no visible effect, so he returned to Glynco. His report was marked TOP SECRET and sent to Navy intelligence, where it was filed as an "Unconfirmed Incident." Years later, naval blimp historian Richard van Treuren tracked down the commander of the U-boat, Volker Zimmermacher, who confirmed the veracity of the encounter that had occurred so close to the US mainland. Because Bautzer was a senior officer, it is certain that he was briefed on the incident and sworn to secrecy.

In late 1943, Admiral Rosendahl, who was the LTA division's chief liaison to the motion picture industry, called on Bautzer for a different kind of military assistance. MGM wanted to make a film about the blimp fleet to be called *This Man's Navy*. Bautzer wrote to studio manager Edward Mannix to learn more. "Borden Chase, who wrote *Fighting Seabees* for Republic, *Destroyer* for Columbia, and *The Navy Comes Through* for RKO, is working on the script," replied Mannix. "As for the cast, at present it looks like Wallace Beery as the Mate, and we need a good boy to play opposite him." Mannix also thought that a song might help to put over the story. This intrigued Bautzer, who then wrote to Rosendahl offering to travel to New York and enlist the services of his friend Irving Berlin. If the world's most famous tunesmith wasn't available, then Bautzer had ideas for other Broadway composers who could pen the music, many of whom he said were his clients.

This Man's Navy was directed by William Wellman, a World War I fighter pilot who had made the aviation epic *Wings*, winner of the first Academy Award for Best Picture. In one scene in the new film, shot at Moffett Field in Sunnyvale, California, Wellman and his crew filmed a spectacular formation of ten blimps, the largest ever caught on film. Admiral Rosendahl sent Bautzer the positive reviews of *This Man's Navy* in the *Hollywood Reporter* and *Variety*. Unfortunately, Bautzer had not been able to convince MGM to create a theme song. But he was able to give Rosendahl another kind of gift. "Not until I heard you express a desire for a Norwegian Elkhound the other day . . . ," wrote Bautzer, "have I had the opportunity to, in some small measure, evidence my sincere gratitude to you for your assistance in helping me get into LTA. With the help of the Norwegian Consul in New York, I finally located what is supposed to be the best of a litter from a breeder of champions in Bethel, Connecticut." Bautzer also gave Rosendahl a Tourneau wristwatch.

In early 1944, Bautzer was ordered to Recife, Brazil, a strategic command center for Atlantic operations. But before he was detached from Squadron 15, there was some personal business to which he needed to attend. He was getting married again.

Buff Cobb was the stage name of aspiring actress Patrizia Chapman. She was born in Florence, Italy, in 1927 to Frank Chapman Jr. and Elizabeth "Buffy" Cobb. Chapman's father had been dean of the American Museum of Natural History. Elizabeth's father was the writer and actor Irvin S. Cobb, who was famous for the Kentucky humor of his *Saturday Evening Post* stories. Frank and Elizabeth divorced in 1930. Two years later, Chapman married the Metropolitan Opera star Gladys Swarthout. In 1936 (the same year Bautzer was finishing law school), nine-year-old Patrizia moved to Santa Monica with her father and stepmother. Swarthout had signed a contract with Paramount Pictures. She made five films, but could not compete with Jeanette MacDonald and Grace Moore, so she returned to concert work. Patrizia's grandfather did better in films; Irvin Cobb sold his Judge Priest stories to Fox Film, acted in movies there, and hosted the 1935 Academy Awards. Hoping to follow in his footsteps, Patrizia adopted both her grandfather's surname and a variation of her mother's nickname.

Buff Cobb was sixteen when she met Bautzer. They were introduced at the Washington home of Henry Luce, publisher of *Time*, *Fortune*, and *Life* magazines. The Luces were like family to Buff. Clare Boothe Luce, the acclaimed playwright of *The Women* and a congresswoman from Connecticut's Fourth District, was Buff's mother's best friend from their boarding school days. No doubt Bautzer saw the advantages of knowing the Luces—to marry Cobb would be to "marry up." Likewise, it is possible that Cobb viewed him as another avenue to Hollywood, although he made a point of telling her that he had no interest in being married to an actress. They were lucky to meet at all, since Bautzer's leaves were both infrequent and short, a two-day pass in August 1943 and a ten-day pass the following month. They made the most of these interludes and announced their engagement in February 1944.

Clare, whose own daughter had been killed in an auto accident the month before, helped Elizabeth with Buff's wedding. The modest event took place on February 22, 1944, at the Episcopal Church in Rockville, Maryland. Army captain Bentley Ryan, Bautzer's law partner, served as best man. The reception was held at the Raleigh Hotel and featured entertainment by Gladys Swarthout.

Bautzer had planned a week-long honeymoon in Sea Island, Georgia, but it was not to be. "The day I was married, I received a telegram from the squadron advising me my orders had arrived," Bautzer wrote Jean Rosendahl, Admiral Rosendahl's wife. "I spent my wedding night trying to convince my wife that I really didn't know they were on their way. I hope I convinced her. I tried!" The newlyweds spent only two nights together before Bautzer left Washington to report to Miami for a transfer to Brazil. In his March 7 letter to Jean Rosendahl, Bautzer enthused about his new wife, calling her his "child bride" and praising her sense of humor, intelligence, and tolerance. "I guess I sound pretty much like a bridegroom—and after only a couple of nights—but Buff's so wonderful I just have to tell you about her." Bautzer thought he had found a perfect navy wife.

Shortly after the wedding, Buff's grandfather, the "man who made millions laugh," died on March 11, 1944. Irvin S. Cobb's funeral was attended by over twelve hundred people. Bautzer's duties in Brazil prevented him from attending.

A few months later, Bautzer wrote to Admiral Rosendahl, requesting a new assignment. "If we are proceeding to the Pacific, I'd like to be in on it," wrote Bautzer. "Fortunately, Buff is reconciled to my desires and the fact that I won't be able to spend much time with her until after the war's over. Maybe she prefers it that way!" Bautzer filled out two military insurance slips designating his wife as beneficiary (but neglecting to provide a name).

In Bahia, Brazil, Bautzer befriended a fellow pilot, Lieutenant Charles McDougall. Bautzer's piloting duties were a puzzler for McDougall. "He was always in the Officer's Club," recalled McDougall. "In the four months we were friends, I don't think I ever saw him go on a mission." Bautzer's military duties included entertaining Admiral J. H. Ingram, commander of the Atlantic Fleet in South America. "Ingram liked having Bautzer around," said McDougall. "He was ten years older than most of the guys and already a celebrity." When Ingram came by on a two-day inspection of the base, Bautzer invited McDougall to play cards with them. "The admiral liked to play bridge, so Bautzer asked me to be his bridge partner. They played for ten cents a point, which was a lot of money in those days. I told Bautzer that I couldn't afford to gamble that much. He said, 'Don't worry. These guys aren't any good. I'll cover your losses.' Well, I won more money in those two days playing with the admiral than I did in my entire life."

McDougall figured out why Bautzer had taken a shine to him. "Because, first, after Greg, I was the second-best bridge player in the outfit. And, second, Greg was clearly smarter than everyone else, and since I had attended Caltech, he thought I was the only one who was on his intellectual level." McDougall enjoyed Bautzer's stories about Hollywood and his law career. "For a guy who was in his early thirties," recalled McDougall, "he seemed like he already had a lifetime of experience."

Being newly married didn't keep Bautzer from having a pretty girl on his arm. "Bautzer was about the most handsome guy I ever met, and he certainly didn't have to try hard to get girls," said McDougall. "There was one woman I remember in particular who was a very famous entertainer in Brazil. She had an act like Carmen Miranda at the Copacabana Palace Hotel in Rio with a big headdress. Bautzer was dating this Brazilian star like there was nothing unusual about it."

Bautzer's wartime marriage did not last long. In August, he received a "Dear John" letter from Buff. She had met someone new and fallen in love. She wanted a divorce. Although Bautzer wrote Rosendahl saying he was emotionally upset by the break-up, it is doubtful that his depression lingered. Cobb did not achieve a film career, but her stage work led to a stint on television's first talk show. Her cohost, Mike Wallace, was her second husband. She would remain friends with Bautzer long after their brief marriage ended, even throwing him a party upon his return from service and introducing him to her roommate, whom he briefly dated.

In late 1944, Bautzer saw the war coming to an end and wanted to serve overseas while he still could. He requested a transfer to Mediterranean operations in North Africa. His request was granted, and he was put in command of a blimp in Squadron 14 at Port Lyautey, French Morocco. Once in Morocco, Bautzer resumed a routine of sun, sports, and privacy. "Bautzer was a lot older than the other guys in the group," recalled Fred Kroll, who was then a twenty-five-year-old ensign. "He had a lot of self-confidence and a certain air of superiority." Kroll never saw Bautzer flying, just playing volleyball behind a Quonset hut. "He kept himself in excellent physical shape, and he could beat just about anyone on the volleyball court." Kroll believed Bautzer's duties mainly involved handling legal documents. One day Kroll went to the legal department to help a local boy with US immigration procedures and saw Bautzer working on what he thought were legal papers, although they could have been training manuals.

Bautzer knew what the LTA program meant to Admiral Rosendahl, and he constantly looked for an opportunity to express his enthusiasm. On one occasion he managed to learn one of the best-kept secrets of the war. An officer had confided to him what he heard from a captured German, and Bautzer conveyed it to Rosendahl. "I was talking to an officer while passing through Recife, and he told me that several of the German survivors who had served on U-boats reported that blimp coverage on a particular convoy—observed through the periscope—had precluded the U-boats from attacking the convoy. . . . Apparently the sub saw the blimp several times while at periscope depth, and the submarine commander would not attack, permitting the convoy to escape."

Bautzer's letter to Rosendahl may be one of the earliest written reports that U-boat commanders avoided attacking convoys when escorted by blimps. Rosendahl was pleased to hear this news. "I do hope their statements go into the official files in Washington," he wrote Bautzer, admitting the possibility that they would not. Additional confirmation of the blimps' effectiveness could have been provided by a military intelligence unit known as the Tenth Fleet. The name was a misnomer, since it had no ships—it was a top-secret operation that spied on U-boats. Not even senior officers such as Rosendahl had access to Tenth Fleet files. Years later, under the Freedom of Information Act, researchers found documents in those files confirming that blimps had deterred U-boat attacks. This information never reached LTA commanders, possibly because the program was held in low regard by navy traditionalists, who preferred funding to go to ships and airplanes.

On May 8, 1945, Germany surrendered and the war in Europe came to a halt. After a stopover in Cairo, Bautzer was put in charge of the LTA base at Pisa, Italy, where he was promoted to the rank of lieutenant commander on July 10. A little more than a month later, on August 26, Bautzer received telephone orders to report to Naval

Operations in Washington. On October 26, Bautzer was given two months and twenty-seven days of leave, at the expiration of which, at midnight, January 22, 1946, he was to be released from all active duty. He gave his law firm's office address as his home address.

Bautzer returned to Los Angeles in late 1945 to await his formal discharge. In the wee hours of Sunday, December 16, he was taken into custody by two radio patrol officers, Charles Cirker and Stuart Morton. The *Los Angeles Times* reported that Bautzer "got heavy" during a conversation with them, which may have meant that he was belligerent, possibly violent. After spending a few hours in jail, he was bailed out by three unnamed lawyers and scheduled to appear at a hearing the following morning. He failed to show up. Municipal Judge Ben Rosenthal ordered his twenty-dollar bail forfeited. The newspaper article described Bautzer as the "squire of numerous screen stars around Hollywood's night spots." He was thirty-four. Like thousands of other returning soldiers, he would need to create a new life.

IV

PLAYERS

8

TOE TO TOE WITH
BUGSY SIEGEL

Gregson Bautzer grew up on the waterfront and went to war in the air. The next phase of his life would drop him in the desert. After his discharge from the navy, he returned to his law practice—and to a surprise. Bentley Ryan was leaving to become an associate director of the Del Mar Beach Club in Santa Monica. Bautzer and Bernard Silbert removed Ryan's name from the office door in the Equitable Building and got back to work. Bautzer had no residence to return to, so he moved in with Billy Wilkerson at his mansion on Sunset Boulevard. By this time, Wilkerson and Joe Schenck were more than mentors to Bautzer. They were his adopted family. They were also both troubled.

Joseph Schenck was recovering from a major scandal. In 1940, a federal grand jury found that he had paid a bribe of $100,000 to a man named Willie Bioff so that the racketeer would call off a nationwide strike of the International Alliance of Theatrical and Stage Employees (IATSE). Schenck was indicted on charges of conspiracy, perjury, and income tax evasion. In April of 1941, he was convicted on the tax charge and sentenced to three years in prison. He had testified against Bioff, so his sentence was suspended, but he still had to serve four months and five days. It is widely believed that all the studios paid Bioff, but Schenck was the only mogul to be charged. President Truman pardoned him after he'd served part of his sentence. Bioff later testified against his Mafia cohorts, ending an ugly period of racketeering in Hollywood. Schenck returned and signed a ten-year contract as head of production at Twentieth Century-Fox.

Wilkerson had helped Bautzer meet Schenck; now Wilkerson needed his help. "The first thing I know," recalled Bautzer, "on the first day I was home, Billy Wilkerson wants to send me over to Las Vegas to buy a chunk of property." There was a compelling reason for this errand. Though Wilkerson's restaurants and the *Hollywood Reporter* were doing well, he was not. His gambling was out of control. His daily schedule was determined not by business but by cards, craps, and the racetrack. In the first quarter of 1944, he gambled away the newspaper's annual profits. In the second quarter, he devoured the advertising receipts of his paper and his restaurants. By the third quarter, his gambling losses were approaching $1 million. Not even he could deny his addiction.

Schenck gave him some advice. "Be on the other side of the table if you're going to suffer those kind of losses," he said. "Build a casino. Own the house."

The idea struck a chord. Building a casino would gratify Wilkerson's two passions—entrepreneurship and gambling. He already had experience running a casino. In 1939, he helped Schenck and CBS founder William Paley with the ailing Arrowhead Springs Hotel, a resort in the California town of Lake Arrowhead in which they had both invested. Signing on as owner-operator for a year, Wilkerson improved the hotel's appearance and it began to show a profit. But there was another explanation for its rising word-of-mouth popularity: it had card games. In 1938, authorities had cracked down on gambling in Los Angeles. Wilkerson and his partners hoped that Arrowhead was not too far from the city for frustrated gamblers to make the trip but sufficiently remote to elude detection. Before long, gamblers started making the three-hour drive to Lake Arrowhead. The setting was sublime, but they saw little of it. Their eyes were fixed on the gaming tables. The makeshift casino didn't last long. In less than a year, the tables were smashed. US marshals raided the hotel, destroyed gaming paraphernalia, and shuttered the premises. Wilkerson barely avoided charges, and he vowed that he would never again run an illegal operation.

Fortunately for Wilkerson, gambling was legal in Nevada. In 1945, it was the only place in the country where it was. Most of the games were in Reno or Carson City, the capital. Las Vegas had a few gambling halls in the downtown area, but the only quality establishments were El Rancho Vegas and El Cortez. Both had opened in 1941, introducing Las Vegas to the concept of a combined hotel and casino. Wilkerson was drawn to the two properties' gambling parlors but not to their hotels. They were quaint, Western-themed, and dull. Other than gambling, there was nothing to attract wealthy travelers to Las Vegas, inside or out. It was hot and windblown, only a stop on the way to someplace else. Still, Wilkerson saw its potential.

One day in January 1945, Wilkerson had just left the tables at El Rancho and was headed for the airport. "When I feel the table turn cold," he said, "I leave the casino." His business associate Tom Seward was with him. Seward was used to seeing Wilkerson bet the *Reporter* payroll. "I watched Billy gamble my future away," Seward said later. Looking out the window of their taxicab, Wilkerson saw a FOR SALE sign at the corner of a lot on Highway 91. The large parcel of land was distinguished by nothing more than the ruins of a motor hotel. "Take that number down," Wilkerson directed Seward.

The lot consisted of thirty-three acres located several miles from the other gambling dens. Wilkerson began negotiating with its owner, one Margaret M. Folsom, who had formerly operated a brothel in Hawaii. By early March, she and Wilkerson had reached an agreement, sealed by a check for $9,500—though the exact nature of this deal is unclear. According to Wilkerson's son, W. R. "Willie" Wilkerson III, author of *The Man Who Invented Las Vegas*, the lot was divided into two separate parcels. Willie Wilkerson believes that his father first bought a ten-acre parcel with the $9,500, leaving the remaining twenty-three acres in the hands of Folsom. What is known for certain is that Wilkerson would not conclude the purchase of the entire lot until Bautzer's return from the war later that year. Meanwhile, Wilkerson hired architect George Vernon Russell and decorator Tom Douglas, both of whom had worked on his Sunset Strip niteries. This commission was more ambitious. What Wilkerson envisioned was something like the casinos he had seen on the French Riviera in the 1920s: a lavish, exclusive resort. He had already brought Paris to Hollywood. Bringing Monte Carlo to Las Vegas would pull the high rollers from Beverly Hills. His vision included a hotel, shops, a casino, a nightclub, a restaurant, a café, a gymnasium with steam rooms, an outdoor swimming pool, and courts for tennis, badminton, and squash. This array of entertainment would make the gambler stay longer and spend more. The resort would be a pleasure dome in the desert.

The project needed a name. Wilkerson thought of the fabled watering holes he had known in New York. One of his favorites was the Stork Club. He thought about birds. He came up with the name Flamingo.

Before he could begin construction, he had to finalize the purchase of the land. Even though Bautzer was still technically in the navy when he arrived back in Los Angeles in November 1945, Wilkerson saw him as the ideal negotiator. "So there I was," recalled Bautzer, "still in my lieutenant's uniform, trying to buy up this property. In those days there wasn't much. Just a lot of bare land." Apparently Folsom had become more difficult to deal with since Wilkerson paid her $9,500 for the first ten-acre parcel. Perhaps she had realized the full extent of Wilkerson's plans and that he could not complete his

dream project without the twenty-three acres she still held. Whatever
the reason, she now wanted much more per acre. Negotiating directly,
without a lawyer representing her, Folsom drove a hard bargain. The
madam and the lieutenant commander went back and forth for an
entire day and then haggled into the night. By the next morning, Folsom had agreed to a selling price of $84,000 for the rest of the land.

Two deeds were signed on November 21, 1945. The first was
recorded under the name of Moe Sedway, and the second was signed
by Gregson Bautzer, acting as agent for William R. Wilkerson. Who
was Sedway? He was not part of Wilkerson's Hollywood contingent.
He was the owner of El Cortez. Why was he involved in the transaction? Wilkerson, for all his entrepreneurial savvy, knew relatively little
about operating a large-scale gambling den. He was also encountering
permit problems and shortages of material due to wartime restric-
tions. He needed contacts in local politics, so he turned to Sedway
and his business partner, Gus Greenbaum. It is not known if Wilkerson researched his new associates. If he had, he would have learned
that Sedway worked for Meyer Lansky, a major East Coast gangster,
and that Greenbaum was an Arizona bookmaker with a police record.

At first, Wilkerson merely contracted with these men to secure
permits, oversee construction, and operate the gambling concession.
But before long, it became obvious that Wilkerson's concept would
require more cash than he had budgeted. Worse, his gambling debts
were growing. At one point, in an act of self-abnegation, he transferred
the first parcel of land to Sedway—hence, the name on the first deed.

Schenck thought this ill advised and helped Wilkerson buy it
back. Still, Wilkerson needed more capital. In February 1946, a mysterious businessman named G. Harry Rothberg approached him with
a timely, tantalizing offer. A New York firm wanted to invest in the
Flamingo, and a consortium of investors would fund the project in
exchange for a two-thirds interest. In reality, G. Harry Rothberg was
fronting for Meyer Lansky. Wilkerson was willing to accept the offer,

but only if he could control the hotel and own the land. His terms were accepted. Although he later professed ignorance, Wilkerson may have known that Rothberg, a former bootlegger, was representing Lansky. After all, Wilkerson had run a speakeasy during Prohibition. Regardless of his new partner's questionable affiliations, Wilkerson signed the deal, and in March 1946 took delivery of $1 million.

A month later, Wilkerson was at the construction site when Sedway and Greenbaum arrived with a friend who was visiting from Los Angeles. Wilkerson immediately recognized the man as someone who frequented his establishments on the Sunset Strip. Benjamin "Bugsy" Siegel was a fixture on the Strip, often escorting starlets such as Wendy Barrie and Lana Turner. But he was known for more than where he ate or who was on his arm—he was a notorious criminal, arrested in 1940 for the murder of mob informant Harry Greenberg. And Siegel was no small-time crook; he was a powerful figure in organized crime. While awaiting trial and being defended by Jerry Giesler, Siegel's meals were catered by Ciro's, and he was spirited out of jail for conjugal visits to girlfriends. Two witnesses were murdered, and the case was closed for lack of evidence, so Siegel returned to mob business, which in his case meant importing drugs from Mexico. His presence in Las Vegas confirmed that Lansky was behind Rothberg's Flamingo investment. Beyond that, Wilkerson did not ask questions. When interviewed years later, Bautzer gave a defense lawyer's explanation for Billy's decision to continue doing business with known mobsters: "It was Billy's decision to concern himself with the eventual outcome and success of the project rather than with connections his business associates might have had."

When Siegel was not in trouble with the law, he was on the fringes of Hollywood, hobnobbing with stars like his childhood friend George Raft and romancing society matrons like Countess Dorothy Di Frasso. He was good-looking, well-dressed, and charming. "A real gentleman," recalled George Kennedy, general manager of

Wilkerson's *Hollywood Reporter*. "He could charm the wrappings off a mummy." Underneath the calculated charm was a reptilian killer with a hair-trigger temper. The slightest misstep was sufficient to send him into a violent rage. "His face would darken when he got angry," recalled Bautzer, "and his blue eyes were known to turn a slate gray color." Legend had it that he shot a newsboy for doing nothing more than hawking a newspaper with the name Bugsy on it. This was the nickname he had earned for his fits of temper. He loathed it and warned associates never to use it. "Anyone who knew Siegel took his threats seriously," said Bautzer.

Siegel respected Wilkerson, but neither man was happy when Lansky assigned Siegel to monitor the project. Siegel disliked Las Vegas for its heat and isolation. "Why would anyone want to come here?" he asked.

"People will go anywhere, endure almost anything, where there is legal gambling," replied Wilkerson.

Siegel assured Wilkerson that Rothberg's investors would not interfere in the building of the Flamingo, yet Siegel himself began telling workmen how to do things. Wilkerson was first astonished, then annoyed. In the beginning, Siegel had been deferential, treating Wilkerson like a sage. Now he was competitive and obstreperous. Siegel demanded more say in the project, so Wilkerson let him oversee construction of the hotel, providing him with architect Richard Stadelman and Phoenix contractor Del Webb. Wilkerson continued to oversee the casino, restaurant, and amenities. There were two discrete companies. Siegel began to see them as rivals. He convinced himself that he—not Wilkerson—had conceived the project. He forbade mention of Wilkerson's name in his presence.

"Billy was sticking to his budget," recalled Bautzer. "Siegel was out of control." In May 1946, Siegel demanded that the original agreement with Rothberg be changed to give him full control of construction. What he offered in exchange was 5 percent additional ownership.

Wilkerson agreed, and Siegel blundered ahead, making needless, costly changes to the plans, and completely mismanaging the project.

Siegel was obsessed with owning the entire concern, but Wilkerson still owned the land. Siegel offered to buy it from him for another 5 percent of the Flamingo. Wilkerson agreed to sell half the land. Siegel used the land as collateral for a loan but quickly ran through the money. In late November, Siegel pressured Wilkerson to cosign for a $600,000 loan using Wilkerson's remaining half-interest in the land as collateral. "Billy was in a difficult spot," said Bautzer. If Wilkerson signed, he would be sucked into a whirlpool of corruption and insanity. If he did not sign, he might kill the project and lose his investment. Wilkerson signed, hoping that the hotel would be finished by early 1947. To his dismay, Siegel decided to open the day after Christmas 1946. Wilkerson enumerated the reasons not to open during the holidays. "I'm the one who makes the decisions!" Siegel shrieked at him.

For all his foibles and missteps, Wilkerson remained a devout Roman Catholic, attending Mass regularly and saying the Rosary in times of crisis. He believed in miracles. He also had earthly patrons. In early December, he received a call from J. Edgar Hoover, director of the FBI. Hoover quietly warned Wilkerson that the mob was contemplating a takeover of the Flamingo project and that his life might be in danger. The syndicate was most likely interested because Siegel had lost control. He was calling attention to himself and, more to the point, had spent $6 million without having a hotel to show for it. An accounting was due. Siegel sensed it and decided to take up the slack.

Siegel called a meeting at the construction site. With him were his lawyers, Louis Wiener and Clifford A. Jones, the latter of whom was also the lieutenant governor of the state of Nevada. Wilkerson brought Bautzer with him. Siegel wasted no time. He had none to waste; the Christmas opening was two weeks away. He addressed Wilkerson. "You're gonna have to part with your portion of the interest," said Siegel. "You're not gonna be paid anything for it, and you'd better have all the interest in hand."

"Just a minute," said Bautzer. "Are you telling this man, who has a legal and valid right to that interest, that he's gonna have to part with it? Cause he's not gonna 'have to do' anything."

"He's gonna have to do this," Siegel explained. "I've sold one hundred fifty percent of this deal, and I don't have one hundred fifty percent—only one hundred percent—and everybody's gonna have to cut, including Wilkerson."

"Well, you'd better figure another way out," snapped Bautzer, "'cause he ain't gonna cut."

Siegel jumped to his feet and snarled at Bautzer. "I can only tell you if I don't deliver the interest to the people in the East, I'm gonna be killed." Then he turned to Wilkerson. "And before I go, you're gonna go first. And don't take that lightly. I'll kill you if I don't get that interest."

Bautzer leapt to his feet also. "Sit down and shut up!" he yelled at Siegel. For a moment there was silence. Everyone was shocked to see Bautzer confront Siegel toe to toe. Even Siegel was surprised. Bautzer told Wilkerson to leave the room for his protection, then addressed Wiener and Jones. "You'd better shut this guy up 'cause I'm gonna make an affidavit—on the remarks Mr. Siegel has made at this meeting and who was present. I'm sending one copy to the district attorney of Los Angeles. I'm sending one copy to the district attorney of the county here in Las Vegas. I'm sending one copy to the attorney general. And I'm sending one copy to the FBI. And if Siegel is wise, or his 'associates' are, they'd better make sure Mr. Wilkerson doesn't accidentally fall down a flight of stairs. They'd better make sure he doesn't sprain an ankle walking off a curb, because that affidavit is going to be in the hands of those men, and I'm going to be prepared to testify—like all the rest of you are going to have to testify—as to the statements Mr. Siegel has made. So you'd better be goddamned sure Mr. Wilkerson enjoys a very long and happy life."

Siegel's attorneys tried to calm Bautzer. They didn't want their names in an affidavit alongside Siegel's. "Nothing is going to happen to him!" They sputtered assurances. "Take it easy, Greg! There's no need for affidavits!"

"That's what I'm gonna do and he'd better be made aware by you gentlemen that represent him of the consequences if anything does happen to Mr. Wilkerson."

Bautzer stormed out of the meeting. As he and Wilkerson left the building, Wilkerson turned to him and said, "I have something very unflattering to tell you—I just wet my pants."

Bautzer went back to the hotel where he and Wilkerson were staying and wrote his affidavit. The usually ebullient Wilkerson was quiet. In a few days, he went to Paris and hid out in the Hotel George V. He told Bautzer that the best thing to do was to wait for Siegel to foul up the opening and anger the syndicate. Bautzer thought he'd do better to sell. "Forty-eight percent of this deal is rightfully mine," said Wilkerson. "Why the hell should I sell?" That he had to hide out might have reminded him why. He spent Christmas in Paris.

The Flamingo opened, on schedule but unfinished. The opening was both poorly organized and executed. Reviews were curdled. Siegel continued to spend. His attorneys asked Bautzer what Wilkerson would take to relinquish his share. Bautzer asked for $2 million and a release of all liability. Siegel agreed to the release, but only offered $300,000. At Bautzer's recommendation, Wilkerson dropped his demand to $1 million. When Siegel rose to $600,000, Wilkerson accepted. His partner Tom Seward went to retrieve the first installment. Siegel was droll. "If your partner were here right now," said Siegel, "I'd blow his fucking brains out."

By April, the Flamingo had begun to show a profit. Wilkerson returned to Beverly Hills, where he received an anonymous call from a woman who claimed to be the wife of a man hired to kill him. "There was every chance that it was a bluff," said Bautzer, "but I advised Billy not to take the risk." He sent Billy to hide out again in Paris. Back at the Hotel George V, Wilkerson received a cable from Seward. On June 20, 1947, Benjamin Siegel had been shot to death in the rented Beverly Hills home of his girlfriend, Virginia Hill. While the murder was taking place, Bautzer was enjoying dinner with actress Greer Garson at the Bel-Air Hotel a short distance away. Siegel's murder was never solved, although there was speculation that the syndicate wanted satisfaction for its misspent millions. The Flamingo passed quietly into the hands of Sedway and Greenbaum.

"Siegel was not the right choice to head an operation like the Flamingo," said Bautzer. "He was a paranoid man who had no business masterminding a multi-million dollar deal. He exhibited no experience building anything. He was in way over his head. I blame the principals associated with Siegel, who let him get away with it, as much as I do Siegel. The Flamingo wound up being the most expensive hotel ever built in the world at the time."

Bautzer was back in action. The town was abuzz with talk of his courage in dealing with Siegel. His practice started to thrive again. As for Wilkerson, he never set foot in the Flamingo. He would conquer his addiction in an unexpected way. In October 1951, his sixth wife, Tichi, gave birth to a son, William R. Wilkerson III, whom they called "Willie." Fatherhood calmed Wilkerson's spirit, and he never gambled again.

9

LOVER DEAREST

On March 7, 1946, Joan Crawford won the Academy Award for Best Actress. Her sensitive, nuanced performance in *Mildred Pierce* had revived her stalled career and lifted it to new heights. Once again, Hollywood was hers. Since shooting to stardom in silent films, she had survived the transition to talkies, the label "box-office poison," three husbands, and an ouster from her home studio, MGM. After twenty years, she was the only silent star still packing them in.

Upon his return from the navy, Bautzer briefly dated Lana Turner again, but it didn't last long, and soon he was looking for another star to date. His thoughts turned to Crawford. He had, of course, secretly been involved with her before the war while he was engaged to Turner. He had also provided legal services to Crawford, helping the single working woman adopt two children from out-of-state adoption agencies. Now, Bautzer was free of entanglements, and he liked the idea of dating an Oscar winner. Crawford was forty-one, at the height of her beauty, and divorcing her latest husband, actor Philip Terry. "The rest of the world may think that the life of a Hollywood bachelor girl is the best ever," said Crawford, "but I get lonesome." Bautzer was thirty-five and ready for a major conquest.

Crawford needed a rest after the flurry of Oscar publicity and she chose La Quinta, a desert resort north of Palm Springs. Bautzer had tried to reach her for weeks before she left town. He sent bouquets and gifts, but she ignored his calls, perhaps still resentful about the Turner episode. Upon learning Crawford was going on vacation, Bautzer bribed her secretary for her itinerary. He knew that driving to La Quinta to surprise the diva would make a big impression. He arrived shortly after Crawford checked in and called her room from the lobby. "Look, Joan," he said, "I can't break through that telephone guard of yours. You're either busy, or not in, or not talking. But I'm here. You're here. It's a beautiful night. Let's go dancing." The grand gesture worked. A romance ensued again—this time as intense as it was sudden.*

Bautzer was the consummate bedroom strategist. He sensed that Crawford would grow bored if he was too accommodating. "She liked men who gave her a hard time," said Adela Rogers St. Johns, the trailblazing journalist who was also the daughter of famed attorney Earl Rogers. "If a guy was always available when she called, she dropped him." Bautzer also knew that Crawford expected the deference usually reserved for monarchs. Greg "treated her like a star," recalled actress Rosalind Russell. "When they entered a room, he remained a few steps behind her. He often carried her dog or her knitting bag—she was always knitting—and, at the dinner table, Bautzer did everything

---

*An alternative story exists about Bautzer and Crawford reuniting. In that version, it is Crawford who invites Bautzer into her life again upon hearing that he had defended her honor in a barroom brawl with cowboy actor Don "Red" Barry. Crawford had briefly dated Barry after her marriage to Franchot Tone. Bautzer supposedly overheard Barry describe Crawford sexually as "fresh meat," inspiring Bautzer to challenge Barry to a fight in which Barry punched out some of Bautzer's teeth. Joan was so impressed with Bautzer's chivalry that she paid for his dental work and welcomed him back. While Bautzer may have fought Barry, the rest of the story is dubious, since Bautzer had already lost all of his front teeth years earlier. If Barry knocked out any teeth, they were most likely dentures.

but feed her." William Haines, the silent star turned Beverly Hills decorator, had been Crawford's close friend for twenty years. "To be Joan Crawford's boyfriend," said Haines, "a man must be a combination bull and butler." Bautzer played the role perfectly. "Crawford expected her escort to place her napkin in her lap, light her cigarettes, and open doors for her," said Russell. "Not many men would put up with it. Bautzer did all these things without losing his masculinity. He made it seem the natural thing to do." Bautzer sublimated his ego in the service of a great romance. "They were nuts about each other," recalled Russell. Bautzer's buddies heard a frank explanation. "A night with Joan is better than a year with ten others," he would say, grinning.

On April 25, Crawford's divorce became final. On May 15, Hedda Hopper wrote in her column, "It would surprise no one if Greg Bautzer became the next husband of Joan Crawford." In October, they were still dating, but no plans had been announced. Hopper spotted them at a party given by skating star Sonja Henie. "Joan Crawford has reached the 'I'll-dance-only-with-Greg-Bautzer' stage," wrote Hopper. When asked by the press about marriage plans, Bautzer replied, "I wish I could be so lucky." Hopper read this and saw through the smoke screen: "That son of a bitch can really come up with the one-liners." To Henry Rogers, cofounder of the public relations firm Rogers and Cowan, Bautzer confessed the truth behind his answer to the frequent question about marriage: "I've been trying for a long time to think of something that would make Crawford come off like a queen and still make me look good," he explained. "This makes people think that I want to marry her and she won't have me, but my friends know the truth. They'll laugh and say, 'Bautzer scored again.'"

Bautzer demonstrated his affection for Crawford in his customary way, with thoughtful, costly gifts. He gave her a cigarette case, encrusted with rubies, engraved FOREVER AND EVER. This was a quote from the song "Always and Always," which she sang in her film *Mannequin*. The matching lighter said HERE'S MY TORCH AND MY LOVE. Not to be outdone, Crawford presented him with a pair of Cartier diamond cuff links. He visited the salon where she bought them and was told that she had paid $10,000. She also gave him a black Cadillac convertible. Crawford retained Bautzer as her attorney. She also brought him clients: John Garfield, Jane Wyman, Ginger Rogers, and even Crawford's second husband, Franchot Tone.

Publicist Henry Rogers represented Crawford at the time and witnessed many an entrance made by her and Bautzer. "There was a decided hush when they walked into a room," recalled Rogers. "It was as though a genie had cast a spell over the place. They knew the impression they were making, and they took full advantage. They stopped in the entrance. As people stared at them, they smiled indulgently. They paused. And then, on the fifth beat it seemed, they glided into the room. The King and Queen had arrived."

What did the king and queen eat? A great deal, according to maître d' Kurt Niklas of Romanoff's restaurant. "First they ordered a bottle of 100-proof Smirnoff vodka packed in ice, with a four-pound tin of Beluga caviar," said Niklas. "They put a pretty good dent into both. Then came a bottle of Dom Perignon which they drained very leisurely. Then with their double Chateaubriand they drank a bottle of Romanée-Conti Burgundy. I had never seen a man and woman dine so extravagantly."

In July 1948, Bautzer and Crawford hosted a formal dinner for two hundred at Le Pavillon—the *Hollywood Reporter* named the party the event of the year. Guests included Irene Dunne, Barbara Stanwyck, Robert Taylor, Gene Tierney, and Marlene Dietrich. Noel Coward, in town to see Tallulah Bankhead in his play *Private Lives*, was there as well. Designer Billy Haines transformed the restaurant into a small garden of Versailles with showers of pink gardenias, the flower to which Crawford had a legendary devotion. Tony Martin and Dinah Shore sang, Jack Benny played his violin, and Coward performed a number with Celeste Holm.

The always outrageous Bankhead titillated onlookers when she announced that Bautzer and Coward were "simply made for each other" and then suggested "Why don't you two go someplace and fuck!"

"Sorry, Tallulah darling," said Coward, "but the gentleman's teeth are far too big for my liking!" To everyone's surprise, Bautzer laughed. He and Coward became lifelong friends. In years to come, whenever they met, Coward would greet Bautzer with "Incidentally, my dear chap, I still think you have too many teeth!"

Bautzer and Crawford were at the apex of their romance, but behind the glossy facade were two very competitive individuals. Bautzer frequently played tennis with talent agent Dick Dorso. "Greg was the most ferocious player I ever encountered," said Dorso. "There was nothing that meant so much to him as winning. At tennis or at anything, winning was all-important." Crawford had likewise clawed her way to the top, and the ruthlessness with which she had achieved fame was applied to her relationships. "She was predatory and possessive," said the British writer Barry Norman. Hedda Hopper chided Crawford for a dinner party at which there were six spare men. "Is it a sin for a girl to have fun?" asked Crawford. "You go find your own men, Hedda."

Oscar Levant, who appeared with Crawford in *Humoresque*, brought his wife June Levant to Crawford's home on Bristol Avenue in Brentwood. June found Crawford terrifying. "She was drunk with glamour," said June. Lana Turner had also been there years earlier. "Those parties were all the same," wrote Turner. "After dinner the guests would be herded into a screening room to watch movies. Joan knitted constantly. During the film, you could hear her needles clicking." Bautzer made the mistake of falling asleep during one of Crawford's screenings. She rose quietly and whispered to her guests not to wake him, explaining that he had had a difficult day at the office and that they should let him rest. They dutifully tiptoed out of the room. "Greg woke up at seven the next morning, alone, with the door locked," wrote Hedda Hopper. "The theater had a kitchenette, so he cooked some breakfast, smashed a window, and went home. Crawford called him later in the day and screamed at him. 'How dare you leave my home without washing the dishes!'"

"Crawford liked to be treated rough, and she made sure that Bautzer obliged her," recalled Adela Rogers St. Johns. "One Saturday morning I ran into her at the Farmer's Market and she pulled me aside. 'Look, darling,' she said. Lowering her sunglasses, she displayed a black eye. I sympathized, but she wasn't having any of that. 'He loves me,' she said, showing off the shiner like it was a medal of honor." Bautzer earned his own medals. Interviewed in 1981 by Richard Last of the *English Daily Telegraph*, Bautzer pointed to four facial scars. "She put them there," he said. "She could throw a cocktail glass and hit you in the face—two times out of three."

In addition to mutual laceration, the couple also engaged in a hostility-charged kind of foreplay. The ritual would begin with Crawford haranguing Bautzer for some peccadillo, then demanding an apology, then refusing to accept it, and then disrobing in front of him—finally driving him to the point where he was so frustrated, angry, and aroused that he would tear off her underwear and force himself upon her.

Publicist Henry Rogers received a description of their lovemaking style firsthand from the actress. Crawford recalled the details of a particularly memorable night: She was already in bed when she heard noises outside her window. "I quickly identified them as footsteps and thought immediately of pushing the alarm next to my bed," she told Rogers. "But I decided it was just one of the security guards patrolling the grounds. Then the noises got louder. Like the cracking and breaking of bushes or trees. Someone was climbing the lattice outside my bedroom window. I heard scrambling, grunts, and cursing from whoever was out there. I was terrified. Paralyzed with fear. I knew I should scream and push the alarm, but at that very moment there was a horrendous crash. Someone had smashed my window and was climbing through. It was Greg! I was still terrified as I watched him take off his clothes and charge toward me. He threw off my covers, ripped off my nightgown—and then— the son of a bitch raped me!"

"He didn't really rape you," Rogers said as she related the story.

"Of course not. But it sounds better that way. I'll never forget how he grabbed me with his bloody hands. In a moment, his blood was all over my body, all over the bed—and I want you to know, Henry—it was the most exciting sexual experience of my life!"

Jealousy over each others' infidelities created an on-again off-again ritual that also fueled their passion. In late 1947, Bautzer dated stars Sonja Henie and Joan Caulfield, as well as MGM starlets Marilyn Maxwell and Ava Gardner. When Crawford learned of the Gardner affair, she froze him out, but when he apologetically came back, she celebrated by buying new matching his-and-hers Cadillacs. After an all-night card game, Bautzer drunkenly crashed his Cadillac into a lamppost and mailbox on Wilshire Boulevard. The front-page news revealed that he was with another woman. Crawford went ballistic and began dating Lana Turner's ex-husband, restaurateur Steve Crane. In turn, Bautzer dated Merle Oberon. Crawford flew to New York for a four-month stay at the Hampshire House. Bautzer saw it as another opportunity for a grand gesture and chased her across country. They made up. He took her shopping at Saks and they returned to Los Angeles, only to break up again when Crawford heard that he was seeing Rita Hayworth on the side.

Crawford took up with British actor Peter Shaw, but the romance was short-lived and soon she was back on Bautzer's arm. Then Crawford heard that Bautzer was seen holding hands at lunch with Lana

Turner. She confronted him about it and he countered that he knew she was sleeping with writer-director Charles Martin. A battle royal ensued. As Bautzer stormed out of her house, he tore off the Cartier cuff links and handed them to her. Furious, she flushed them down the toilet, forgetting how much they cost. A plumber answered her late-night summons and was able to retrieve them from the bend in the pipe, charging $500 for the emergency visit. Bautzer did his own damage. He jumped into the second Cadillac that Crawford had given him and crashed it into a wall.

With all the publicity they were getting in the press, keeping score on the Bautzer-Crawford romance was becoming Hollywood's favorite pastime. Crawford's jealous vengeance was now public knowledge. Hedda Hopper wondered why Paulette Goddard was so often out with Bautzer. "You know," said Goddard, "it's strictly business."

"Yes, but when you go out with Greg," warned Hopper in her column, "never turn your back on a certain star. You might get a stiletto in it."

Actress Arlene Dahl experienced Crawford's venom as a seventeen-year-old ingénue at a black-tie party in honor of Cole Porter. It took place at 1018 Benedict Canyon Avenue, the home of Sir Charles and Lady Mendl. The latter, the former Elsie de Wolfe, was America's premier interior decorator and Hollywood's leading hostess. When Dahl arrived, she was awed by the number of stars in attendance: Joan Fontaine, Fred Astaire, Clark Gable and his wife Sylvia, Norma Shearer, and Janet Gaynor and her husband, couturier Gilbert Adrian. "I felt like Alice in Wonderland," says Dahl. "And there at the end of the living room were Joan Crawford and Greg Bautzer." Dahl nervously approached and then blurted out "Miss Crawford, it's so nice to meet you! You're my mother's favorite actress." She immediately sensed that she had said the wrong thing. "And mine, too," she hastened to add, trying to cover her mistake. She was too late. Crawford hated being reminded of her vintage.

"She was livid," said Dahl. "Greg, on the other hand, thought it was funny. He started to flirt with me. And that only made things worse. She 'accidentally' spilled a glass of red wine on my white dress." Joan Fontaine saw it and loudly exposed Crawford to the entire party, exclaiming, "You did that on purpose, you bitch!"

The volatile relationship was pure gold for newspaper writers. "These two battle any time, anywhere," wrote Dorothy Kilgallen. "They quarrel in Hollywood and make up in New York. They kiss in the Catskills and feud again at Malibu." During one fracas, Crawford dashed onto her balcony, yelling for the police. When Bautzer went after her, she climbed onto the roof. Neighbors witnessed the episode.

Bautzer's tennis chum Dick Dorso was taken aback when Crawford invaded the tennis court at the Wilkerson mansion. "Mr. Bautzer, is it going to be your tennis game or me?" she demanded. "Give me an answer."

"I'm sorry, dear," came the answer. "I can't leave now. I'll come by as soon as I'm finished."

Dorso described the meeting of two immovable forces. "There would be a moment's pause between the two of them, he returning her steely-eyed glare with a similar steely-eyed glare. She would then realize that this was a battle that she couldn't win. Finally, she would mutter 'You can go to hell,' and walk off the court determinedly. Then we would hear a screaming of tires as she roared off."

Radio personality Johnny Dugan also witnessed an uncomfortable scene when he tried to go on a double date with the volatile couple to an MGM charity luncheon. Bautzer chauffeured Dugan and his girlfriend over to Crawford's home, but when they got there, Crawford was still dressing. Bautzer fixed drinks and they all got comfortable in the living room. Twenty minutes went by, which turned into forty, and Crawford still hadn't come downstairs. Bautzer became agitated as the minutes ticked by. This wasn't right, he told them. She shouldn't treat her guests this way. He decided to hurry the prima donna along and climbed the stairs to her bedroom, leaving Johnny and his date alone on the couch.

It wasn't long before Dugan heard Crawford's voice bellowing, "Get out of here, you son of a bitch! I'll be down when I'm good and ready. And if you don't like it, you can go to hell!" This was followed by the sound of crashing furniture and objects hitting the walls. Dugan sprung off the couch, not knowing what to do. A moment later, Bautzer bounded down the stairs with a bleeding lip. Without a word to Dugan, he bolted out the front door and slammed it behind him. Within seconds, Dugan heard a window open in Crawford's room and loud footsteps banging across the floor. He looked outside and saw articles of men's clothing falling onto the driveway.

"And don't you come back, you lousy prick!" Crawford shouted as Bautzer's car peeled away. Dugan and his date realized the party was over and took a bus home.

While Bautzer handled Crawford by night, by day he was handling a bustling legal career. In late 1946, as Bautzer was helping his close friend Billy Wilkerson grapple with Bugsy Siegel, he also represented the publisher of the *Hollywood Reporter* in a libel suit. Wilkerson was being sued by actress Myrna Loy for $1 million. Loy was the star of the *Thin Man* series and had done exemplary work entertaining troops during the war. Earlier that year, the *Reporter* had printed an article that listed actors who were supposedly "part of the Communist fifth column in America . . . serving a possible treasonable purpose." The list included Edward G. Robinson, Orson Welles, Burgess Meredith, James Cagney, Lionel Stander—and Myrna Loy. It was the beginning of an anti-Communist fever that would eventually grip the nation, accusing Hollywood filmmakers of trying to infuse motion pictures with Communist propaganda.

Loy knew the actors named. "One or two may have got involved with the Communist Party briefly," she wrote in her autobiography, "just as I might have if my intellectual curiosity had run in that direction, but none was a committed Communist. And even if they were, isn't political freedom an American right?" Wilkerson did not think so. Loy was determined to clear her name.

"You want to sue?" Martin Gang, her attorney, asked her.

"Probably," she answered, "but first let's try for a retraction."

Wilkerson refused to recant. Instead, he reprinted the list. On October 4, Gang filed suit against the *Reporter* and Wilkerson, stating twelve causes of action for libel. Bautzer took Loy's deposition, grilling her about alleged Communist publications. "No, I'm sorry," she answered repeatedly. "I don't know anything about that." Bautzer believed her. He had investigated her background prior to the deposition and told Wilkerson he could find no evidence of Communist affiliations. In the end, Bautzer convinced Wilkerson to admit his mistake. Sometimes the best advice a lawyer can give his client is that he or she is in the wrong.

In early November 1946, he represented rubber-faced actress Martha Raye in her divorce from dancer Nick Condos on the grounds of cruelty. Raye wanted custody of their two-year-old daughter, Melodye, but not alimony or child support. This was Raye's fourth marriage. After less than a week she decided to reconcile, and the marriage lasted for eight more years.

At the same time as he represented Raye, he also represented actress Laraine Day in her divorce from airport executive James R. Hendricks, just six weeks after they had adopted a thirteen-year-old son. She also had two children from a prior marriage. Day was best known for her recurring role as Nurse Mary Lamont in the Dr. Kildare films. Rumor had it that an in-flight flirtation with Leo Durocher, manager of the Brooklyn Dodgers, was the reason for her divorce. This was confirmed when Day wed Durocher—one day after she divorced Hendricks.

In March 1949, Bautzer's client and occasional date Paulette Goddard wanted to divorce producer-director-actor Burgess Meredith. Bautzer told the *Los Angeles Times* that Goddard had not decided whether to file suit in Mexico, seeking a Mexican decree, or in California Superior Court. In 1942, Bautzer had taken a different stance. While representing Sally Wright Bernheimer against her husband Earle Bernheimer, he questioned the validity of a Mexican divorce decree, dismissing it as "mail order divorce." But in the late 1940s the Mexican divorce was becoming a common practice.

Goddard told the press about her divorce action before she told her husband, who was three thousand miles away. "I have not yet talked with Burgess," she claimed, "nor received any communication from him. I have requested from him a consent decree. I intend to fly to New York to talk things over with Burgess, and then go to Mexico where I have been asked to preside at the Easter festival in Acapulco." The press speculated that she was romantically involved with author John Steinbeck, but she denied it. Bautzer supported her story, saying he was negotiating for her to star in a film titled *Cup of Gold* and Steinbeck was writing it. Backing for the project was contingent upon the involvement of actor James Mason. The up-and-coming English actor was overbooked, so it was never produced. Bautzer also packaged a film for Goddard entitled *Enamorada*, but it never got off the ground.

Goddard's star had faded. Her divorce took time, during which she dated both Bautzer and Clark Gable. Gossip columns also hinted that Bautzer was seeing Ann Sheridan, the "Oomph Girl," at this time. As he often did, Bautzer explained that their dates were merely business meetings. He claimed to be negotiating a contract for her for a picture titled *Torch Song*. As with Goddard, Sheridan's career was on the way down, and no such project materialized. Saying dates were "strictly business" was becoming a cliché.

As the decade came to a close, the Bautzer-Crawford romance was reaching its limits. In October 1949, Bautzer and Crawford attended a party given by Louis B. Mayer. During the evening, Bautzer committed the faux pas of paying too much attention to another female guest. Crawford didn't say anything at the party, but she was not pleased. When the party was over, Crawford offered to drive.

Bautzer described what happened after they left the party in an interview for a 1978 BBC documentary profiling Crawford: "I lived at the Bel-Air Hotel, and she lived in Brentwood, and my car was parked at her home. We were driving back along Sunset Boulevard to go to her home in Brentwood. That was before they built the freeway, and there was very little there, very few homes, very little traffic. About equal distance between the Bel-Air Hotel and her house, which is a pretty good ten to twelve miles, she slowed the car and said, 'Darling, I think there's something wrong with the right rear tire. Would you be a dear and go out and look at it?' I said 'Of course, darling.' I get out and go around and boom! The car takes off. That was my discipline; that was to serve as my penance for having paid some attention to this very lovely actress whom I had known for quite some time. And so I proceeded to walk home to the Bel-Air Hotel."

Bautzer told the BBC interviewer that in situations like this, when Crawford would cause a scene, he usually called the next day to apologize "just to get things back to status quo." But this time, he said, he didn't call to apologize and claimed that he never called her again. Other sources contradict his statement. Crawford biographies maintain that he did call her the following day to ask for forgiveness. According to these reports, he arrived at her home at five o'clock with his arms full of long-stemmed roses.

"Is this to apologize?" Crawford asked.

"Yes."

"Then kneel as you make your apology."

"Bullshit!" said Bautzer. And with that, he flung the flowers across the room and stalked out. He had finally had enough.

A little later, Bautzer ran into Crawford's ex-husband Franchot Tone at the Polo Lounge in the Beverly Hills Hotel. Bautzer told Tone the story and asked if anything like this had ever happened to him while he was married to Crawford. "Yes, it did," said Tone.

"What did you do?" asked Bautzer.

"I knelt."

Months later, Crawford reportedly came unannounced to Bautzer's office. He had instructed his secretary to say that he was out. Crawford glared at her for a moment, pushed past her, and strode into Bautzer's office. He was nowhere in sight. Crawford realized her error and left in a huff. The secretary was baffled. Where had he gone? As she was standing in the doorway, she saw something move outside the window. It was her boss, creeping along the window ledge. He had hid outside his office window, two floors above Hollywood Boulevard.

In the years to come, Crawford would mend fences with Bautzer and continued to seek his legal counsel. Reflecting on his long affair with Crawford in the interview he gave for the BBC documentary, he admitted that he was "stuck" on her, but he also revealed that the role he played embarrassed him. "A hostess would always be pretty assured that the guests for a dinner party would be on time if word got out that Joan and I were coming to dinner. Because the ritual was that [when we arrived] I would be two to three steps behind Joan carrying a knitting bag in one arm and a small white poodle in the other. And the guests used to all get there so they could look at me with a kind of smile that said, and sometimes they did say, 'geek.'"

In 1978, Crawford's daughter Christina would publish a book called *Mommie Dearest*, which contrived to tell how her mother abused her. She referred to Bautzer simply as "Uncle Greg" in the memoir and said she liked him a lot, although she also recalled their arguments. In 1981, *Mommie Dearest* was made into a movie starring Faye Dunaway. Her performance pushed Crawford's persona into the realm of camp grotesquerie. Bautzer's portrayal by Steve Forrest as "Greg Savitt" was more flattering.

Crawford fans have questioned the accuracy of Christina's version of her mother as an abusive parent, asserting that Christina had motives for misrepresenting her childhood. But an incident reported by Bautzer tends to confirm Christina's point of view. Christina's brother Christopher was left-handed. Crawford was training him to use his right. One evening at dinner with Bautzer, Christopher forgot and used his left hand. "Joan leaned across the table, knocked the food out of his hand, and hit him across the face," recalled Bautzer. "He started to cry. So I immediately went over and put my arms around the boy. As I was holding him—we were having a roast leg of lamb—I got it right in my face." By "it" he meant the lamb.

Regardless of the way the film showed Crawford as a mother, it ably captured the essence of the Bautzer-Crawford relationship without the gory details. Bautzer is shown making passionate love to her in the shower, dealing with her obsessive whims, and finally walking out on her when the hurt-me-if-you-love-me act gets to be too much. After viewing the film, he was interviewed by the *Washington Post*. "If anyone was abused, it was me," said Bautzer. "I guess I was big enough to take it."

So was his career. In 1950, it would grow far beyond even his expectations.

10

DIVORCE OF THE CENTURY

GET ME GIESLER! read the big, bold headline on May 3, 1949. Bautzer marveled at it as he ate breakfast at the Bel-Air Hotel, where he lived in a bungalow. GET ME GIESLER! That said it all. The headline could mean only one thing. A star was in trouble. Bautzer read on and then stopped. Scandal was his stock in trade, but this story gave him pause. Movie star Ingrid Bergman was seeking a divorce from her husband of twelve years, Dr. Petter Lindström. And she admitted having an affair with Italian director Roberto Rossellini.

Ingrid Bergman was not merely a movie star. She was the biggest movie star in the world. In the past five years she had been nominated for four Academy Awards. She had won the best actress Oscar for her performance in *Gaslight*. She took top billing over her costars—even over Cary Grant, a rare feat. She projected an almost saintly integrity, which producers exploited in films like *The Bells of Saint Mary* and *Casablanca*. Virtually every film she made was a massive hit.

Producer David O. Selznick had brought her from Sweden in 1939, along with her neurosurgeon husband and young daughter. Contemplating a publicity angle, Selznick fixed on her natural beauty. "David said he'd work on the idea of a natural girl," recalled Bergman.

"We did tests in color with no makeup on at all. He told makeup he'd kill anyone who touched my eyebrows. I looked very simple and I acted like the girl next door. So I became the 'natural' star." The public responded to the ungilded lily and she was a hit in her first film, *Intermezzo*. Her most recent was *Joan of Arc*. Playing saints and nuns was natural for someone whose private life was seemingly exemplary. An adulterous Bergman was unthinkable.

As a law student, Bautzer had idolized Jerry Giesler, but he was wrong for this case. Short, bald, and brusque, Giesler played fast and loose in the courtroom, distorting facts and making irrelevant pleas for sympathy. He tried cases on the courthouse steps, insulting prosecutors and judges. Colleagues derided his tactics but admired the results. He had successfully defended Busby Berkeley, Errol Flynn, and Bugsy Siegel. He had recently gotten Robert Mitchum's marijuana conviction reversed. Impressive as Giesler's track record was, it presented a problem. His cases showed the seamy side of Hollywood. Bugsy Siegel and Ingrid Bergman could not be mentioned in the same breath. If Giesler represented Bergman, she would be associated with Giesler's other notorious clients. Bergman and Giesler made no sense. She had dignity; he had none. Still, the articles that were covering the story did not say that Bergman had retained Giesler. They said an American lawyer living in Italy named Monroe MacDonald had flown in from Italy to hire local counsel on her behalf. Perhaps he would not hire Giesler.

MacDonald needed to hire someone good. He was making a mess of the case. MacDonald had released Bergman's written account of her marital problems to the press. This was an inexplicable legal faux pas. Although she cited Lindström's overbearing behavior, she took most of the blame for the breakup. She even went so far as to state that she was through with Hollywood. Henceforth, she would only make films in Europe, which was a disloyal, ungrateful thing to say. Much worse, the newspapers said Bergman was offering her husband a "fortune" to free her. MacDonald may have thought a public confession would garner sympathy; instead, it deprived Bergman of negotiating leverage.

MacDonald did not hire Giesler. Instead, he called Bautzer, who recognized an opportunity. This divorce could be the biggest the industry had known, with yards of publicity. It could be a springboard to legal superstardom. How MacDonald chose Bautzer is not exactly known. It is likely that MacDonald called Selznick, who in turn recommended Bautzer. Selznick and Bautzer had known each other for many years and frequently played cards together. Selznick may even have provided Bautzer with client referrals to settle gambling debts. The producer of *Gone with the Wind* had a ferocious gambling habit and lost virtually every penny he made pressing his luck.

At his first meeting with MacDonald, Bautzer did not criticize the unsophisticated lawyer. Instead, Bautzer complimented his handling of the press, praised his strategy, and otherwise flattered him. Bautzer knew how to win friends and influence people. MacDonald warmed up and gave Bautzer the facts. Rossellini, Bergman's partner in adultery, was a husband and father, revered in his country as an artist and a national hero for advancing the cinematic style later dubbed Italian neorealism. Bergman had been so impressed by his 1948 film *Roma, Città Aperta* (*Rome: Open City*) that she wrote him, offering her services. Rossellini came to Hollywood and stayed with the Bergman/Lindström family in their home, and he invited her to visit him in Europe. They decided to work together. With a star at his disposal, Rossellini obtained financing from Howard Hughes and RKO Radio Pictures to make the film *Of God's Earth*. In the spring of 1949 Rossellini took Bergman to the island of Stromboli to make the film.

Bergman found Rossellini's continental attention a pleasant change from the reserved, critical nature of Dr. Lindström. As a young woman, Bergman had been attracted to men who took control of her affairs and allowed her to exist as an almost childlike artist. She wanted

Lindström to be a father figure, to handle her money and other business matters. But now, the mature qualities she had once admired in her husband, his coolness and self-possession, irritated her. Lindström kept the wealthy star on an allowance so small that she had no cash for household items. She had to obtain his approval before agreeing to an interview. "You shouldn't talk so much," he sniped. "You have a very intelligent face, so let people think you are intelligent, because when you start to chatter it's just a lot of nonsense." Away from his controlling ways, she became involved with Rossellini. When she told Lindström about the affair, he traveled to Italy to win her back, but she had no interest in continuing a loveless marriage.

Bautzer asked MacDonald the usual questions. Were there any children? Yes, a daughter named Pia, age ten. What was the amount of the community property? It was believed to be several hundred thousand dollars, but the exact amount was unknown; Lindström withheld financial information from Bergman. Why was Bergman in such a rush to get a divorce? Despite her public confession, no one could prove that she had committed adultery, and, based on her husband's mental cruelty, she had an excellent chance of winning the court's sympathy. Why was she so eager to give up her share of the marital property without a fight? MacDonald was not at liberty to explain. All he could confirm was that his client was in love with Rossellini and required an immediate divorce. Bautzer could tell that MacDonald was concealing a key piece of information. Bautzer assured MacDonald of his discretion, and MacDonald disclosed the truth: Bergman was very pregnant with Rossellini's child. She was due to deliver in just a few months. Bautzer's springboard began to look like a torn trampoline. How could he get Bergman divorced in a matter of months?

Back in Italy, Bergman and Rossellini were appalled at MacDonald's handling of the case. Bergman's written description of her marriage was meant for her attorney's eyes only, not for the press. She was dismayed that MacDonald had made her affairs public, especially her offer to pay top dollar for a speedy divorce. But most of all, Bergman was "horrified" that MacDonald had hired Bautzer. She had expected MacDonald to enlist a wise, older attorney with lots of experience. All she knew about Bautzer was that his picture was constantly in movie magazines for dating different actresses. Bergman fired MacDonald, but before she could fire Bautzer, Selznick told her not to. Behind the flashy image was a consumate professional. He never lost a case. Bautzer called Bergman and gained her confidence. But he was in a tight spot and he knew it.

One of the maxims of any lawsuit is that the best defense is a strong offense. The usual tactic in a case like this was to blame the husband. But Lindström was holding all the cards. If Bautzer attacked him publicly, Lindström could easily just delay the proceedings. Bautzer had to pacify Lindström in the hope that he would cooperate in a timely manner. Unfortunately, Bautzer could not control the press's handling of the material MacDonald had released. To make matters worse, John Vernon, Bergman and Lindström's business manager, sided with the latter, telling the press that Lindström would not negotiate with Bautzer over money. "I do not think he would ever consider 'selling his wife,'" said Vernon, who claimed that Lindström's greatest concern was for their daughter Pia, whom he described as "a lovable child who now knows of her mother's determination and is accepting her fate with sadness, but with reality."

As late as December 1949, no progress had been made. Lindström would not accept his wife's terms, and rumors of a pregnancy were beginning to circulate. Rossellini and Bergman said the rumor was "preposterous." Art Cohn, the film's screenwriter, weighed in on it. "I saw her less than two months ago," he said. "If anybody would notice that, I would."

In late December, a settlement appeared imminent. "We've just turned over the formal document by messenger to Dr. Lindström's attorney, Lawrence Brinn, in New York," Bautzer reported to the press. Brinn confirmed that he was in settlement discussions with Bautzer. Besides property issues, the settlement would resolve the custody of Pia.

In reality, however, Bautzer was nowhere near a settlement. In fact, he was dealing with an impossible situation. Bergman had offered Lindström a settlement of half her holdings, provided that funds were set up to care for Pia. Lindström would have none of it. He wanted all her property—and sole custody of Pia. Lindström knew he was negotiating from a position of strength. His wife was desperate for a quick divorce; he had no reason to rush. He may not have known for certain that Bergman was pregnant with Rossellini's child, but there could hardly be another explanation for her urgency. All Lindström had to do was sit and wait. It was inevitable that Bergman would give in.

Bergman and Rossellini were desperate in more ways than one. They were strapped for cash. Bergman sought the assistance of her friend and publicist Joe Steele, who had worked for Selznick and helped build her career. Rossellini's film, now retitled *Stromboli*, was ready for release. Steele discreetly approached Howard Hughes, describing Bergman's situation, and asked for RKO to release *Stromboli* immediately. That way Bergman could realize some income before the newspapers found out the truth about her love child. Steele asked Hughes to keep the pregnancy a secret. Hughes agreed, but after Steele left, he phoned gossip columnist Louella Parsons and told her. Hughes thought a scandal would make *Stromboli* a sensation. His plan backfired. When the news broke, a chorus of opprobrious churchmen, cheered on by American newspapers, condemned Bergman and Rossellini. "They have been guilty of the most contemptible and outrageous conduct in centuries," preached the Most Reverend C. E. Byrne, bishop of the Roman Catholic diocese of Galveston, Texas.

In early January 1950, Rossellini obtained a Vienna annulment of his current marriage "under a friendly arrangement." A few days later, an Italian court in Turin recognized the validity of the Vienna annulment, even though it was considered a violation of pacts between the Vatican and Italy by the Catholic Action Organization in Rome. Meanwhile, settlement talks between Berman and Lindström had come to a halt. Dr. Lindström denied that he was the cause of the delay. "Dr. Lindström is not holding up negotiations," said Vernon. "It's just the distance that slows things down."

By late January, Bergman could not wait for Lindström to grant her a divorce. She was about to deliver. Bautzer had no option but to advise a quickie divorce in Mexico, even though its validity might later be questioned. Bautzer hired the firm of Gomez, Trevino & Cocke in El Paso to file divorce papers in Juarez, Mexico. Lindström refused to acknowledge the Mexican action and instructed the firm of Shepherd & Shepherd to file for divorce in Los Angeles on his behalf. Attorney William Cocke in El Paso said that the Mexican courts would not dismiss Bergman's divorce action merely because Lindström had filed in Los Angeles. Bergman and Rossellini continued to deny the pregnancy.

On February 2, 1950, the inevitable happened. Bergman gave birth to a boy named Robertino. One week later, her Mexican divorce was granted. This may have resolved the Lindströms' marital status, but it did nothing to resolve issues of property or custody. At least the pregnancy crisis was over. Bautzer no longer needed to dance around the issue and be polite to Lindström hoping he would capitulate. In fact, the tables were turned. By delaying so long, Lindström had overplayed his hand. Now that the child was born, the scandal had peaked. The damage was done. Bergman had nothing left to lose. More significantly, she felt that Lindström had purposefully punished her by refusing to agree to a divorce before she gave birth. She wanted revenge.

On March 16, Bautzer filed an action on behalf of Bergman in Los Angeles Superior Court seeking custody of Pia and child support.

The thirteen-page petition said that Lindström had served as Bergman's manager and received $154,000 of her earnings from *Stromboli*. He had made an oral agreement to hold the money in trust and deliver it to his wife, but after numerous requests, he had not. Instead, he had invested it and received profits from the investments.

Bautzer also listed assets controlled by Lindström that, he argued, should be given to his client in their entirety since the Mexican court had awarded the divorce on the grounds of cruelty. Because Lindström had not contested the Mexican divorce, the default being entered against him was based entirely on Bergman's side of the story. She was therefore entitled to all of their marital assets: government bonds, jewelry, furs, furniture, automobiles, and royalties from her recent films *Under Capricorn* and *Joan of Arc*. Bautzer also wanted the court to order the sale of their home at 1220 Benedict Canyon, splitting the proceeds between them, plus other real and personal property in Sweden. He maintained that Lindström had threatened to put property beyond his client's reach and requested that the court restrain Lindström from defrauding her.

Bautzer also employed the tactic of threatening to depose Lindström, who was loath to be cross-examined. He knew that Bautzer would try to make it seem that he mishandled Bergman's affairs and bullied her. Lindström would be on trial, not the adulterous Bergman. Howard Shepherd, Lindström's attorney, saw that Bautzer could easily drag the physician's private life into the papers. Shepherd was out of his depth. He withdrew from representation. Lindström promptly engaged the experienced Los Angeles trial attorney Isaac Pacht.

Lindström couldn't have hired a more worthy adversary to oppose Bautzer. At age fifty-three, Pacht was only fourteen years older than Bautzer, but he had been practicing law since age sixteen, giving him more than thirty-five years experience to Bautzer's thirteen years (or nine considering lost time in the navy). Pacht was one of the most respected lawyers in Los Angeles and had been handling celebrity divorces since 1915, when at age eighteen he represented the wife of silent movie star Theodore Roberts, who played Moses in Cecil B. DeMille's silent version of *The Ten Commandments*. Pacht had also been a judge for several years in the early 1930s, regretfully leaving the bench to return to private practice because he couldn't support his family on a judge's salary.

Pacht was nearly a foot shorter than Bautzer but packed twice the punch. Photos of the two lawyers taken at an impromptu press conference in court reveal how different the two men were. Pacht's weathered face gives him the look of a battle-scarred veteran. He seems completely relaxed as he answers questions, hands tucked nonchalantly in his suit pockets. In contrast, Bautzer appears uptight and nervous, clutching a briefcase and avoiding eye contact. It is clear who was in command. Pacht even grabbed Bautzer's arm as they walked through a doorway, like a parent escorting a child.

Lindström dreaded having his deposition taken by Bautzer, but Bergman had more to fear. To win custody of Pia, she would have to return to the United States and be cross-examined about her fitness as a mother. "We know that Miss Bergman at all times has been prepared to come here to appear on an action concerning the custody of Pia," said Bautzer, but this was mere posturing. The last thing he wanted was Bergman on the witness stand. Pacht would delve into her affair with Rossellini and try to make her admit other affairs. Lindström suspected his wife of affairs with all her leading men, and while that may not have been true, she did have affairs with actor Gary Cooper, photojournalist Robert Capa, and director Victor Fleming. As her counsel, Bautzer advised her of the risks of continuing litigation. Her public image might recover from her recent impropriety, but a habit of "adulterous immorality" would make her unemployable. There was a morals clause in every movie actor's contract.

Public opinion did not favor Bergman. When *Stromboli* opened, it was poorly attended. Edwin Johnson, Democratic senator from

Colorado, called Bergman "a horrible example of womanhood and a powerful influence for evil." He denounced Rossellini as a Nazi collaborator, a black market operator, and a well-known cocaine addict. He criticized RKO for distributing *Stromboli*. A rumor circulated that the US Immigration Service planned to deny Bergman entry on the grounds of "moral turpitude." California senator Sheridan Downey came to her defense and said the idea was preposterous. Bautzer issued a formal statement. "We have not been advised of any prohibition that would preclude Miss Bergman from coming to California to protect her interest insofar as her daughter Pia is concerned."

Bautzer and Pacht spent most of March trying to reach a settlement. Pacht requested a short extension to April 12 to file an answer to Bergman's complaint. Bautzer refused, forcing Pacht to file a motion for extension. The court granted the motion. Bautzer kept the case in the news by implying that Lindström had stolen from Bergman. "We still want to know what happened to all that money," said Bautzer, "and where the records of it are." Lindström fired back that he was offering "reasonable custody" of Pia so long as the visits occurred in California and Rossellini was not allowed near her. Bautzer responded that Lindström's settlement offer was no offer at all, because they could expect to get such terms from the court even if they lost.

Meanwhile, Lindström's business manager, John Vernon, had disappeared from his home in Sherman Oaks and turned up in a San Francisco hotel, apparently a victim of amnesia. He was admitted to a hospital. In his possession was a briefcase which was said to contain important papers regarding the financial and personal affairs of Bergman and Lindström. Bautzer wanted it opened in court. A hearing was set for April 5. There is no record of that hearing, but Bautzer did discover a mysterious $80,000 deposit in Vernon's name in an obscure Los Angeles bank. Vernon would commit suicide in a downtown hotel several months later, leaving many questions unanswered.

As talks between Bautzer and Pacht continued, the likelihood of either Lindström or Bergman taking the witness stand faded. By April 14, an out-of-court settlement appeared imminent. Six days later, after seven months of litigation, the terms of divorce were completed. Property division and custody rights were settled. The physical custody, care, and protection of Pia were placed in Lindström's hands. Bergman would have Pia with her during half of Pia's school vacations.

Almost immediately a dispute arose about whether the wording of the agreement required that Pia leave the country to be with her mother or that Bergman come to California. Bautzer maintained that it required that Pia go to her mother wherever she might be. Pacht said that by its intent it did not. The ambiguity of visitation rights was a hanging question.

Despite her initial doubts, Bergman was pleased with Bautzer's services and wrote him a letter thanking him for both his good work and for the extreme modesty of his fees. True to her word, for the next six years Bergman would make films solely in Europe. This was not so much a matter of preference as a surrender to circumstances. Ingrid Bergman had been excommunicated from Hollywood filmdom.

The Bergman-Lindström case was a milestone in Bautzer's career. It provided him with months of national publicity. In his 1962 autobiography, Jerry Giesler wrote that "Get Me Giesler!" became a catchphrase at the time of the Bergman headline. It also signaled the beginning of the end of his dominance in Hollywood. Bautzer had become a formidable rival for noncriminal business. In recounting the Bergman anecdote, Giesler inadvertently revealed the extent of his jealousy. He couldn't bring himself to credit the young lawyer who had once been his apprentice.

Soon after the Bergman case was settled, Bautzer, Bernard Silbert, and a new lawyer named Gerald Lipsky joined attorneys Arnold Grant and Gordon Youngman to form the firm of Bautzer, Grant,

Youngman & Silbert. In 1951, they moved from the Equitable Building at Hollywood and Vine to 356 North Camden Drive in Beverly Hills. The Hollywood lawyer was now a Beverly Hills lawyer.

11

CHANGE PARTNERS
AND DANCE

Lana Turner would later call Bautzer "Hollywood's greatest escape artist" for his ability to disentangle himself from the arms of starlets. It
was an apt description. In the sultry summer of 1949, while preparing the Lindström-Bergman divorce case, Bautzer was seen dancing
with filmdom's most famous hoofer, Ginger Rogers. Hedda Hopper
phoned Bautzer for details and got the standard press release: he told
her his dinner with Rogers was strictly business. His client, producer
Walter Wanger, was planning a circus film, he explained, and Rogers
was interested. Hopper didn't believe it. "Greg Bautzer, who's usually
quite truthful, threw me a curve when he said that he and Ginger
Rogers were merely talking a business deal," wrote Hopper a few days
later. "Their dancing at Mocambo was such a closed corporation, you
couldn't have squeezed in a bit of tissue paper." It was the beginning
of something big.

Like Joan Crawford, Rogers had first attracted attention as a teenager in the Roaring Twenties, when she won numerous Charleston
contests. Rogers was born Virginia Katherine McMath in Independence, Missouri, in 1911, the same year as Bautzer. Her cousin gave

her the name Ginger. Her mother Lela gave her determination. Two years of singing and dancing in vaudeville brought her to Broadway. Being at the right audition at age nineteen got her into George and Ira Gershwin's *Girl Crazy*, in which Ethel Merman introduced "I Got Rhythm" and Rogers introduced "Embraceable You" and "But Not for Me." Lela decided that the next move for her daughter was to Hollywood. For two years, Rogers was stuck in second-string movies until, once again, she found herself in the right place at the right time.

In 1933, RKO cast Fred Astaire, who was a Broadway star but a Hollywood unknown, as a second lead in *Flying Down to Rio*. Dorothy Jordan, who was not known for singing or dancing, was cast opposite him, but she opted to marry RKO boss Merian C. Cooper instead. After Jordan dropped out, Ginger Rogers got the part. The pairing of Astaire and Rogers was magical. Their dancing was elegant, graceful, and sexy. They stole the film from leads Dolores del Rio and Gene Raymond and became overnight sensations. They were given their own film, *The Gay Divorcee*. "Ginger Rogers is the most effective performer with whom I've ever worked," Astaire said. "She can sell a number in a unique way. She's a showman." Eight Astaire-Rogers films followed. Then Rogers did the unexpected: she tried straight dramatic roles. In 1940, she won an Oscar for her performance as a working girl in *Kitty Foyle*.

Bautzer was obviously attracted to Oscar-winning actresses, and Rogers was likewise attracted to the trim, tanned attorney. They were well matched. The fresh-faced blonde with the stunning figure had been married three times and had dated Howard Hughes, but Bautzer was in his own category. "Greg was Bachelor Number One in Hollywood," wrote Rogers in her 1992 autobiography. "Not only was he tall, dark, and handsome, but he was also a prominent lawyer and superb athlete, one of the best tennis partners I'd ever competed with or against. He was a terrific dancer too, my social Fred Astaire." In fact, he was such a good dancer that she said he was one of the three best dancers she had ever known and compared him to Astaire's choreographer, Hermes Pan. Rogers also admired Bautzer's self-assuredness. It reminded her of her mother, the most important person in her life. Bautzer was one of the few people allowed to call her Virginia.

The Bautzer-Rogers romance was followed almost as closely by the press as the Lindström-Bergman divorce. On September 2, 1949, Bautzer and Rogers attended the opening of Patti Moore and Ben Lessy's burlesque show at Ciro's. Also present was Rogers's soon-to-be ex-husband, Jack Briggs, escorting actress Ann Miller. According to Hopper, Bautzer was "as nervous as a cat." Two weeks later, Bautzer took Rogers to a party thrown by former law partner Bentley Ryan and his wife, actress Marguerite Chapman, at their apartment in the new Bel-Air Gardens. Lana Turner attended with her husband, Henry J. "Bob" Topping. Hedda Hopper wrote in her column that Bautzer and Rogers were thinking of marriage, because they were overheard discussing the purchase of a desert retreat. On November 20, Bautzer and Rogers won the mixed doubles Pimm's Cup Tennis Match at the Racquet Club in Palm Springs, beating Gussie Moran and the ubiquitous Pat Di Cicco. Bautzer also made it to the men's finals with partner Art Drummit, losing only to the club's owner, Charlie Farrell, and his partner, Dr. Lew Morrill. "Greg Bautzer almost came out on top in BOTH mixed and men's doubles," the *L.A. Times* reported. "And that Ginger Rogers plays such a magnificent game that it's almost symphonic in its rhythm."

In early 1950, the romance appeared to be turning serious. Bautzer and Rogers went to church together, first attending the Hollywood Christian Science Church and then moving to the Beverly Hills Church, the same one attended by Joan Crawford. Bautzer took Rogers out regularly to events such as the season opener of the Hollywood Stars minor league baseball team, and he was seen buying an Easter bonnet for her at Rex Clothiers by—who else?—Hedda

Hopper, who was there with her granddaughter. Hopper complimented Bautzer's taste in hats.

Rogers had four months to wait for her divorce decree from Briggs. It was shortly after her divorce became final that sightings of the couple started to dwindle. The romance had apparently cooled. Hopper saw Bautzer at one of those so-called business dinners in September. He was with another thrice-divorced Oscar winner.

Jane Wyman had recently won the Best Actress Oscar for her performance as a deaf and mute rape victim in *Johnny Belinda*. Prior to that she had been a well-regarded leading lady, married for eight years to a well-regarded leading man, Ronald Reagan, who was also president of the Screen Actors Guild. Wyman blamed their recent divorce on his politics, but her alleged affair with actor Lew Ayres while making *Johnny Belinda* may also have been a factor. There were only a limited number of stars in Hollywood, and lives intersected constantly. Ayres had been married to Ginger Rogers fifteen years earlier. Rogers was working with Reagan on a film called *Storm Warning*. Crawford's second husband, Franchot Tone, was working with Wyman on *Here Comes the Bride*. There was no such thing as six degrees of separation in Hollywood.

By the spring of 1951, the Bautzer-Wyman romance was in bloom. The couple graced the premiere of her film *The Blue Veil*. Ronald Reagan attended with his future wife, Nancy Davis. Bautzer and Wyman also attended the Academy Awards ceremony together in March. Wyman wondered why a little boy across the room was staring at her and Bautzer the entire evening. She later learned that he was Joan Crawford's son.

In the summer of 1951, movie magazines were speculating that Bautzer and Wyman would marry. Unbeknownst to everyone, the couple had taken blood tests in order to get a marriage license. It looked like Bautzer might finally wed a star. A journalist from *Modern Screen* magazine saw them at George Sanders's party for British producer Gabriel Pascal. The writer printed a conversation between two female guests. "Look at them," said the first. "They're obviously in love. What a pity he won't marry her."

"How do you know they won't get married?" asked the second.

"Come now. You've been around. Does Greg Bautzer marry any of them? Did he marry Lana Turner? Did he marry Dorothy Lamour? Did he marry Joan Crawford or Ginger Rogers? I admit he's been married twice before, but that was when he was young."

The July issue of *Photoplay* magazine carried an article examining Wyman's relationship with Bautzer.

> The guy has something, there's no doubt about that. Ask any man what it is and he'll tell you. "Bautzer's a man's man, virile, successful, a gentleman where he works, or where he plays. And he's out to win, wherever he is, in the courtroom, at the poker table, or on the tennis court. Yet somehow, once he has won, he seems to lose interest—as though the fun were all in the battle, and the victory anticlimactic."
>
> Ask any woman what it is about Bautzer and she'll tell you. "He's a woman's man . . . thoughtful, considerate, attentive. If you ask him to the most informal dinner party, he'll send flowers the next day with a sweet note. If you go nightclubbing with him and are separated from him for so much as one dance, he'll send a waiter with a scribbled message: 'Miss you.' When you're with him you know that for him—at that moment at least—you're the only woman in the world, and the most beautiful."

Bautzer and Wyman never did become engaged. The only explanation came from Wyman, who simply said that Bautzer enjoyed his bachelor life too much to give it up.

By May 1951, Bautzer and Ginger Rogers were dating again. They attended Lena Horne's show at the Cocoanut Grove and were reported to have danced "like a couple of school kids" and "looked like love in bloom." The romance continued into 1952. In April, Rogers threw a surprise forty-first birthday party for Bautzer in Perino's private dining room. Guests included Van Johnson, Edgar Bergen, and Dore Schary, the new head of MGM. But Bautzer's relationship with Rogers had turned prickly. "Our dates would go from pleasant to tepid to cool to argumentative," wrote Rogers. Actress Ann Savage lived down the street from Rogers. "If they were getting along," recalled Savage, "they would drive down the hill together in his car. If they were fighting, he would fly down the hill about ninety miles an hour by himself. She would fly by even faster a few minutes later in her car."

In late July, Rogers went to France for an unplanned vacation. She met a twenty-four-year-old actor named Jacques Bergerac. "It's a little premature to speak of marriage," she was saying two weeks later when asked about her relationship with Bergerac. When she returned to Los Angeles, Bautzer went to her home to find out her intentions. "What about this fellow Bergerac," he asked. "Is he important?"

"I don't know exactly. Why?"

"Look, do you want to get married? Is that it?" In a moment Rogers realized that the elusive bachelor was actually proposing marriage. She was taken aback, unable to formulate a response when she thought she should. There was an awkward silence, and then she caught her breath.

"Well, Greg, you're just three years too late."

It was Bautzer's turn to be surprised. He gathered himself. "You've changed, Virginia. Yes, you've changed. That episode with that, that . . . [she thought he was going to say 'frog'] . . . that Frenchman, had more meaning to you than appears on the surface."

Rogers didn't respond.

"Well, I hope you will be very happy," he said. And that was the end. He stormed out.

Rogers knew Bautzer as well as any of his previous girlfriends. Her appraisal was perhaps the most perceptive. She saw a complex individual who was as warm in private as he was dazzling in public. But there was a dark side. "Greg liked to get his own way," wrote Rogers. "If he didn't, he'd flare up. I had had a few experiences with him when he lost his cool, and these episodes stuck in my mind. If we had married, I would always have suffered the disadvantage of being an adversary to one who earns his living by winning arguments. I always hated to see Greg angry. It changed his handsome demeanor." Six months later, Rogers married Bergerac. The marriage, like her others, lasted about four years.

The next star to enter Bautzer's life was Peggy Lee, who had achieved fame in 1943 singing "Why Don't You Do Right?" with Benny Goodman's orchestra. Bautzer would often come to Ciro's to watch Lee perform. He sent her unusual gifts, including a small sculpture of an ostrich that had a ruby eye and a black-pearl-and-diamond tail. She felt that the most romantic thing he ever gave her was a book of her poetry that he had privately printed, entitled *Softly, with Feeling*. After dating Bautzer for a time, Lee considered Bautzer "running first" in her affection, but when he asked her to marry him, she turned him down.

She had grown tired of having their dates, whether in a restaurant or at home, interrupted by calls from Howard Hughes, who by 1952 had become one of Bautzer's clients. "I am so sorry," Bautzer would say. "I have to leave." Lee surmised that the billionaire aviator disliked her because she had once insulted the *Constellation*, one of his planes. She was traveling with actor Burt Lancaster when an engine caught fire. Hughes had also tried to date her when she was still married, but she rebuffed him.

Years later, remembering Bautzer, Lee felt pangs of regret. "What a fool I was!" she wrote, citing low self-esteem for her failure to marry him. Hughes felt that he had ruined the relationship. To apologize he gave Bautzer a white Cadillac convertible, which Bautzer promptly drove onto Lee's front lawn in a rage over her dating another man. Once the anger had cooled, he and Lee agreed to stay friends, which was the pattern of Bautzer's breakups.

In late 1952, Bautzer and actress Mari Blanchard became an item. A former fashion model, Blanchard had dark curly hair and a body so voluptuous that she reportedly inspired the character of Stupefyin' Jones in Al Capp's *Li'l Abner* comic strip. Stupefyin' Jones is so gorgeous that men become paralyzed at the sight of her. Blanchard was also the alleged cause of Marguerite Chapman's 1950 divorce from Bentley Ryan.

Blanchard was not a star. When she met Bautzer, she had only played bit parts and a supporting role in *Overland Telegraph*. She soon progressed to leading roles in *Abbott and Costello Go to Mars* and *Destry*. Never a studied actress or model, she was nine units short of earning a degree in international law at USC when she dropped out to pursue an acting career. Hedda Hopper asked Blanchard why she had done this. "Because," answered Blanchard, "most men would rather look at a girl than listen to her."

"Since Greg's an attorney and you almost became one, who wins the arguments?" asked Hopper.

"We don't argue," said Blanchard. "I do my huffing and puffing alone. When I become irritated, I go home and beat my head against the wall."

"Gal, you ought to marry and get some masculine touch around the house," said Hopper. "Why don't you put the old clamps on Bautzer?"

"We're not getting married. We seem to fit each other's plans nicely." Blanchard tried to be philosophical about Bautzer's unavailability. "Dogs and men are very much alike. The trick is to catch them young and train them."

"You're not going to train Greg."

"No, I wouldn't hold my breath for that." Fortunately, she did not, because Bautzer was soon off and running.

In October 1952, Bautzer represented actress Arlene Dahl in her divorce from actor Lex Barker. Since suffering the embarassment of Joan Crawford pouring a glass of wine on her in retaliation for flirting with Bautzer, she had gone on to star in such films as *Reign of Terror* with Robert Cummings and *Three Little Words* with Fred Astaire. Born in Minneapolis, red-headed Dahl was known for her Nordic beauty. She worked at MGM for several years before marrying Barker, who had succeeded Johnny Weissmuller as Tarzan. Barker was a direct descendant of the founder of Rhode Island, Roger Williams, and played football at Fessenden and Phillips-Exeter Academy. When he left Princeton to become an actor, his family disowned him. He ordered Dahl to give up acting and keep house. This she would not do. "When I needed a divorce from Lex, my first husband," said Dahl, "I called Greg." Bautzer suggested that he introduce in court some unflattering things he knew about Barker. "I don't want to say anything bad about Lex," said Dahl.

"Then how are you going to get a divorce from him?" asked Bautzer. "Let's go to dinner to talk about the case." Though Bautzer was still involved with Blanchard, he saw nothing wrong with treating Dahl to one of his famous "business" dinners; this one took place at Perino's restaurant. Bautzer impressed the actress.

"He was such a good-looking man. He could have been a movie star if he wanted to. He had a wonderful deep voice and he would talk softly to get you to lean in and listen. He really knew how to make a point. Well, at the end of our dinner he said, 'Arlene, I would like to date you.' I was uncomfortable dating my attorney, and so I said: 'Greg, I don't like to mix business with pleasure.' He laughed and said 'I always do!' He had a wonderful laugh."

Today, dating clients is strongly discouraged. The American Bar Association's Model Rules of Professional Conduct expressly prohibit

sexual relations between a lawyer and client unless the sexual relationship existed prior to representation. In California, sex between a lawyer and client is deemed to impair the lawyer's professional judgment
and can be used as evidence against the attorney in a malpractice
lawsuit or disbarment proceeding. However, during the first thirty
years of Bautzer's career, lawyers were rarely sued for malpractice, and
dating a client was not considered much of an ethical problem.

In court, Bautzer coaxed Dahl to tell Judge Stanley Mosk that
Barker had called her a "hick from Minnesota" when she refused a
cocktail. Barker was often sullen, refused to speak to her, and had
once locked her out of their home on Fox Hills Drive. His behavior
made her so nervous that she required medical care. Bautzer called her
sister, Evelyn Rolin, to the witness stand to corroborate Dahl's story.
Barker did not contest the divorce. In the property settlement, Dahl
received the house and furnishings, but no alimony.

Barker was another celebrity with very few degrees of separation
from Bautzer. After Bautzer handled Dahl's divorce, Barker went on
to marry Lana Turner. Barker later starred with Mari Blanchard in
Jungle Heat.

12

THE BERGMAN SEQUEL

In the spring of 1952, Ingrid Bergman's daughter Pia Lindström was thirteen. Summer was approaching, the time for her annual trip to Europe. Her parents' divorce settlement called for her to visit her mother during time off from school. The previous year, Pia's mother had seen her in England. This year, Bergman wanted to see her in Italy, at the home she shared with director Rossellini. Pia's father, Dr. Petter Lindström, thought this custody arrangement was potentially dangerous. He was concerned that Bergman might not return her; courts in foreign jurisdictions were not required to follow other courts' orders regarding custody. He also thought that Pia should not be forced to spend time in an environment he considered amoral. Bergman disagreed. In 2011, Pia Lindström recalled the dispute: "My mother rejected a proposal to meet in Sweden, and my father was concerned that they would not be able to guarantee my return from Italy, because an Italian court would not force a mother to send her child out of the country. Then my father offered to have Phyllis Seaton, wife of director George Seaton and one-time mayor of Beverly Hills, take me to see my mother someplace else. But that was not accepted. My mother insisted on Italy. I was told I needed to say something definite."

Bergman instructed Bautzer to file a suit that would clarify visitation rights. She was able to do this because the divorce settlement agreement had failed to specify where visitations were to occur. Like the sequel to a blockbuster movie, the Lindström family went to court again. This time there would be a full-blown trial.

Bautzer knew he was taking a major risk going up against Lindström's lawyer Isaac Pacht in a rushed trial. It was like stepping into a boxing ring with a heavyweight champion. Pacht wasn't just a wily trial lawyer with nearly forty years legal experience; he had been a judge himself. This not only gave him insight into the way evidence would be received but also earned him respect from sitting judges. Any advantage the court could give, he would get. Why Bautzer didn't run away from the fight is an enigma. Perhaps he couldn't resist the publicity. Perhaps he was prideful and considered himself infallible. After all, he had never lost a trial. Or perhaps he had no choice, and Bergman demanded that the matter go to trial. Whatever the reason, when Bautzer walked into the courtroom, he knew he was in for the fight of his life. He had handled many public scandals, but he had never handled anything like this. If he lost, it would be reported on the front pages of every paper in the country.

From the start, he knew there was a potentially fatal flaw in his case. Bergman could not come to the United States to attend the trial, because she was nine months pregnant with twins. Celebrity lawyers know that it is difficult to win a trial without the client present. It gives the impression that the star doesn't care about the outcome—that she thinks she's superior and not subject to the same rules as common folk. Even with a good reason for not attending the trial, it is hard to shake the prejudice. As always, Bautzer exuded confidence, but inside he had to be scared.

The hearing began in early June with Judge Mildred L. Lillie presiding. The outcome would be determined by the judge herself; custody matters are not for a jury to decide. In order to enter the courtroom each day, Lindström and his daughter had to run a gauntlet. "There were dozens of reporters and cameramen, gawkers, fans," Pia recalled. "I hadn't seen anything like that before. To me they looked like crazy people who were going to trample us."

Bautzer anticipated an attack on Bergman's fitness as a parent, so on June 9 he called two character witnesses. The first to testify was Superior Court judge Thurmond Clarke, a fellow USC Law School alumnus who had been the presiding judge in the divorce proceedings. He had visited the Rossellinis in Italy the previous year and had observed the director demonstrate "kindness and devotion" toward both Robertino, his child by Bergman, and Lorenzo, his child from his prior marriage. "Did you observe anything detrimental to the children?" asked Bautzer.

"I did not," replied Clarke.

Judge Lillie did not give much weight to Clarke's testimony. Only two weeks before, Clarke and his wife had sat with Bautzer and Ginger Rogers at a benefit dinner for the Pasadena Children's Hospital. This was an error on Bautzer's part. The judge's presence at the dinner was picked up by the press. It was clear that the judge was starstruck and potentially influenced by the company he was keeping.

The next to testify was producer David O. Selznick, who had also visited the Rossellini home. "I have seldom seen a man who was more a playmate with his children," said Selznick. "I was enormously impressed. While we were at dinner, he had a desperate anxiety to get back to the boy Robertino. Ingrid seemed a very contented wife. It was characteristic of Ingrid that she helped with the chores, served the guests, and seemed to be the same person as when she was here."

Pacht cross-examined Selznick about Bergman's salary from 1940 to 1945. "I'm sure Dr. Lindström has the figures," Selznick answered. "He took care of her money." Pacht asked Lillie that the remark be stricken from the record. Selznick tried to clarify his dig at Lindström, saying that his primary interest was in defending Bergman. "I think her standing is first rate," he said. "Her public is with her. I think she's been persecuted enough, and I'm interested in her as a human being. Rossellini is extraordinarily generous and talented, a fine father, a good husband, and generous. He's given money to the poor. They regard him as a god in the south of Italy." Pacht moved to the question of morality. This touched a nerve, causing Selznick to raise his voice. "His morals I know nothing about, and neither do you, and neither does that Dr. Lindström, or he wouldn't have had him in his house as a guest!" Pacht then read from the July 1950 Congressional Record in which Senator Edwin O. Johnson had accused Rossellini of Nazism and drug addiction. "May I ask who wrote this script?" snapped Selznick.

On June 12, it was time for Pia Lindström to be called to the witness stand. Since there had been no pretrial discovery, this was the first time she had encountered Bautzer. "My impression of him was that he was very handsome and very confident," said Pia. "But he was condescending and I felt he thought of me as a child he could manipulate." Pia saw Bautzer as someone unaccustomed to dealing with children. "He made me uncomfortable. He was not interested in what I was saying, only in what he could make me say to fit his purpose. I thought he was setting traps for me to damage my father. I did not want to help him in any way."

Bautzer's examination was reported in *Time* magazine:

Q. Miss Lindström, do you understand what this case is about? What your mother is seeking?

A. Yes. She wants me to go to Italy. And I don't want to go to Italy. I just saw her last summer in England.

Q. You realize that your mother is not making a request that you go to live with her, don't you?

A. Yes.

Q. When you told your mother that you loved her and missed her when you saw her in England last summer, you said it only to be polite?

A. I don't believe I said I missed her. Well, I—I guess I did. We saw each other several days. Mother asked me: "Are you happy?"

Q. Didn't you say you had missed her and would like to see her?

A. I don't believe I ever said that. She never really asked me: "Do you miss me?" And I never said: "Yes, I do." Even if she did, I couldn't very well say that I didn't love her.

Q. Don't you love your mother, Pia?

A. I don't love my mother. I like her. I don't want to go to Italy to be with her. I love my father.

Q. Have you ever written your mother, telling her that you love her?

A. I always sign my letters "Love, Pia."

Q. Does that express the way you feel about her?

A. No. That's just the wording of the letter.

Q. Do you feel that your mother doesn't care about you now?

A. Well, I don't think she cares about me too much. . . . She didn't seem very interested about me when she left. It was only after she left and got married and had children that she suddenly decided that she wanted me.

Bautzer then questioned her about the period in 1949 when Rossellini had been a guest in the Lindström home.

Q. Did you have any conversations with Mr. Rossellini at that time?

A. Well, he lived in our house, so I guess I talked to him, but I don't remember anything we talked about.

Q. Did you find him to be a considerate, gentlemanly man?

A. I don't remember. I didn't find him anything.

Q. What sort of discussions have you had with your father about Mr. Rossellini?

A. We discussed that he used to stand in front of the fireplace and tell us how religious he was, and he used to . . . he borrowed all my father's money and bought presents for me with my father's money.

Bautzer finally asked Pia if she missed her mother. "No," she answered. "I'd rather live with my father."

After Pia stepped down from the stand, the court reporter, Ms. Breska, said Pia had delivered her testimony "like a little Ingrid." Bautzer's cross-examination had backfired and he knew it. Trial lawyers typically avoid asking questions that they don't know how the witness will answer. Unfortunately for Bautzer, due to the speedy nature of the case, he had not had the opportunity to take Pia's deposition beforehand. As such, he had no choice but to wing it. The result was disastrous. Each time Pia answered a question, the judge lost sympathy for Bergman. The thirteen-year-old had beaten him.

For her part, Pia did not view her testimony as a victory. "I felt ashamed and embarrassed," recalled Pia. "I felt sad for my mother and regretted that I hurt her. I felt sad for myself, too. But I wanted to be faithful to my father. Having seen the personal and professional humiliations suffered by him, I felt a strong need not to add to his sorrow. My father was a serious and accomplished neurosurgeon. The scandal was a shattering experience. It changed the course of his life. And after my mother left to go to Italy, my father had been both mother and father to me."

Next, Dr. Lindström was called to the witness stand. For the first time, the public got to hear all the lurid details of his divorce from Bergman. In testimony that lasted four days, he gave a step-by-step description of the events. It started with his going to Messina in May 1949 and attempting to convince Bergman to give up Rossellini. He had then spent weeks in England hoping she would change her mind or at least meet him to discuss Pia's future. Marta Cohn, wife of *Stromboli* screenwriter Art Cohn, had told the court she had met Lindström in Paris on July 15, 1949, and begged him to give Bergman a divorce. Lindström further testified that Mrs. Cohn had warned him that Rossellini had threatened suicide if Bergman saw her husband again. "She said she had to take the revolver away from him," Lindström testified. "I said, 'This sounds like nonsense. If he would wave a pistol and then let a woman take it away from him, there's not much substance to the man.'"

Lindström also took Bergman to task for not meeting Pia in person to break the news of their divorce. "I told her it is impossible to write a ten-year-old child and tell her you're not coming home," said Lindström. He had also told Bergman that he would meet her anywhere she liked so that she could talk to Pia in person.

Pacht offered into evidence newspaper reports that Bergman had become pregnant with Rossellini's child while still married to Lindström. Bautzer objected, calling the articles "scandalous." Pacht explained that the articles were offered to show that the publicity had affected Pia. Showing deference to Pacht, and trusting her own abilities to separate which facts were significant and which weren't, Lillie overruled Bautzer's objection and allowed the papers into evidence. Lindström testified that Pia's schoolmates were taunting her. "When some boy had done something bad," said Lindström, "he'd 'done a Rossellini' or he 'was a Rossellini.'" Pia had complained to him several times.

"This is something we can't do anything about," he told her. "Just pretend you don't understand or hear. Go on about your play. Time will take care of it."

Without his client present to defend herself, there was little Bautzer could do to counter Lindström's testimony. He sat there for four days knowing that he was fighting with both hands tied behind his back. He needed Bergman by his side, not thousands of miles away in Italy. Whatever remained of the public's sympathy for Bergman was lost. It was frustrating and humiliating, and there was no way to stop it.

Finally, all that remained to be done was to have expert witnesses testify. Pacht called Dr. Charles O. Sturdevant, a psychiatrist, to the stand. He characterized Pia as a normal, healthy child who had nonetheless been traumatized by her parents' separation and by the scandal. Bautzer called psychiatrist Dr. Mandel Sherman, who told the court that Pia's trauma could be cured by seeing her mother. It was a very mild counter at best.

On June 24, Judge Lillie issued her ruling. For a half hour, she read her eleven-page opinion, which counted points in both Lindström's and Bergman's favor but chastised both of them for their "pride and selfishness." Lillie ruled that the child could not be forced to go to Italy against her will. The determining factor in her decision was Bergman's failure to visit Pia in the United States since her divorce. This was an unpardonable sin. There had been nothing to prevent Bergman from exercising her right under the divorce settlement to visit Pia in California. Lillie expressed regret that Pia or "any child must be subjected to publicity of the kind arising out of litigation such as this. Unfortunately, the parents in this case seem to be more interested in what each deserves or what each is entitled to under the law than in what would be for the best interests of the child, regardless of the law."

Lillie was critical of Bergman's much-quoted claim that she had "bargained and paid for" visitation rights. "The court wonders how long it will take her to realize that although she and the plaintiff might be able, between themselves, to place a dollar-and-cent sign on the rights of visitation and custody of a child, neither she nor anyone else can bargain for and buy the affection, love, and respect of a child." Lillie had interviewed Pia privately and found her charming, well mannered, and vital, but indifferent to her mother. In Lillie's opinion, Pia was almost lost to Bergman. Lillie urged Bergman to visit Pia and she cautioned both parents against ever again exposing her to protracted litigation. "The court is not alone in its belief that a reconciliation must take place between mother and child in order to give Pia proper security."

After the judgment was read, Bautzer fled the courtroom immediately. He did not want to answer questions for the press. He hated losing more than anything, and now he had lost badly. Moreover, he had to call Bergman to tell her the news before someone else did. Lindström stayed and gloated over his victory. For the first time, he allowed the reporters to take photos of Pia. He told the press he planned to take Pia to Pennsylvania, where he had accepted a position as chief neurosurgeon at Aspinwall Veterans Hospital.

The next day, Bautzer realized that he needed to make a statement to try to repair Bergman's image. The divorce had made her seem to the public like a cheating wife; now the fight over visitation rights convinced the world that she was also a terrible mother. Bautzer told the *Los Angeles Times* that Bergman intended to visit Pia in the United States for six weeks. Bautzer also tried to give the impression that the fight wasn't over. He added that he had hired Jerry Giesler as consultant. Giesler made his own announcement: "All I can say now is that there undoubtedly will be some sort of action." The prediction was a hollow one. Neither lawyer could think of a way to appeal the court's decision or put pressure on Dr. Lindström to send Pia to Italy. The Bergman-Lindström visitation rights case would go down as the only major courtroom defeat in Gregson Bautzer's career.

It should not have happened. The location of Bergman's visitations was probably never discussed by Bautzer and Pacht during the final negotiations of the divorce settlement. It is not unusual for a court to refuse to allow a divorced parent to take a child outside the state in which the court resides, let alone to another country. Perhaps it didn't occur to Bautzer until after the divorce settlement was signed to ask Bergman if she wanted to see Pia outside California. Perhaps Bergman, not knowing how courts treat such issues, assumed that she could see Pia in Europe at her discretion. The bigger question is how Bautzer could have counseled Bergman that she could win this dispute.

He knew the odds were against him. For three years Bergman had not visited her oldest daughter in the United States. The inescapable impression was that she was too absorbed in her new husband and baby to spend time with her daughter. It also appeared that she was trying to hurt her ex-husband by yanking their child away from him. Her sincerity was suspect. How much time could she spend with Pia in any case? She was nine months pregnant. The trial was still in session when, on June 18, she gave birth to twin daughters Isabella and Isotta.

It is conceivable that Bautzer continued with the case on Bergman's terms because she forced him to do so. Bergman was known to be stubborn. The production of her last Hollywood film, *Joan of Arc*, was unnecessarily difficult and expensive, in large part because of her temperament. It is also conceivable that Bautzer didn't tell his client that she had a bad case. Lawyers who represent major stars are frequently afraid they will lose a client if they tell them things they do not want to hear.

In the end, however, it was not Bergman's intractability or Pacht's cleverness that lost Bautzer the case. It was the testimony of one witness. Pia Lindström had, with her simple, honest answers, won Judge Lillie's support.

The decision could not, unfortunately, resolve the family's discord. Contrary to Bautzer's statements to the press, Bergman did not come to visit Pia in Pennsylvania or anywhere else. In the five years that followed, her only contact with Pia was in writing. "I had no communication with her except for a few letters," said Pia in 2011. "By then, she had three children with Roberto Rossellini and a new home in Italy that she said she loved. In spite of Mr. Bautzer's statement, my mother did not come to the United States. I went to Paris to meet her when I was eighteen." Bergman remained in Europe, making films there. Despite her self-imposed exile, American audiences forgave her, and she won her second Oscar just five years later for *Anastasia*. Bergman did not return to Hollywood for the ceremony; Cary Grant accepted the award on her behalf. She went on to win her third and final Oscar in 1974 for *Murder on the Orient Express*. "I've gone from saint to whore and back to saint again all in one lifetime," she said.

The next time Pia Lindström saw Bautzer was many years later, at a party in Beverly Hills. By this time, she had a career in broadcast journalism. Bautzer walked up to her and proclaimed, "You are the only person to ever lose a case for me." This was hardly an icebreaker, given the trauma the trial had caused her. Pia was surprised he didn't take more responsibility for the outcome. "I did not lose the case. He lost it. He might have suggested a compromise like visiting in Sweden or England. My father was willing to take me there." There is no way of knowing whether Bautzer did suggest a compromise and Bergman refused. Oddly enough, despite her displeasure at being reminded of a painful time in her life, Pia could not help noticing that Bautzer had retained his charm. "He was just as handsome. Later, when I read how many women fell in love with him, I could see why."

13

BATTLING BOGIE

The pressure of a burgeoning law practice took a toll on Bautzer's psyche. His famous clients were paying a lot of money for his services; they expected a lot in return. Because of their celebrity status, many felt they deserved special treatment. Temperamental and spoiled, they called at all hours of the day and night to dump their latest problem in his lap, whether large or small. They expected him to stop whatever else he was doing and fix their troubles immediately. Bautzer took these responsibilities seriously and prided himself on giving his clients his total attention.

Like an emergency room doctor, he was on call twenty-four hours a day. In a time before mobile phones, Bautzer made certain his secretary knew which restaurant, nightclub, or party he would be attending in the evening so she could contact him. Waiters frequently brought a telephone with an extension cord to his table so he could take his clients' calls. While he enjoyed the excitement of nonstop action and the aura of importance it gave him in the community, his big-shot status came at a price. He constantly needed to let off steam.

To relieve the tension Bautzer played as hard as he worked. He gambled at card games, engaged in serial romances with starlets, and drank heavily. At the time, drinking copious amounts of alcohol was not only tolerated, it was considered a sign of maturity and manhood. The cocktail hour officially started at 5 PM and lasted all evening. Executives bragged about having "three-martini lunches" and kept private bars stocked in their offices for daytime "pick-me-ups." Inebriation without appearing too drunk or getting sick was called "holding" your liquor, and it was considered a virtue.

Bautzer thought he could hold his liquor, but often he couldn't. When he drank, his personality changed, reverting to the barroom brawler of his youth on the docks of San Pedro. "Watch out for him," Howard Hughes warned publicist Paul MacNamara. "When he gets on the sauce, he can be trouble." That his uncle had died of alcoholism at age thirty-two should have been a warning.

Lawyers are disproportionally high candidates for alcoholism, and Bautzer was a textbook example. Current studies show that nearly 30 percent of lawyers who have been practicing for twenty years or longer have an alcohol-use disorder—triple the average for the general population. The situation is so prevalent that the California State Bar requires all lawyers to take a one-hour educational course in preventing substance abuse once every three years. Most lawyers who drink heavily are able to get away with it because their careers do not suffer. They are known as "highly functioning alcoholics." The same personality traits that allow them to succeed professionally make it possible for them to keep their drinking from affecting their jobs. They are typically perfectionists and overachievers, with a competitive workaholic nature and a strong physical constitution. Bautzer possessed all of these traits, and so he never thought he needed to stop drinking. Moreover, he didn't always drink too much. Sometimes he could consume one or two glasses and go home without incident. But as his practice grew, his consumption of alcohol increased, and so did the frequency of bad behavior under the influence.

The trouble would start in the most innocuous way. Bautzer would be talking with his dinner companions, apparently unaffected by the number of cocktails he had downed. His attention would move to an adjoining table where other diners were engrossed in conversation, oblivious to their renowned neighbor. Suddenly Bautzer would take umbrage at something—anything. It could be a sidelong glance, a laugh, a word. In an instant he was on his feet and moving toward an innocent person.

For much of the twentieth century, fistfights were part of the code of manhood, a holdover from the days when gentlemen fought duels to settle disputes and defend their honor. "Real men" weren't afraid to march onto the battlefield and back up their words with action. Celebrities like Ernest Hemingway, Norman Mailer, Frank Sinatra, and even studio boss Louis B. Mayer were renowned brawlers. Nevertheless, Bautzer's drunken battles went far beyond the bounds of the era's social norms.

Friends tried to stay ahead of Bautzer, but it was difficult. "Greg wasn't a staggering, falling-down drunk," remembered MacNamara. "You might not even know he was in trouble. He simply turned off his lights when he got a certain amount of firewater aboard, and when that happened, look out. He would change in the blink of an eye from a charming, gentle fellow to an enraged bull."

MacNamara explained the problem further: "Greg had a faulty connection in his radar set that would sometimes snap and give him incorrect messages, and the message that he would receive would be from some total stranger who wasn't trying to send him a message at all. The message he mistakenly received was to the effect that he, Greg Bautzer, was a son of a bitch. This, of course, would enrage Greg, and he would turn on the stranger, who would be sitting in all innocence a few tables away, sipping his wine, oblivious that a Pearl Harbor attack was on its way. This led to all kinds of misunderstandings, spilled drinks, and uncalled-for blows. Usually there wasn't too much damage, but it would be difficult for Greg's friends to explain to the victim and his friends."

MacNamara was with Bautzer at the Racquet Club bar one night when he saw Bautzer take a sudden dislike to a stranger across the room. The man was doing nothing but sitting there, finishing a drink. Bautzer's face clouded. His eyes narrowed. He began insulting the man, and then he challenged him. A bartender named Tex whispered to MacNamara, "Get your friend outta here. That guy he's monkeying with is trouble." Sure enough, the stranger was arming himself with a glass ashtray and was flanked by two bruisers. Just when it looked like all hell was going to break loose, the club's bouncer walked in, carrying a club. "Bautzer cooled off," said MacNamara, "but it had been close, and it had been his fault." Bautzer was fortunate someone stepped in to stop it. The formidable stranger was on the Los Angeles Rams football team. The next day MacNamara told Bautzer how lucky he had been. "He looked at me funny and wanted to know what I was talking about," recalled MacNamara. "He had no recollection of what had gone on. And when I gave him the details, he just shook his head."

Bautzer was relatively sober the night he encountered Humphrey Bogart in a bar. The star enjoyed needling people. He would cast witty insults to see just how far he could push someone to provoke a reaction. "Bogie thought of himself as Scaramouche," said writer-producer Nunnally Johnson, "the mischievous scamp who sets off the fireworks, then nips out." In a town crowded with oversized egos, he found many targets. Bogart was democratic; he insulted friend and foe alike, and no one was safe, neither stars nor executives. "Bigwigs have been known to stay away from brilliant Hollywood occasions rather than expose their swelling neck muscles to Bogie's banderillas," said Bogart's favorite director, John Huston. Irving "Swifty" Lazar, Bogart's agent, thought that the star occasionally hurt people but believed that his usual target was someone who could defend himself. No doubt Bogart took one look at Bautzer and saw a bull's-eye. In a few minutes, he had gotten the unflappable debater angry. "I'm going to beat you to a pulp," Bautzer told him.

"You're not going to hit an old man, are you?" asked Bogart, who was then in his fifties.

"Well, stop needling me," said Bautzer.

"You know, Greg, you have a bad pattern to your life," said Bogart with mock sadness.

"That does it." Bautzer got to his feet and ordered Bogart to step outside.

"Go on," said Bogart. "You go first. Everyone will follow us if we both go out together. Let's fight in private." Bautzer stormed out. Bogart watched him go, paused, finished his drink, and then ordered another. Five minutes went by. Bautzer walked back in, puzzled. "You look cold," Bogart said to him. "Come in. Warm up. Have a drink." Bautzer stared at him for a moment, then he got the joke. He laughed. Laughter could change Bautzer's mood.

Actor George Hamilton had a number of run-ins with Bautzer. The first was at the New York nightclub El Morocco, where friends were helping him get over a breakup with actress Susan Kohner. To the great displeasure of her father, talent agent Paul Kohner, Bautzer had lured the dark-haired young beauty away from Hamilton by serenading her bedroom window with a musical quartet. "And who should come in but Susan, and with Greg Bautzer," said Hamilton. "He kept dancing her by my table, dipping her dangerously close to me, rubbing her in my face. I got upset and called him aside. 'You've got no manners,' I told him. He jumped into action and put up his dukes. 'You want it right here, kid? How do you want it? Fists? Guns? Karate? You name it.' I backed off. I couldn't do a duel in front of Susan, not at El Morocco."

Hamilton got a second chance at a dinner at Hedda Hopper's home. When Bautzer gave him the opportunity, he took Bautzer outside and knocked him flat. To Hamilton's surprise, Bautzer admired him for it. When Hamilton ran into Bautzer on the street in Beverly

Hills, Bautzer smiled, called him "compadre," and hugged him. After that, whenever the two met, Hamilton was Bautzer's compadre.

Bautzer's favorite way to relieve tension was to seduce beautiful young actresses. When he wasn't drinking, fighting, gambling, playing tennis, or arguing a case, Bautzer was wooing. He was a master at giving a woman what she wanted. MacNamara analyzed his system. "His looks were enough to get him started, and his technique was always the same," said MacNamara. "First, long-stemmed roses came in two-dozen bunches. They were followed by a small but expensive fur piece. Then came an invitation to Acapulco for a long weekend. It never failed to work."

There is no way to know how many actresses Bautzer dated, but there was certainly a long trail of stems and fur between Hollywood and the beach at Acapulco. In December 1941, after breaking up with Dorothy Lamour, he had stepped out with the legendary Marlene Dietrich, who would also one day be a client. In 1942, he paid actress Carol Bruce some attention. In 1946, he courted the gorgeous Marguerite Chapman, who later married and divorced his former law partner Bentley Ryan. In June 1947, Bautzer was reported to be "stardusty" with Audrey Young, the future Mrs. Billy Wilder, at the same time that he was seeing Greer Garson. In New York one month later, he was "cruising the glitter spots" with *Cat People* actress Jane Randolph. In the early 1950s, Bautzer dated buxom blonde Barbara Payton. She had a reputation for sleeping with every man she met, including Howard Hughes, who supposedly said she would perform any sexual act a man desired. Bautzer stopped seeing her after just a few weeks when he realized she was mentally unstable. Her bohemian lifestyle shortened her career and led to an early tragic death after a degrading drug-addicted existence as a street prostitute. It has been reported that she and Bautzer were engaged, but there is no evidence of it.

Bautzer's style didn't work on every woman, though. In 1953, he tried his technique on Ann Rutherford, who had played Carreen O'Hara in *Gone with the Wind*. She was hesitant to accept his invitation to dinner and asked a friend, actress Ann Miller, what she thought. Miller had been out with Bautzer. "He was suave, gallant, and eloquent," said Miller, "and he had the smoothest line of blarney I've ever heard."

"Do you think he'll give me the same line?"

"Let's have some fun," said Miller. "I'll tape record what I remember him plying me with, and then let's compare it with what he tells you."

"Will you bring the tape to my house?" asked Rutherford. "I'll play it back as soon as I get home and make the comparison."

Rutherford had dinner with Bautzer that night. About midnight she called Miller laughing hysterically. "You told me, but I really didn't believe it," said Rutherford. "It's true! It's true! I played your tape as soon as I came home and it's just as you said. He gave me the same flowery line—how beautiful I was, how he would walk on water for me, how he loved me more than life itself—all the bunk. I had fun, though. He really is a charmer."

Bautzer enjoyed his status as a famous playboy. It is cliché to say that variety is the spice of life, but Bautzer had his pick of the most desirable women in the world. According to his secretary, Lea Sullivan, some actresses even pursued *him* seeking a date. They saw no reason to stand on ceremony and called his office to ask him out. Sometimes these ladies became so insistent, Sullivan had to tell the switchboard operator not to put the calls through. In truth, for most of his life Bautzer's first love was his career, and that commitment always came first.

In 1951, Bautzer turned forty. By no means middle-aged, he had nonetheless been a Hollywood fixture for fifteen years. His status was beginning to provide him with leadership opportunities in the community. In 1953, Bautzer was named by Conrad Hilton to the Citizens' Committee for Major League Baseball, which hoped to bring the St. Louis Browns to Los Angeles. In 1954, he joined the board of directors of National Theaters Inc., a company created to control Twentieth Century-Fox's former theaters after the federal government's 1948 determination that studios owning theaters constituted a violation of antitrust laws. In 1955, he was elected to the board of the Pepsi-Cola Bottling Co. of Los Angeles. Alfred Steele, chief executive officer of Pepsi, had recently become Joan Crawford's fourth husband. Crawford used her influence to put Bautzer on the board of directors.

Bautzer was also a board member and chief counsel of the Fidelity Pictures Corporation, which produced low-budget films for release through Republic Pictures. The company made several interesting pictures employing top-notch talent, including *House by the River*, directed by veteran director Fritz Lang; *Woman on the Run*, starring Ann Sheridan; *Rancho Notorious*, also directed by Lang and starring Marlene Dietrich; *The San Francisco Story*, starring Joel McCrea and Yvonne De Carlo; and *Montana Belle*, directed by veteran director Alan Dwan and starring Jane Russell. Bautzer had a hand in casting the films. Ann Sheridan and Marlene Dietrich were both his clients and romantic interests. His former steady girlfriend Ginger Rogers also made a comedy for Fidelity called *The Groom Wore Spurs*. In it, Rogers plays a lawyer trying to rescue a cowboy actor from gangsters to whom he owes gambling debts, only to end up marrying him. *New York Times* critic Bosley Crowther panned the picture, saying, "The only thing funny about this picture is that it is called a Fidelity film." Hollywood could laugh at itself. When the trade paper *Hollywood Box Office* ran an article about Fidelity's production slate of six films, the title read: FIDELITY WILL FILM SEX FEATURES IN 18 MONTHS. It was most likely a misprint, but there were those who thought it alluded to Bautzer's reputation with the ladies.

V

EMINENCE

14

AN ELEGANT WIFE

When the firm of Bautzer, Grant, Youngman & Silbert moved to Beverly Hills in the early 1950s, its new offices were nothing special. The space they leased at 356 North Camden Drive was just a hallway on the second floor, with a door to each office. Gordon Youngman left after only a few years and formed a new firm with attorney Fred Leopold. Together they did the legal work for Disneyland. In gratitude, Walt Disney painted the name of YOUNGMAN & LEOPOLD on a second-story window on Main Street, which remains more than half a century later.

After only a few years on Camden Drive, Bautzer, Grant & Silbert moved to 190 North Canon Drive, also in Beverly Hills. When Bernard Silbert left, the firm became simply Bautzer & Grant. Arnold Grant's offices were in New York, but he frequently came to Los Angeles; similarly, Bautzer frequently traveled to New York. Also practicing in Los Angeles with Bautzer were partners Gerald Lipsky, Woody Irwin, and Jerald Schutzbank. By this time, Bautzer was representing producers, directors, and actors in contract negotiations. The firm's clients included Katharine Hepburn, Jack Benny, Cyd Charisse, Judy Garland, Farley Granger, Rock Hudson, Gene Kelly, Mario Lanza, Sophia Loren, Robert Mitchum, Patti Page, and Merle Oberon. They also represented producers such as Walter Wanger, Jerry Wald, and Ray Stark.

The new offices were as glamorous as the firm's clientele. They occupied the four-story building's entire penthouse suite. Bautzer's secretary Lea Sullivan recalled, "You got off the elevator and went into a beautiful circular lobby with a door leading to each partner. There were other attorneys there, but their offices were down a hallway." The Beverly Hills Brown Derby delivered lunch every day, which Bautzer usually ate in his office when he wasn't taking business lunches.

Bautzer had been living at the Bel-Air Hotel for the past ten years, in a bungalow off a courtyard at the corner of Stone Canyon and Chalon Roads. While there, he socialized with superstar Clark Gable, who also occasionally lived at the hotel. Both men had been involved with Joan Crawford and were still friends with her. They would take long drives together in Gable's Jaguar to unwind. Bautzer's hair had started to turn prematurely silver, a dramatic contrast to his youthful physique.

In September 1955, Bautzer and his partner Arnold Grant went to a cocktail party at the Beverly Hills Hotel. The event was a swanky one. The famed hostess Cobina Wright was honoring Madame Wellington Koo, ex-wife of the Chinese politician V. K. Wellington Koo. Bautzer stood with Grant, surveying the party. "You see that girl over there?" asked Bautzer. Grant spied a tall, slender brunette across the room and nodded. "Her name is Dana Wynter," said Bautzer, "and I'm going to marry her."

Bautzer's interest in Wynter was picked up by the *Hollywood Reporter*: "Greg Bautzer came stag, took one look at Dana Wynter, and sparks flew. Wynter was with someone else, but Bautzer chums noted that he didn't leave the affair until he had her phone number." But getting her phone number was not enough to get him a date. Wynter had just finished a film and she was leaving town to publicize it. She declined his first invitation.

Dana Wynter was twenty-four, five-foot-seven, with raven hair. She was born Dagmar Winter in Berlin, the daughter of a German surgeon and a Romanian mother, raised first in England and then

Southern Rhodesia (now Zimbabwe), where her father took his practice after Britain nationalized heath care. She studied medicine at
Rhodes University in South Africa, the only girl in a class of 150. The
school's drama society sparked her interest in acting, so she returned
to London. While learning her craft, she played bit parts in a few
films, acted on London radio with Orson Welles in *The Private Life
of Harry Lime*, and met composer Richard Rodgers, who wanted her
to play Liat in the Broadway revival of *South Pacific*. She lost the part
because she was taller than Herb Banke, the actor playing Lieutenant
Joseph Cable; Carol Lawrence got the job instead.

Wynter went to New York anyway and got her first role on television in *Robert Montgomery Presents* when Eva Gabor dropped out at
the last minute. After appearing on other "golden age of television"
shows such as *Suspense* and *Studio One*, she was signed by Charles K.
Feldman's Famous Artists Agency and was approached by Columbia
and MGM. She turned them down and signed a seven-year contract
with Twentieth Century-Fox.

The cultured young woman created a stir upon her arrival in
Hollywood, a community that was susceptible to a British accent. She
was sponsored by Samuel Goldwyn's wife Frances, who sat her next
to composer Cole Porter at a dinner party. Soon Porter was throwing
a party for Wynter. When Darryl F. Zanuck, who ran Fox, called her
to his office, she feared that with his reputation for casting-couch
moves, he would make a pass at her. To Wynter's relief, he kept his
hands to himself. "You know," said Zanuck, "you are the last woman
I've signed as a contract player. I haven't had much luck with women.
I hope I will with you." He was referring, no doubt, to Bella Darvi,
the Polish starlet whom he had launched with great fanfare, and to an
utterly hostile reception, both critically and commercially.

When Wynter got home from her meeting with Zanuck, she was
surprised to receive a call from him. "You know, Miss Wynter," he said.
"I think you're in luck. You're going to have a lead in a picture, but I

can't tell you what it is yet." It turned out to be a drama of Southern bigotry called *The View from Pompey's Head*. Zanuck left town, tired of Hollywood politics and gossip, so producer Buddy Adler, a longtime friend and client of Bautzer's, took charge of the studio and *The View from Pompey's Head*.

While on the press junket for the film, Wynter stopped at the William Morris Agency in New York. There she met the independent producer Walter Wanger. He had recently signed Vera Miles for his next project, a science-fiction movie based on Jack Finney's novel *The Body Snatchers*. He took one look at Wynter and saw a body worth snatching. "There's somebody new in town called Dana Wynter," he told the owners of Allied Artists. "I want her." In short order, Miles was out and Wynter was in. *Invasion of the Body Snatchers* had just finished shooting when Wynter met Bautzer.

Bautzer launched his own campaign. As Wynter passed through Philadelphia, Boston, and Chicago on her publicity tour for *The View from Pompey's Head*, she was met by masses of flowers and by long-distance invitations from her new admirer. Bautzer offered to fly to wherever she was just to take her to dinner. Wynter declined, saying she was too busy, but he kept calling. Her last stop was at the premiere in New York. She was being entertained there by former beau Viscount Esmond Rothermere, who had flown from London to see her.* Bautzer called and asked to meet her at the airport upon her return to Los Angeles. She weakened momentarily and told Bautzer her estimated time of arrival. "I'll be there," he said. "I'll be at the plane and I'll take you to dinner."

She returned the first week of November. As promised, Bautzer met Wynter at her plane. He then took her to the Traders, an exotic Tiki restaurant in the newly opened Beverly Hilton Hotel. They ate a

---

*Rothermere was thirty-two years older than Wynter. At the time they dated, he was a twice-divorced former member of Parliament who owned the second-biggest-selling newspaper in the United Kingdom, the *Daily Mail*.

Chinese-themed meal and then went to Ciro's. To her surprise, Wynter found herself disarmed by Bautzer's sense of humor and charm. Later she would understand that the secret to his seductive skill was his ability to concentrate on the woman he was with. He listened carefully to everything she said and spoke little about himself. It made her believe she had his complete attention, as though she was the only person in the world. "Every woman fell for it," said Wynter.

However, even with all his charm, when Bautzer got to "You know, Dana, I'm going to marry you," she nearly fell off her seat laughing. After she composed herself, she replied, "You're a terribly nice man, but you're the last man in the world that I would ever marry." Bautzer was hurt.

"Why?" he implored. "Why do you say that?"

"Well," she said, "we have nothing in common. And you have an appalling reputation. It's very nice of you to say it, but there's no way." Finally it was time to call it an evening. "Look, I really have to go. I'm a bit tired."

Despite laughing at his marriage prediction, she and Bautzer started to date. Even years later, Wynter could not completely explain the mutual attraction. They were so fundamentally different. Their backgrounds, interests, and tastes were poles apart. She was well read. He rarely read anything other than legal journals. On the rare occasions when he did read for relaxation, he read detective novels by Raymond Chandler. Wynter knew that Bautzer had the capacity for more worthwhile pursuits, but she also knew that his life revolved around work. That meant shoptalk and gossip. Who was doing what to whom. Who was in power. Who was out.

Wynter was very different from other women Bautzer dated. Bautzer's previous romances had been with forceful, domineering movie stars. To carve a career and become a star, each of them had climbed from an unfortunate background and fought their way to the top. When Bautzer went on a date with such a woman, he felt that she was constantly jockeying for position, competing with him for the limelight. Not Dana Wynter. In conversation she let him take the lead. If at times she appeared reticent, it was more from reserve than aloofness. She had little in common with the power brokers who exchanged shoptalk with Bautzer and who knew only the business side of movies. She was fascinated by the aesthetic aspects of filmmaking. She enjoyed meeting Hollywood personalities who thought of film as art, innovative directors like Rouben Mamoulian, who had made the masterly *Dr. Jekyll and Mr. Hyde* and *Queen Christina*. When she met studio executives, she was disappointed to learn that most of them cared nothing for the creative side of filmmaking; they were interested only in a product—in financing, packaging, and selling it.

Despite her misgivings, Wynter liked that Bautzer was a lawyer and not an actor; she could never imagine being involved with an actor. Bautzer was twenty years older, but this did not faze her; she preferred the company of older men. And when Wynter spent time alone with Bautzer, she found him enchanting. "He was an original," she would say years later.

They shared an offbeat sense of humor. Hers was "dark and wicked." His was "loony." On a plane trip to New York with Bautzer and David O. Selznick, Wynter took part in a practical joke played on talent agent Ray Stark. While Stark slept, Bautzer and Selznick dared her to take a pair of scissors and cut Stark's trouser legs above the knees. To their delight, she did it. When the plane landed in New York, Stark had no choice but to wear his newly shortened pants onto the tarmac, even though there was snow on the ground. Reporters meeting the plane were mystified. What made the prank even more satisfying was that Stark never suspected Wynter. He blamed a flight attendant who he thought resented him for not getting her into the movies after he had gotten her into his bed.

In another airborne prank, Bautzer and his screenwriter friend Charles Lederer goaded Wynter into sitting next to Random House publisher Bennett Cerf disguised as a flashy French actress, complete with blonde wig, fake eyelashes, and an excess of lipstick. Traveling next to Cerf, Wynter learned that blondes really do have more fun: the publisher paid her an inordinate amount of attention. When she removed her disguise, Cerf was embarrassed.

Bautzer also encouraged Wynter to be more spontaneous. "Let's go to Mexico," he would say at the spur of the moment. She would protest, saying that she needed to pack for the change in weather. "For heaven's sake," Bautzer would cut in. "Don't bother about that. We'll pick up a few bits and pieces. Let's just go!" So she went, and it was laughter all the way. When they arrived, there was more laughter, as Bautzer impressed her by water-skiing backwards. Bautzer thought Wynter had the "nerves of a burglar," and he liked the way she handled a car, driving as fast as he did. In fact, Bautzer liked most everything about Dana Wynter.

What Wynter did not like about Bautzer was the intrusiveness of his social circle. When she entered a room with him, she sensed that there were women who had dated him, or who were friends with women who had. They regarded her as nothing more than the latest in a long line of conquests. Even so, she found herself responding to him. He was attentive and generous. One time he sent a parasol covered with fresh gardenias. Another time he sent a phonograph with a romantic record on it. According to Hedda Hopper, he also sent a $12,000 full-length black mink coat and a sable stole, and he put at her disposal both a chauffeured limousine and an airplane. "How can you not marry a man like that?" asked her coworkers.

They conducted their romance discreetly. Bautzer had recently moved from his bungalow at the Bel-Air Hotel to the Beverly Hilton, as the first occupant of its penthouse. Wynter was living in a two-story wood-shingled cottage nestled behind the Mormon Temple above Santa Monica Boulevard. Bautzer also owned a house in Palm Springs. Wynter spent weekends there with him, hanging out at his favorite celebrity hot spot, the Racquet Club, which was just across the street. In January 1956, he won a mixed doubles tennis tournament there with partner Nancy Kiner against a field of eighty other teams. The pair defeated Barbara Kimbrell and Marion Hawkes 6–3, 7–5 in the semifinals and then trumped Pat Heard and Tommy Cook 6–4, 6–1 in the finals.

In April 1956, over a Chinese dinner at the Palm Springs Beachcomber restaurant, Bautzer proposed to Wynter. She accepted, contingent on her parents' permission. She flew home to Africa, and on May 3, announced her engagement at a government reception for her and her father in Salisbury, Southern Rhodesia. A reporter asked Bautzer if he really planned to marry Wynter. After all, he had been engaged numerous times. Bautzer trotted out the well-rehearsed reply. "I hope I'm that lucky!" This time he meant it. "Greg intended to go to Africa with me to ask my parents formally for my hand in marriage," Wynter explained to Louella Parsons, "but some unexpected business came up and he couldn't make the trip. But he talked to my parents in Africa by long-distance telephone and they gave their blessing." When Bautzer met Wynter at the airport on her return, he surprised her with a string trio that played "I've Grown Accustomed to Her Face," from the recent hit musical *My Fair Lady*.

Being engaged was one thing; getting married was another. Like his father, Bautzer winced at the idea of staging a large-scale wedding in a caste-conscious community. He asked Wynter to plan a small wedding with him. He even asked her to forgo an engagement ring. She did not object, because she had never accepted jewelry from men. Bautzer was perhaps worried that a long, conspicuous engagement might draw unwanted interference—that there were people who would try to break them up. His fears were not mere paranoia. Bautzer's past did invade their lives at Teddy Stauffer's newly opened Villa Vera Hotel in Acapulco, where Bautzer and Wynter were celebrating their engagement. At first it seemed innocent. A mariachi band came out of nowhere and began serenading the lovebirds with "Piel Canela."

"The moon was high and the stars were shining and it was absolutely magical," recalled Wynter. "Greg went forward to give the man some money. The man said 'No, no, no, no. We wouldn't dream of accepting any money for it.' At that point I burst into tears because I thought it was extraordinary, a beautiful gesture, and, oh my gosh, the Mexicans, aren't they sensitive and lovely." As it transpired, they had already been paid—by Mari Blanchard, who was staying at the hotel. The leader of the band handed Bautzer a note from his former lover. She had hoped to lure Bautzer to her cabana. "I was shocked," said Wynter. "It was the first time I had been at the receiving end of something quite as unattractive as that. Greg, of course, was furious. Absolutely livid."

When Wynter shopped for a wedding dress, she went to Saks Fifth Avenue on Wilshire Boulevard in Beverly Hills. She swore the sales personnel to secrecy and chose a Victorian-style gown, short in the front and longer in the back, with leg-of-mutton sleeves. A thoughtful salesperson lent her a blue garter from her own family.

On June 10, 1956, Bautzer and Wynter were married by the Reverend Charles H. Burrill at the Church of the Wayfarer in Carmel, California. The only friend present was Joe Schenck, who served as best man; the aging mogul had encouraged Bautzer to marry Wynter. Ashton A. Stanley, owner of La Playa Hotel, where they were staying, gave the bride away. "Now, what about the ring?" asked the minister.

"Oh my God!" exclaimed Bautzer. "I've forgotten the ring!" He called around the Monterey Peninsula for a ring. When Wynter saw it, she was disappointed. It had baguette diamonds, which she disliked, but it was the only ring available, so they proceeded with the ceremony.

After the ceremony, the newly married Bautzers realized that they had a problem. They needed to alert the press, and that meant calling one of the two gossip columnists who ruled Hollywood. But which one? If they called Hedda Hopper, Louella Parsons would be furious and they might be blackballed in the Hearst press. If they called Parsons, Hopper would lash out at them in the *Los Angeles Times*. "You know," said Bautzer, "I think we had better call Louella." Wynter pointed out that Hopper had become a great pal. "Well," he said, "you can't call them both. There's always one who has to be told first. So I think we had better make it Louella." The decision was likely influenced by Bautzer's business relationship with Marion Davies, mistress of the late William Randolph Hearst and a major stockholder in the Hearst publishing empire. As might be expected, Hopper was piqued and immediately told her syndicated readership that the marriage would not last.

A few weeks after the wedding, jeweler Herb Tobias called the bride. "Dana, there's a wedding present for you down here," he said, "but you've got to choose it yourself."

"Well, for heaven's sake. Who is it from?"

"I'm not allowed to tell you. It's a secret."

"Well, I can't accept jewelry from someone I don't know. So, no, thank you. I'm not coming down."

"Oh, Dana!" he sniffed. "All right, I'll tell you, but don't tell him I did. It's Joe Schenck. He's very eager to give you something, but he thinks you should have the choice. He's picked out three things." There was a heavy diamond bracelet, a watch set in a diamond bracelet, and a ring in the form of a daisy. This last intrigued her. It had a round central diamond that was surrounded by petals made of diamonds; the curled stem formed the ring. It was not as valuable as the bracelet or watch, but she was taken with it. "I'm so glad you chose that," Tobias smiled. "It was Joe's first choice." Wynter liked her husband's best friend very much. She was impressed by Schenck's lack of pretension. "He was what he was," she recalled. "I liked him for that, and I think he felt that." On occasion Bautzer would have a jeweler call to say that he had found an engagement-style ring for her. "No thank you, Greg," she would say. "It's too late now, and anyway, I don't need it. I have this lovely ring that Joe gave me. And how many rings does a person need? So thank you very much, but no thank you."

The newlyweds purchased a house at 750 Lausanne Road in Bel Air. But when they were ready to move in, the previous owner was still there. For several weeks they lived in Bautzer's old bungalow at the Bel-Air Hotel. When they finally did move in, they found that the owner had taken all the door handles with him, inside and out. Still, Wynter was relieved that the house was fresh, with no memories of Bautzer's former lady friends. Other than clothes, Bautzer had few possessions. The only thing Wynter recalled him owning was an eighteenth-century figurine of a man in a long yellow jacket.

Wynter found married life with Bautzer different from their courtship. The fireside intimacy was replaced by a sparkling conviviality. He was always entertaining guests. It took Wynter a while to accustom herself to the social whirl. She hired a chef named Francis Simini to cook Italian food for parties. She got to know the people whom her husband counted among his closest friends, industry veterans such as director Mervyn LeRoy, producer Jerry Wald, and screenwriter Charles Lederer. It was as though Bautzer existed in the center of the motion picture industry. One evening Wynter enjoyed a rare treat: Ben Hecht, considered to be among the greatest screenwriters and playwrights in the business, read a new play of his to her in their living room.

Bautzer was fond of comedians and sometimes he would introduce new talent to Hollywood. Bob Newhart was performing at the Crescendo in San Francisco when he got a call asking if he would come to Los Angeles a day early and perform at a party being thrown by the Bautzers at Romanoff's.

Newhart recalled the occasion: "My record was just starting to get noticed at the time. I got a call from my agent saying that Bautzer was offering me $1,500 to perform. That was how much I was getting paid for an entire week, doing eight shows, so of course I said 'yes.'

Before the show I went to his house on Lausanne in Bel Air and met him and his wife Dana. We discussed the kind of material I would be doing, and that was it. But Bautzer didn't prepare me at all for who would be in the audience. Before I went on he introduced me, and when I stepped out and saw who was there I was in shock. It was the cream of Hollywood. They were all his clients. It turned out to be an informal audition to the big time. I looked one way and there was George Burns. Seated in the back of the room was Danny Kaye. Up front was Jack Benny. When I got to the 'Driving Instructor' routine, I looked over to where the imaginary student was supposed to be, and Benny is right in my line of sight and I know he knows I'm timing it wrong, but Jack was laughing anyway. He was a wonderful audience."

Another swell party was the one the couple gave for King Hussein of Jordan. It was thrown together on a minute's notice at the request of the US State Department. The king was fed up with formal dinners and wanted to relax one evening, meet movie stars and, if possible, some pretty girls. The Bautzers' home was besieged with security people, and they were asked not to invite any Jews, a request they refused to honor. King Hussein enjoyed meeting the stars and was enchanted with a petite brunette actress named Susan Cabot, who had recently appeared in the "B" picture *The Wasp Woman*. After the party, the king asked if he could borrow the Bautzers' home in Palm Springs for the weekend, which he spent with Cabot. In real life, Cabot was no WASP. Her real name was Harriet Shapiro, and when the king found out she was Jewish, he had to end the affair.*

---

*In the book *Next to Hughes*, Robert Maheu asserts that it was he who was first contacted by the government to arrange the party for King Hussein, and that he asked the Bautzers to host it at their home. Maheu was an ex-FBI agent and covert CIA operative hired by Howard Hughes to serve as head of his operations. Regardless of whether Maheu's account of the party's origin is correct, Maheu confirmed the Cabot affair, adding that she had actually traveled with the king all the way to Jordan, and that Bautzer was called upon to sneak her out of the country to avoid an international scandal. Maheu could not say how Bautzer got her out of Jordan unnoticed, but Maheu was very impressed that he accomplished the delicate maneuver.

Dinner parties were an essential part of the Hollywood social scene. As Wynter soon learned, the typical dinner was different than the one at which she had met Cole Porter. The purpose was not to relax and entertain but to grease the wheels of commerce. Guests ate quickly. After dinner the women retired to one room for gossip. The men went to another for cigars, cards, and shoptalk. Wynter was at first bored, then irritated by the ritual. She wanted people to mingle and chat as they did at the home of David Selznick and Jennifer Jones. Wynter regarded Selznick as the last of the intellectual producers, in whose home she could meet the multitalented Leonard Bernstein or Vladimir Nabokov, the author of *Lolita*.

Wynter also had to adjust to her husband's culture of gambling. After Bautzer finished a day at the office, he inevitably slid into a game of gin rummy at Charles Lederer's home. Wynter was hard-pressed to understand the custom. Bautzer explained that he needed to unwind from the day's pressures. Playing cards cut him off from his worries, like the dropping of a theater curtain. Wynter understood his need to relax, but she was appalled by the stakes: tens of thousands were wagered. During stays in Palm Springs, Bautzer joined the same kind of games. He even bet on his tennis matches at the Racquet Club. Everything was a gamble and not for fun. Wynter saw friendships endangered and careers jeopardized. "The games were too fierce," she said. "It wasn't just competition on a friendly, sporting level. It became much more complicated than that. 'Macho.' The winning of points off people, testing their nerve." Dick Dorso had been playing tennis with Bautzer for years. "Let me tell you about Bautzer," he warned one opponent. "At one point in the set, when he feels it's apropos, he's going to give you a bad call. Don't blow up. That's what that call is designed to do, to get you so mad that your game goes downhill." After seeing her husband do this a number of times, Wynter had had enough. "I couldn't bear to watch it," she said. "I told Greg I wouldn't go to the Racquet Club any more."

Wynter found Palm Springs society equally unprepossessing, a parade of sunbaked old men escorting young girls and leather-skinned biddies wearing short pink tennis dresses and socks finished at the ankle with a bauble. To her there was nothing worse than a Racquet Club dowager dressed in a bathing suit and wearing an enormous diamond ring. At first she had been fascinated, for she had never seen "this kind of showing off." But then she became disenchanted. "I just missed that period when there was style and there were beautiful people there. I came in at the end of that. The place seemed to be full of old furriers."

Back in town, as the 1950s came to a close, there was still glamour. Stars dressed to the nines for premieres and parties. In July 1957, the Bautzers attended the Paramount premiere of *Beau James*, Bob Hope's dramatic debut. Also attending were Lucille Ball and Desi Arnaz, Fred MacMurray, Burt Lancaster, Ann Miller, and Anthony Perkins. Indicative of Bautzer's social standing was his presence at two Romanoff's restaurant events. The first was an A-list gathering hosted by Mike Romanoff himself. Guests included Frank Sinatra, Edward G. Robinson, Lauren Bacall, Dean Martin, William Holden, and Elizabeth Taylor. The second was a society event hosted the next evening by Mr. and Mrs. Cornelius Vanderbilt Whitney. Motion picture people were not invited. The Bautzers were.

It was at another party at Romanoff's that then-actor Ronald Reagan sought Bautzer's advice on going into politics. Reagan had served numerous one-year terms as president of the Screen Actors Guild, and he frequently attended the same parties as the Bautzers. Wynter thought Reagan dull. Whenever she saw him he told her the same story about teaching his son to swim. One night in the early 1960s, the Reagans cornered Bautzer: "Greg, we'd like to ask your advice on something," said wife Nancy. "Could we go upstairs for a quiet moment? You and Dana come up with us." The upstairs room at Romanoff's was empty. "Listen, Greg," said Reagan, "I know your involvement in politics. I know that you ran Earl Warren's campaign [for governor].* I'd like to ask your advice about something. I'm thinking of running for governor. I wonder what you'd think about that."

Bautzer paused and looked at him. "You know, Ronnie," he said, "I don't know anything about you. I don't know what you stand for. You have no shape. People don't have an image of you, of what you stand for. So—I wouldn't vote for you." Nancy Reagan sucked in her breath. Her cheek bones protruded. She grew rigid. "But if you want that office," Bautzer continued, "then I think you have to sit down and figure out what you're going to stand for and then make that clear—to everybody."

A short time later, in early 1963, Bautzer was appointed by Governor Edmund "Pat" Brown to the State College Board of Trustees. After Reagan was elected governor in 1967, the future president removed Bautzer from the Board of Trustees and appointed his own replacement. Despite this, when Reagan defeated Jimmy Carter in the presidential race of 1980, he sent Bautzer an invitation to the Presidential Inaugural Ball. Bautzer declined.

During the early part of their marriage, Wynter's film career was thriving. In 1956, she received the Golden Globe Award for most promising newcomer. In 1957, she starred with Rock Hudson and Sidney Poitier in *Something of Value*. The next year, she made *In Love and War* with Robert Wagner, another Bautzer client. In 1959, she starred with James Cagney in *Shake Hands with the Devil* and was cast in Twentieth Century-Fox's *Sink the Bismarck*. But Dana did not get all the parts she thought she deserved. Studio chief Buddy Adler, her husband's client and friend of twenty years, offered her inferior parts and suspended her when she turned down unsuitable scripts.

---

*Bautzer was not tied to either the Republican or the Democratic Party. He backed candidates he admired regardless of their affiliation. He supported Republican Earl Warren in the 1940s and '50s and Democrat Pat Brown in the 1960s, soliciting large donations for each of their campaigns. He gave donations to both parties for his entire life.

His action was inexplicable. Wynter later came to believe that he was holding a grudge from their first meeting, when he had made a pass and she had deflected it. Wynter wanted out to work in television. Adler eventually relented, and she was allowed to appear in the prestigious *Playhouse 90* on CBS.

Her career took a backseat, though, to planning a family. In late January 1959, Wynter was admitted to Cedars of Lebanon Hospital to deliver a baby. Wearing a mask and gown, Bautzer went into the operating room to get her consent for a Caesarean section. On January 29, 1959, Wynter gave birth to a ten-pound baby boy. He was named Mark Regan Bautzer. The hospital tried to accommodate 137 floral arrangements. While it might be thought that the flowers had more to do with Bautzer's power in the industry than Wynter's career, she was in fact a star in her own right, receiving abundant amounts of publicity in movie magazines on a monthly basis. On February 3, Bautzer showed up at the hospital in a new station wagon to drive his family home.

Unfortunately for Bautzer, the demands of his career would always create competition for the time he spent with his family. And when it came to his wealthiest and most important client, it was always difficult for Bautzer to say no.

15

THE RICHEST CLIENT
IN THE WORLD

The client who would change Bautzer's life forever was Howard Hughes. For much of the twentieth century, he was considered to be the wealthiest man in the world. During their twenty-five-year relationship, Bautzer would serve as Hughes's adviser, protector, confidant, harem-keeper, and best friend. Having Hughes as a client paid off in more ways than earning high fees from the billionaire. It made other important businessmen want Bautzer to be their lawyer. If he was good enough for Hughes, he was good enough for them. Although Hughes would later become reclusive, at the time Bautzer started as his counsel he was nothing like that. In fact, they had a lot in common. They were both athletic, handsome, competitive businessmen, out to conquer the world and bed beautiful movie stars.

Howard Robard Hughes Jr. was a financial titan, a singular genius who blazed trails in industry, aviation, and filmmaking. Greg Bautzer would most likely have first heard of him in late 1926, when Hughes was winning Los Angeles golf tournaments. Hughes and his wife Ella had recently moved to a home that was adjacent to the Wilshire Country Club on Muirfield Road so he could walk from his back door onto the ninth hole. He was twenty-one, tall, and boyishly handsome. He was also marked by fate. In 1909, when he was three, his father, Howard Hughes Sr., had patented a dual-cone rotary drill bit, which could pierce previously impenetrable rock. The Houston-based Hughes Tool Company (a.k.a. Toolco) would eventually collect massive licensing fees for most of the oil drilling in the world. In 1922, Howard Jr.'s mother died of an ectopic pregnancy. In 1924, his father died of a heart attack. Orphaned at eighteen, Howard Jr. collected his inheritance and took the reins of the company. His uncle, Rupert Hughes, was a successful screenwriter in Hollywood. The wealthy young man decided that he would invest his newfound wealth in film production. In 1926, he moved to the Ambassador Hotel in Los Angeles and opened the film division of his Caddo Company at 7000 Romaine Street in Hollywood.

Hughes knew nothing about making films, but he learned quickly. His third film, *Two Arabian Knights* (1928), won an Academy Award for its director, Lewis Milestone. Hughes conceived his fourth film as a tribute to the British aviators of World War I. While he was filming gruesome air battles, Hollywood made the transition to sound films. As inventive as his father, Hughes was able to keep up. He reshot and recast, discovering Jean Harlow in the process. After spending three years and $3.75 million on the epic *Hell's Angels*, Hughes gave it a monster premiere at Grauman's Chinese Theatre on Hollywood Boulevard. The film was a sensation, but it had cost too much to be profitable. Hughes made a few more films, but when he got into a protracted fight with the motion picture censorship committee over excessive sex and violence in his 1932 film *Scarface*, he left Hollywood, divorced his wife, and devoted himself to a new pursuit: aviation.

In 1932, Hughes founded his own aircraft company. He designed and tested fast airplanes, setting a transcontinental speed record in 1937. He wanted to prove that commercial air travel could be both fast and safe, so in 1938 he flew a Lockheed Super Electra around the globe in ninety-one hours. He was feted with a ticker-tape parade in New York. In 1939, he was honored with a Congressional Gold Medal for advancing the science of aviation. He then bought a controlling interest in Transcontinental Western Airlines (later renamed Trans World Airlines, or TWA for short), upgrading its fleet by means of a secret deal with Lockheed.

In 1941, he returned to moviemaking and produced a film that was so explicitly sexual it could not be released. *The Outlaw* sat on the shelf for six years, but Jane Russell, whom Hughes had tried to showcase in it, became an overnight star based on pinup photos featuring her ample bosom.

When World War II called for the manufacture of military planes, Hughes Aircraft stepped in, and in the process became the single largest employer in Southern California. After the war, Hughes continued to design aircraft, most memorably the XF-11, which he crashed in a residential neighborhood of Beverly Hills during a 1946 test flight. He was almost fatally injured and never fully recovered. The chronic pain he suffered for the rest of his life fostered an addiction to prescription medication.

Hughes came into Bautzer's orbit around the time of Hughes's purchase of RKO Radio Pictures in 1948. Bautzer knew that they had dated a number of the same women, among them Ginger Rogers and Ava Gardner. There are two versions of how Bautzer and Hughes met. The first involves their mutual friend Pat Di Cicco, who worked for Hughes in a capacity that has never been fully explained, but almost certainly involved procuring young ladies. In this version, it is Di Cicco who introduced Bautzer to Hughes in a bungalow at the Beverly Hills Hotel, where the tycoon lived. According to publicist Henry Rogers, when Bautzer and Di Cicco arrived, they found Hughes in the bedroom, stark naked, a telephone in one hand, struggling to put on his trousers. A woman smoking a cigarette lay in his bed. Hughes finished his telephone conversation, zipped up his fly, and walked over to his two visitors.

"Howard," said Di Cicco, "I want you to meet my friend Greg Bautzer, the best attorney in town."

"Let's go down to the bar for a drink," Hughes grunted. The woman remained in the bed.

But the story Bautzer told his son, Mark, was that he first met Hughes in a nightclub. Bautzer was at a table with Lana Turner; by this time, they were no longer dating. A man came up to the table and leaned over to ask a question. "Mr. Hughes would like to know if Miss Turner will give him her phone number," he said politely.

"You tell that miserable son of a bitch that if he wants to talk to Lana, he's going to have to face me," responded Bautzer. "And if he's a man, he'll do it." The emissary retreated. In a few minutes, Hughes walked over and introduced himself.

It is impossible to say whether either of these stories is true. What is known for certain is that by 1947 Bautzer was very good friends with people who were among Hughes's inner circle, and it is likely that one of them made the introduction. In addition to his long-standing friendship with Hughes's girl-getter, Pat Di Cicco, Bautzer was also close to another well-known Hughes bird dog, casting direc-tor Walter Kane. An incident in December 1947, illustrated just how close Bautzer was to Kane.

Walter Kane was a forty-five-year-old talent agent and the former husband of actress Lynn Bari, the so-called "Woo Woo Girl" and the "Girl with the Million-Dollar Figure." Just after midnight on Decem-ber 12, Kane swallowed an overdose of sleeping pills, then had a change of heart and called Dr. Lee Siegel. A rescue squad rushed Kane to the hospital from his home on Doheny Road in Beverly Hills, where Dr. Siegel had found a suicide note and called the persons listed. They gathered by Kane's hospital bed: Bautzer, Howard Hughes, Colum-bia Studios mogul Harry Cohn, and Kane's secretary, Josephine "Pat" Paterson. Kane was on the road to recovery when Bautzer learned that he had been listed as sole beneficiary in Kane's will.

"I was amazed," said Bautzer. "I can't understand it." Kane's suicide note read: "I am sorry to check out like this, but there really isn't any other course to take. I hope you know, Greg, that I am very grateful to you for your friendship and so very grateful to W.R.W. [Billy Wilkerson]. If the following fellows would just sort of get together and have a drink on me, I would like it: [boxer] Jack Dempsey, [singing idol and actor] Rudy Vallee, [socialite] Jonah Jones, Harry Cohn, Howard, and by all means you and Billy." Kane was being sued at the time by a grocery store for $632, so financial difficulties may have had something to do with his attempted suicide, although Bautzer denied it. Kane recovered and continued to serve as one of Hughes's closest advisers.

Regardless of how Bautzer met Hughes, his earliest known legal work for the billionaire occurred in July 1952. Jean Simmons, a twenty-one-year-old British actress, and Stewart Granger, her movie-star husband, were suing Hughes to get out of an acting contract. She had signed the contract, but Hughes and RKO had not. Since then, he had neither given her work nor let her work elsewhere. Simmons asserted that she wasn't bound by the contract. Hughes asserted that they had a binding deal, and that his reason for not signing the document itself was that it included an illegal term.

The offending provision involved tax issues related to a side deal that Hughes made with the couple. In addition to containing the agreement for acting services, the contract Simmons and Granger signed sold Hughes their Bel Air house and motion picture rights to a book owned by Granger. They were trying to report amounts for the house and book as capital gains rather than as income from Simmons's RKO work. Capital gains were taxed at a lower rate than regular income. In order to avoid high taxes on the sale of their home and book rights, the Grangers needed Hughes to agree that the side deal was not part of Simmons's acting contract. Hughes refused to agree to this, claiming it was part of the payment for her acting work, and therefore they would have to pay taxes at the higher rate.

In truth, Hughes was simply inventing an excuse for never having signed the contract. If he had wanted to, he could easily have agreed that the house sale and book rights were a separate deal and allowed them to pay less in taxes. Hughes wanted to hold her to the contract even though he had not cast her in a picture. The trial went on for seventeen days, then it was halted for settlement talks. Bautzer negotiated an arrangement in which Simmons would be under contract to RKO for three more years. In addition, Hughes would pay her $250,000 and her legal fees and would allow her to work for other studios at higher salaries.

Even though Bautzer sat across the table from Simmons in this dispute, he became friends with her after she divorced Granger. Bautzer attended her wedding to director Richard Brooks in November 1960 and he and Dana Wynter threw a party for them. Billy and Audrey Wilder, David Selznick, and Dean Martin attended.

After Simmons's lawsuit was resolved, Hughes kept Bautzer on a monthly retainer. For Bautzer, it was a dream come true. Having Hughes as a client elevated Bautzer's career to a new level. "When Howard Hughes all of a sudden says, 'This is my lawyer,' it makes you kind of important," Bautzer said. But he also knew that keeping Hughes as a client would require more than just good lawyering. He would have to provide services like no other lawyer. He would need to be more aggressive and more creative, work harder, and cater to Hughes's whims, whether business-related or personal. It was an all-consuming task, yet the hardships were worth it. The title "Howard Hughes's lawyer" was priceless. Representing the richest man in the world gave him the kind of prestige few lawyers enjoyed. When Bautzer walked into a room, his standing was unquestioned. When he wanted to get important people on the phone, no matter who they were, they took his calls. Few if any lawyers could claim to have more clout. And the longer his relationship with Hughes lasted, the more powerful Bautzer became.

In the fall of 1952, Bautzer worked on his first major corporate transaction involving Hughes. It was an odd one, almost as odd as the billionaire himself. After only four years of owning RKO, Hughes wanted to sell it. He said that he wanted out because he was under attack by minority shareholders and felt that Hollywood had "grown too complicated." In truth, the company was having the only good year since he had arrived, mostly because independent producers were releasing their pictures through RKO, which was earning Hughes a fee at virtually no up-front cost. When Hughes bought RKO, it was the smallest of the five major studios, yet it was known for brilliant, quirky projects like *Citizen Kane, Cat People, Out of the Past, Crossfire*, and *Murder, My Sweet*. Most of these movies made money, and there was an esprit de corps at the corner of Gower and Melrose where the studio was located. Hughes changed that, first with his paranoia of Communists and then with a purge. Within two years he had decimated the staff, turning the studio into a cross between a ghost town and a bomb crater. He had promised not to interfere with productions, then broken every promise. He meddled in casting and script revisions, and called for endless reshoots. The executives and producers who had not been fired quit. "RKO's contract list is down to three actors and 127 lawyers," said former RKO star Dick Powell.

A group of investors wanted to purchase RKO, and Hughes saw his chance to get his money out of the failing studio. Strangely, Bautzer was retained to represent the buyers in the transaction, not Hughes. Today such representation would be deemed a conflict of interest and would require informed written consent of both parties. Perhaps Hughes suggested that the sale would go more smoothly if his own lawyer handled it. Perhaps there was another reason that was less innocent.

The group of investors was headed by Ralph E. Stolkin, a thirty-four-year-old Chicago financier and industrialist who had reportedly gotten rich by setting up a $15,000 mail-order business and then, after

two years, selling it at a profit of $1 million. Other investors included
Edward Burke and Ray Ryan of San Antonio, Texas, and Stolkin's
father-in-law, Abe Koolish, who was president of the Chicago-based
Empire Industries, another mail-order house, and vice president of
National Video Corp., which manufactured television tubes. Koolish
was also involved with Screen Associates Inc., which financed a Dean
Martin and Jerry Lewis film, *At War with the Army*. A cursory glance
of these men revealed nothing of concern.

Papers were signed on September 23, 1952, pursuant to which
the syndicate purchased 1,012,420 shares of Hughes RKO stock at
a price of $7 per share, for a total of $7,086,940. In reality, however, this was only an option contract. The group was paying Hughes
just $1.25 million up front. The balance was payable over a two-year
period. If the group defaulted, Hughes would get his studio back—
and keep the $1.25 million.

Following the transfer of RKO, Bautzer's firm—which at the
time was still Bautzer, Grant, Youngman & Silbert—was appointed
counsel for the new corporation. Arnold Grant was chosen chairman of the board. Gordon Youngman was appointed to the board.
Other members included the investors Ryan, Koolish, and Burke, and
Sherill Corwin, director of the Theater Owners of America. Stolkin
was named president. Then came the surprise. Chicago lawyer Sidney Korshak was retained as labor counsel for RKO. Korshak would
theoretically help resolve union disputes like the recent one with the
Writers Guild of America over Hughes's refusal to credit writer Paul
Jarrico on *The Las Vegas Story* (1952) because of alleged Communist
ties. But Korshak wasn't just a labor lawyer. He was a well-known
lawyer for mobsters, and his presence was worrisome.

Sure enough, the *Wall Street Journal* published articles in October
that linked board members to the underworld. Ryan was connected
to Frank Costello's bookie operation in Florida. Stolkin sold mail-
order punchboards, a bogus cardboard lottery game used by con men.

Koolish had been indicted in 1949 by the Federal Trade Commission for mail fraud, but the charges had been dropped. He was also accused of bilking the Disabled American Veterans out of charity proceeds, claiming that his hefty withdrawals were "expenses." Minority shareholders of the studio threatened to sue the dubious new administration, asserting they were unfit to run a publicly traded company. To make matters worse, RKO was losing $100,000 a week.

Some think that Bautzer was aware of the mob connection. According to them, Hughes asked Bautzer to have Korshak use his mob ties to set up a syndicate of investors. However, this is very unlikely. For one thing, although Bautzer would later become friends with Korshak, at the time of the RKO sale he barely knew him. Furthermore, Bautzer's law partners would not have willingly served on a board of directors with criminals, and Bautzer would never have put them in such a position had he known about the investors' backgrounds.

On October 23, Stolkin and Koolish resigned from the RKO board. They had no desire to have their past activities brought to light in a court of law or investigated by the Securities and Exchange Commission. By mid-November, Korshak and the remaining members had resigned as well. By February, the investors defaulted on the balance owed to purchase the studio and Hughes regained control of RKO. He pocketed the initial $1.25 million, which the *Wall Street Journal* called "the financial feat of the year." While Bautzer was probably uninformed about the personal history of the purchasers, Hughes likely knew exactly with whom he was dealing. For the rest of his life, Korshak believed that Hughes had leaked the story about the investor's backgrounds in order to induce the default. His suspicions had merit, given that Hughes had pulled a similar ploy on Ingrid Bergman, when he leaked news of her secret pregnancy in order to build ticket sales for her RKO film *Stromboli*.

After the aborted sale of RKO, Hughes kept Bautzer busy with legal work. There was a flurry of lawsuits by minority stockholders alleging Hughes had mishandled the company. There were also numerous contracts to draw up. Hughes had a penchant for doing deals that reduced his tax liability. Bautzer came up with a way to structure talent agreements with actresses that satisfied Hughes's needs. These contracts allowed Hughes to pay sums of money to talent in monthly installments over a long period of time and deduct the amortized cost against other corporate profits. Since Hughes habitually put actresses under contract without using them, the resulting tax break was so great that their contracts cost him almost nothing.

One actress to sign such a deal was Gina Lollobrigida. The Italian beauty came to the United States in 1950 and danced nightly with Hughes for weeks. At one point during her visit, he had her sign a contract. When she got tired of waiting for a screen test, she went home. In September 1954, Hedda Hopper announced that Lollobrigida would work with Gary Cooper in a picture titled *The Wastrel,* an American production to be shot in Italy. Hopper mentioned that her contract with Hughes prevented her from working in Hollywood; in all likelihood, Hopper was repeating what Hughes had told her about their arrangement. Lollobrigida disagreed with Hughes's position, insisting that document she had signed with him was just an option and that they had no true agreement. In the past, Hughes had threatened to sue any studio that wanted to hire her, and fear of a lawsuit from Hughes had successfully prevented anyone from doing so.

But now Hughes had a problem. He needed Lollobrigida to sign a real contract in order to get the favorable tax treatment. When she came to New York for the premiere of her Italian film *Pane, Amore e Gelosia* (US title: *Bread, Love and Dreams*), Bautzer flew to New York and tried to get her to sign an agreement. He also threatened to sue her if she made the Cooper picture. The dispute seemed unsolvable. Then, in 1955, someone recommended that Bautzer hire a New York contact named Bernard "Bernie" Schwartz to help get Lollobrigida to sign the agreement. Schwartz was a television producer who had a reputation for connections to people who could solve virtually any problem. Schwartz went to Italy and within six weeks had found a way to convince the actress to come to terms. Thanks to Schwartz, Bautzer was able to negotiate a new contract. Lollobrigida would star in four pictures at $280,000 each. A payment of $2,000 per week would continue for ten years. She accepted the deal and stayed in Europe, and everyone was happy. Bautzer and Hughes were so impressed with Schwartz's problem-solving abilities that he was offered a position in Bautzer's firm. Schwartz was flattered, but he couldn't accept; he was not an attorney. Bautzer had assumed that he was. Bautzer admired talented businessmen, and he offered to find other work for Schwartz. One day he would make good on that promise.

By 1958, Hughes's Toolco had increased its holdings in TWA to 78 percent and was controlling the airline's day-to-day operations. Since the introduction of jet engines in the 1950s, it was only a matter of time before propeller-engine planes were phased out. The only question for a company was which jet to purchase. Boeing 707 and Douglas DC-8 jets were already on order for Pan American Airlines, United Airlines, and American Airlines. Hughes delayed making a decision, trying to find the most profitable alternative. Hughes finally ordered Boeing 707s, but then threatened to cancel, hinting that Hughes Aircraft might be designing a better plane. He let the Boeing order stand and then placed an order with another manufacturer called Convair for thirty 880 jetliners. The total cost came to $400 million, more than he had in reserve. He would need to borrow much of the money to purchase the planes. Normally, this would not be a problem, but Hughes had complicated matters by insisting that Toolco purchase the planes rather than TWA itself. His game was to lease the planes to TWA so that Toolco could write off the costs of the jets. This would deprive TWA of its own tax advantage and increase the net cost to the airline. Hughes's Toolco would receive a huge financial benefit from tax avoidance, and TWA would be saddled with the real debt.

As the jets were being delivered, Hughes agreed in principle to a partial financing plan devised by investment bankers Dillon, Read & Company. A consortium of banks and insurance companies would furnish $165 million and Hughes would arrange other financing in the amount of $100 million, for a total of $265 million. However, there was a catch. The bankers didn't trust Hughes to manage the airlines. As a condition of making the loan, they required Hughes to place his airline stock in a ten-year voting trust—and allow the lenders to select the majority of a board of directors. Hughes was loath to give up control of TWA. The terms started to gnaw at him. He wanted to find another way.

When it came time to close the deal, Hughes delayed. His longtime Houston attorney Raymond Cook tried repeatedly to get Hughes to answer questions and give instructions, but Hughes would not return calls. Then, on three separate occasions, Hughes tried to back out of the Dillon, Read plan. In response, the lenders imposed stiffer terms, including the insulting stipulation that Hughes sign papers personally. They didn't want there to be any question about whether the man signing had the authority to do so. Hughes, of course, became infuriated by their distrust, and refused to agree to this. He took out his frustration on Cook and fired him. Hughes sent Bautzer in his place to handle the transaction. Bautzer immediately got on a flight to New York and tried to renegotiate the deal and remove the voting trust, but the lenders refused. Bautzer reported back to Hughes that he had no choice—he had to agree to the lenders' terms. In early December 1960, Bautzer announced to the press that Hughes had signed the letters of agreement and he got back on a plane to Los Angeles. This should have been the end of the transaction, but Hughes took his time transferring his stock to the voting trust. After all, he had until December 30. Then the fun began.

On December 28, Raymond Holliday, Hughes's proxy, was to travel to Wilmington, Delaware, to sign over Hughes's stock. Holliday did not appear. He telephoned from New York to say that he was awaiting authorization. The lenders suspected that Hughes was buying time to try to find a way out and warned Bautzer that they would go to court if Hughes reneged on the agreement. They were right; Hughes had not given up hope of retaining control of the airlines. "Mr. Bautzer worked clear through for twenty-four hours," recalled secretary Lea Sullivan. "Then he got on a plane and went to New York. He was there overnight and still on the phone with Hughes in Hollywood the next day and half the night. So for two days he didn't get any sleep." Then Hughes stopped answering his phone. Bautzer frantically tried to get him to answer. "Howard, this is a red alert!" said Bautzer to the answering service. "Mr. Bautzer would call in to the office for his messages," recalled Sullivan. "He sounded very bad. He would call, and he wouldn't be talking. He would be yelling."

December 30 was the last business day of 1960. The lenders threatened that if the documents were not signed, a new set would have to be drafted and approved by all parties. "It was a bad time for us in that office, a very bad time," said Sullivan. "Mr. Bautzer was under such pressure. He felt as if he had the world on top of him." Sullivan tried to get through to him. "If you don't stop and take a deep breath," she yelled at him, "you could get a heart attack."

"Mind your own business!" he snapped back.

"Well, I won't have a job if you get a heart attack and die, so it is my own business!"

On the morning of December 30 Bautzer finally reached Hughes and got his approval for the stock transfer. The deal seemed to be complete. Then, Hughes managed to create another roadblock. At three in the afternoon on December 30, Holliday entered the conference room of the Chemical Bank in New York—and refused to sign the papers. He said he needed a lawyer to review the voluminous documents. The lenders believed this was another stall. They were right. Hughes was still maneuvering for time, thinking he might yet be able to find a way to retain control of the airlines. The bankers called Bautzer's suite at the Hampshire House Hotel. He was not there. He had been taken to Roosevelt Hospital with severe chest pains. Bautzer thought he was having a heart attack. The pressure was too much. Holliday begged for a postponement. The bankers held firm. The deal had to be closed that day. Bautzer called Hughes from the hospital, and convinced him that it was time to close the deal. There were no other alternatives. If Hughes didn't complete the transaction, the airline would go bankrupt.

At seven-fifteen that evening, Holliday announced that Bautzer had obtained Hughes's authority to transfer the stock. Holliday signed the papers. In convincing Hughes to give up control of TWA, Bautzer saved the airline. He had managed the unmanageable, although it nearly killed him.

Unfortunately, TWA's legal troubles had just begun. Using TWA to get a tax break for Toolco led to major litigation. On June 30, 1961, TWA filed a complaint in New York federal court on behalf of the minority shareholders, charging that Hughes had violated antitrust laws by simultaneously owning jets and leasing them to TWA. Hughes had Bautzer hire New York attorney Chester C. Davis of Simpson, Thatcher & Bartlett to defend the case. Davis got the job after every major New York law firm turned it down due to conflicts of interest. Simpson, Thatcher & Bartlett had done work for TWA and was conflicted also, but Davis agreed to leave the firm in order to handle the case. Hughes instructed Bautzer to settle the lawsuit, but the Wall Street lawyer wanted to litigate. Hughes sent Davis on a three-day trip to Houston to get him out of the way. "I want no divided responsibility about these negotiations," said Hughes. "I am placing the matter completely in your hands, Gregson, with the simple request that you make the best deal you can."

When Davis realized that he had been hijacked, he grew angry and told Hughes that a good settlement could not be reached unless he was prepared to fight. Hughes ignored him. By late July Bautzer had reached a tentative agreement with TWA. As part of the deal, Hughes would invest $150 million in the airline over the next two years. TWA in turn would purchase thirteen more Convair jets that Hughes had previously ordered for Toolco, which would of course remove Toolco's obligation to pay for them. Hughes signed the settlement papers and gave them to Bautzer, telling him not to transmit them until some minor points were changed. Davis didn't like the agreement, saying it would lead to more litigation and asked Hughes to reconsider.

In early August, without consulting Bautzer, Hughes had a change of heart and decided to fight the lawsuit "to the hilt." The litigation would continue for decades, eventually making its way to the US Supreme Court. According to Hughes's head of operations, Robert Maheu, Davis had promised Hughes that an adverse judgment would award no more than $5 million. In the end, the plaintiffs got $146 million. The case established legal precedents allowing minority shareholders to sue a board of directors for making harmful business decisions, especially if they benefit another company owned by the majority shareholder.

By delaying, Hughes paid Chester Davis untold legal fees—but when he had other concerns, it was Bautzer he trusted to attend to them. While their relationship was sometimes strained, Hughes would remain Bautzer's client until the day he died. Hughes knew that Bautzer was willing to put his interests first and make great personal sacrifices on his behalf. According to secretary Lea Sullivan, Bautzer went overboard for his biggest client. "Other than being his lawyer, I think that Greg was Hughes's best friend. He must have recognized that. There was nobody else Mr. Hughes could have gotten to do the things for him that Greg did." In fact, when it came to serving Hughes, Bautzer would do virtually anything.

16

BILLIONAIRE SECRETS

In the early 1960s, Greg Bautzer could lean back in his office and make a grand pronouncement. "There are only three things I'm really sentimental about. First, there's my son. Second, there's money. And third, there's Howard Hughes. In that order of priority. I just love that goddamned guy." Hughes had strong feelings for Bautzer, too. Since Hughes rarely went out and kept his distance even from the men who attended to his every need, Bautzer may have been his only friend. He wanted to be able to reach Bautzer at all times. Bautzer had a second private phone installed in his office just for Hughes. The billionaire called Bautzer at restaurants. He called him at home. He called at all hours of the night. He had a second phone installed at Bautzer's secretary's home so that he could reach her if her boss was unavailable.

Hughes's demands were often unrelated to legal work. One Friday at 2 AM, Lea Sullivan awoke to hear Hughes asking her to procure a print of a film. Sullivan called a San Bernardino drive-in theater and got the print, but her job was just beginning. Hughes was not interested in watching the film. He wanted its plot and dialogue transcribed. Bautzer happened to come into the office over the weekend and was surprised to see her there, typing away as a projectionist screened the film for her.

Hughes wasn't the only client that required hand-holding. Celebrity clients called Bautzer's office for all kinds of things that had little or nothing to do with legal work. If Merle Oberon needed airplane tickets on TWA, she called Bautzer. When Jack Benny needed to take his driver's test again at the department of motor vehicles, he called Bautzer to accompany him. Whenever possible, Bautzer asked his secretary to handle these day-to-day favors, but the nonstop people-pleasing was exhausting. "The stress of working in that office was tremendous," said Sullivan. "We were representing the richest, most famous people in the world, and the pressure to meet their needs was incredible."

As early as 1955, Bautzer felt the need to get away from Hughes. "That guy is driving me crazy," said Bautzer. "I've gotta have a vacation." In July he made reservations to travel to Italy and refused to tell Hughes where he was staying, even when Hughes insisted. "Gregson, I just have to know where you'll be," said Hughes, "in case something comes up in the RKO deal." Hughes was trying to sell the studio a second time. Bautzer told Hughes that the RKO deal was dead. Hughes had changed his mind too many times and the buyers had given up. Bautzer left for Italy without giving Hughes his contact information. Lea Sullivan remembered the private line ringing in Bautzer's office while her boss was away.

"Sullivan! Is that you?" Hughes asked loudly.

"Yes, it's me, Mr. Hughes."

"Oh, OK," said Hughes, his voice dropping to a normal register. "Where is Greg?"

"I don't know, Mr. Hughes."

"Do you expect him back today?"

"I don't know, Mr. Hughes. I really don't know." She told Hughes nothing. She was sworn to secrecy. Even if she knew he was coming back early, she could not tell Hughes.

Bautzer was in Reggio, looking at Italian women and drinking wine. After a few days of lounging in the sun, he decided to drive north to Capri. On impulse he stopped at a small village and checked into an inn. It was not planned and he had told no one he was going there. He had been in his room only a few minutes when the phone rang. It was Hughes. From then on, Bautzer kept getting calls, no matter where he drove. Hughes had sent detectives to trail him.

Hughes's ability to locate Bautzer at any time was uncanny. One night when Sullivan was with Bautzer on a business trip to Oklahoma City, the cocktail hour arrived, but there was no watering hole to be found. Oklahoma City was a "dry" town. Bautzer needed a drink. Sullivan thought a cab driver could solve the problem. Sure enough, she found one who knew a private club, far off the beaten track. She and Bautzer had just settled in at a table when the waiter came over with a telephone. "Are you Bautzer?" he asked. "There's a phone call for you." It was Hughes. To this day, Sullivan does not know how he tracked them down.

Hughes and Bautzer shared a closeness that Hughes didn't have with others. After Bautzer married Dana Wynter, Hughes would personally fly him to Palm Springs in a small plane, land at the tiny airstrip that was its original airport, and spend the night with the couple in their home. He and Bautzer would often stay up late talking business. Hughes was totally relaxed at their home. If he arrived without toiletries, Wynter would jump in the car with him and go to a drugstore. According to Wynter, there was nothing unusual about Hughes's behavior at all, except that he required her husband to be available at all hours.

On one occasion, the Bautzers were in Acapulco and Hughes called. Wynter overheard her husband's side of the conversation: Hughes wanted Bautzer to cut his vacation short and travel to Washington. "Yes, Howard. . . . No, Howard. . . . There's no need for me to go to Washington. I can handle it from here." Hughes didn't take no for an answer easily, and the conversation went on like this for a while, with Hughes continuing to demand that Bautzer make the trip.

Wynter finally pulled the phone away from her husband. "Howard," she said, "if Greg says he doesn't need to go to Washington, he doesn't need to go. And if he does, it will break up our marriage. And it will be your fault!" Hughes deferred to Wynter. From then on, when he asked Bautzer to travel on business, he would pause and say, "Now, I don't have to talk to Dana, do I?"

Hughes depended on Bautzer for a variety of services, some legal and some that could be euphemistically described as extralegal. In the mid-1950s, Hughes asked Bautzer to help him date Elizabeth Taylor. "Have you asked her?" Bautzer said.

"No. I want you to ask her," replied Hughes.

"But I wouldn't know how."

"I want you to take a proposal to her mother."

"That you want to screw her daughter?" Bautzer asked.

"No. Not in so many words. You're to say to her mother that I am prepared to pay a million dollars for Elizabeth to be my bride."

"That isn't the way it's done, Howard."

"It's the way I'd like to do it."

Bautzer wanted to placate Hughes, so he went to see Taylor's mother, Sara. "I have a very unusual proposal to make," said Bautzer. "Howard Hughes wants to marry your daughter."

"But she doesn't know Hughes," said Taylor's mother.

"There's an inducement. He's prepared to pay a million dollars for her."

Mrs. Taylor thought for a second then asked: "Tax free?" Bautzer laughed and conveyed her message to his client. Hughes realized it was not to be and moved on. In 1957, he married actress Jean Peters. Hughes had dated the beautiful green-eyed brunette a decade earlier. Some have claimed she was the only woman he ever truly loved, although even with Peters, Hughes was never monogomous.

Hughes frequently used Bautzer's services as a harem keeper. He had Bautzer sign women to acting contracts and pay them out of a corporate entity named Black Gold Productions, an obvious allusion to Hughes's oil fortune. The Black Gold account was kept separate from the ones he used to pay established actresses. Its so-called acting contracts were an elaborate way to seduce a girl and pay her living expenses. Hughes would recruit a kept woman by promising to launch her acting career. He found his targets in various places. He would notice a woman in a restaurant. He would catch a glance of a profile in a passing car and take down the license plate number. He might even see a picture in a magazine. He then hired detectives to locate these women. After an intermediary like Pat Di Cicco or Walter Kane had presented the proposition and gotten the woman's consent, Hughes would rent an apartment for her and provide acting, singing, and dancing lessons. Hughes would not meet the woman for several weeks. He would tease her with the prospect of a visit, and then repeatedly break the date, saying something important had come up. Sometimes he called the woman, saying he was out of town while he was actually in an adjoining room. By the time the woman finally met him, she was willing to do anything to get his attention. Other seduction techniques included buying her a dog and then having it kidnapped, only to pretend that he had found it and triumphantly return it. His tricks were devious but effective. An assistant named Jean Parker kept the books for Black Gold Productions and drafted the checks for Bautzer to sign. Parker technically worked for Joseph Schenck, although Bautzer paid her separately for her Black Gold bookkeeping services.

Bautzer didn't always help Hughes score with women; sometimes he tried to protect the women. Tony Curtis recalled how Hughes once had Bautzer fly the entire Paris Symphony Orchestra to Hollywood on the pretext of a recording session just so could Hughes could "meet" the female violinist. When the eighty members arrived, Bautzer tracked down the violinist and warned her not to sleep with Hughes, but she didn't listen. Once Hughes had made his conquest, he canceled the orchestra's contract and sent her and the orchestra members packing.

In the 1960s, Bautzer's recurring task for Hughes was to quash unauthorized magazine articles and biographies about the billionaire. In 1962, Hughes sent Bautzer, publicist Dick Hannah, and Washington attorney Clark Clifford to the offices of *Life* magazine to suppress an article, or at least get final approval over it. The team of envoys waxed eloquent, but the editors were unmoved. The article ran, emblazoned with the provocative heading "A playboy who became a secretive, besieged, and lonely man." Bautzer was quoted in it complaining to Hughes about his late-night calls. Hughes was furious. Although Bautzer was working hard on his behalf, the magazine article had upset Hughes beyond measure. He wrote Bautzer a rambling memo demanding an explanation.

From the looks of things, it would be difficult to conceive how we could have brought our present relationship to a much more bitter and antagonistic status. I was so upset following our last conversation before my health commenced to recover from the ill effects of my loss of temper and explosion of blood pressure it brought our conversation to a conclusion. I am sure that, like everyone else, it is my tendency to see controversial matters from my side, but perhaps it is your nature, likewise, to look at things from your side.

Now I criticize you for seeming to be more interested in the management of Northeast Airlines than in anything else. You again answer, "I am doing a great job." What good is a great job to me if it benefits Northeast Airlines, which I may only possess for another month at most and when Northeast Airlines is not the place where I desire you to direct your efforts when it is Life magazine and three or four other situations which are cutting into my body like a knife and destroying my efforts to recover my health and putting me daily closer to the grave with unbelievable rapidity and force.

Your great job for Northeast Airlines might as well be a great job for
Henry Kaiser in Honolulu, when I am about to be crucified and I
would say it is an even money bet that they will cause Jean [Peters,
Mrs. Howard Hughes] to take the same route as Marilyn Monroe.

Under these circumstances you may understand why even one
minute of effort on your part devoted to Northeast Airlines evokes
my extreme bitterness when I feel that time and that effort should
have gone to Life magazine.

I await your reply. I don't know if I will be able to answer this
morning as I am about at the end of my rope.

Bautzer calmed Hughes down and stayed in his good graces, but
there were a growing number of aspiring Hughes biographers, and he
wanted Bautzer to stop them all. Film historian Ezra Goodman was
writing a book on Hughes, so Bautzer and New York lawyer Chester
Davis brought him to New York, put him up in the St. Regis Hotel,
and bribed him $38,250 to instead write about silent film director
D. W. Griffith. Goodman's publisher, Lyle Stuart, wouldn't stand for
this kind of business interference and sued Hughes, Bautzer, Davis,
and Rosemont Enterprises, the company that Hughes had set up
to pay off Goodman. Bautzer heard of Stuart's weakness for gour-
met food and invited the publisher to a lavishly catered settlement
meeting at the St. Regis. Stuart appreciated the gesture but stood his
ground. "You're not going to buy me off," he said. "I know you aren't
going to believe this, but I don't have a price. I didn't go into publishing just to make money, but I've made a million. And you're not going
to threaten me. I know that Howard Hughes is a very powerful, very
influential man who has lots of friends. I've got friends, too. And if
we have to fight, I'll fight." As the lawsuit continued, Hughes had the
audacity to sue Goodman for $38,250, claiming that the manuscript
Goodman delivered on the life of D. W. Griffith was unsatisfactory,
but his lawsuit was thrown out.

Bautzer's next antagonist was Random House. Publisher Robert Loomis had signed Tommy Thompson to write a Hughes bio, but the poor quality of the writing caused Loomis to hire another writer, John Keats. Bautzer showed up at Loomis's office and tried to convince him not to publish the book. Loomis was unmoved. Bautzer threatened his colleague Random House cofounder Bennett Cerf with litigation. Cerf ignored him. Bautzer sent a letter to Cerf stating that he needed Hughes's permission. Cerf ignored the letter. Bautzer went to see Cerf and Loomis again. He told them that if Random House would pull the Keats book, Hughes would agree to an authorized biography. Cerf and Loomis doubted Hughes would ever go through with it and declined. *Howard Hughes* by John Keats was published in 1966.

In January 1972, Hughes heard some alarming news. McGraw-Hill was publishing an "autobiography of Howard Hughes." His supposed coauthor was a novelist named Clifford Irving. McGraw-Hill had paid Irving an advance of $100,000 and given Irving a $400,000 check for Hughes, which Hughes had reportedly signed and deposited in a Swiss bank account. Bautzer made a statement: "Irving may have had some tapes, but Hughes didn't give them to him. The autobiography is a complete and absolute fraud. I have represented this man for twenty-five years and the last thing he would ever do—this good American—is deposit a check to a numbered Swiss bank account."

If Hughes planned to discredit Irving, it would have to be done in public. Since 1958, Hughes had kept out of sight. He was not about to appear in person. Bautzer arranged a news conference with seven journalists who had known Hughes for years. The journalists would be televised talking to Hughes over the telephone. At the January 7 conference, Hughes spoke over a public address system in a flat, nasal voice. Every reporter recognized his voice and confirmed his identity. After holding forth on a variety of topics, he clarified his connection with Clifford Irving. "I don't know him," said Hughes. "I never met him."

Three weeks later, Bautzer filed suit against McGraw-Hill. On that same day, Irving confessed to forging Hughes's signature and plagiarizing an unpublished book by Hughes's former business manager Noah Dietrich. The autobiography had been ghostwritten by a writer named James Phelan, with whom Irving shared a mutual friend, and that friend had given him access to the manuscript in the hopes that he would rewrite it. Irving, his wife, and his coconspirator Richard Suskind were convicted of defrauding McGraw-Hill of $939,000. They all served time in prison.

The next flare-up was minor by comparison, but potentially more damaging. Joe Hyams was a respected Hollywood journalist. In 1974, Bautzer learned that he was writing an exposé of the "Howard Hughes personal contract-starlet-call girl system," a setup that provided female escorts for Hughes's business associates. Bautzer took him to lunch in order to promise him a much bigger assignment. "I'm not saying that Howard's going to do his autobiography this month or next," Bautzer said in a confidential tone, "but it will be soon. And when I recommend you as the writer, I don't want him to say: 'Isn't he the fellow who did that unauthorized story about me?'"

Hyams had to think twice. "I estimated the Hughes book to be worth at least $100,000, maybe more," he recalled. He agreed to kill the call-girl story. Of course, he never heard another word about an autobiography. Bautzer had to have been relieved that the story was never published, as he was signing the checks for Hughes's women.

The April 1968 issue of *Fortune* magazine listed Howard Hughes as the richest man in the world, with assets worth $1.4 billion. Bautzer decided that Hughes should use some of his money to purchase the American Broadcasting Company. The television network had been in merger talks with other companies, including International Telephone & Telegraph (ITT), but had broken off negotiations. Hughes thought it was a great idea. "I have no desire to produce a long line of 'Batmen', etc.," he told Bautzer. "I have no desire to be associated with a lot of artistic crap. I have no desire to remake the entertainment policy of TV, as many people want to do. My only real interest is in the very areas in which I understand ABC is really hopeless—news and public events and the technical side of the business, in which field I am equipped to do a really outstanding job."

Bautzer clearly had his own interests in mind when he proposed that Hughes buy the network. Bautzer was friends with James T. Aubrey Jr., who had been fired as head of CBS Television in 1965. In the intervening three years, Bautzer had tried to involve Aubrey in several ventures, including potentially producing feature films together. Prior to CBS, the executive had worked for ABC as head of programming in the late 1950s, when he was credited with lifting the network out of the doldrums. Now he and Bautzer were reported commuting to Las Vegas to see Hughes. If the tycoon bought the network, Aubrey was first in line to replace Leonard Goldenson as president. Having ABC as a client would provide all sorts of high-paying legal work for Bautzer and his firm.

On July 1, 1968, Hughes's Toolco offered to purchase up to two million shares, or approximately 43 percent, of the outstanding common stock of ABC. The offer was $74.25 a share, a big markup from the current trading price of $58.87. The total offer was $148.5 million. Goldenson told stockholders that the offer was "substantially below the intrinsic share value." On July 3, Bautzer met with Goldenson and ABC executive vice president Simon B. Siegel. "Mr. Hughes would like to work this out on a friendly basis," Bautzer told them. According to Bautzer, Hughes had no antagonistic motive and was willing to provide financing to ABC. Its facilities were in need of a $90 million upgrade, which Hughes would be happy to underwrite. Despite Bautzer's presentation, ABC could not visualize Hughes as a benign controlling stockholder. Neither could the Federal Communications Commission. In a letter to Bautzer, the FCC warned Hughes not to seek a controlling interest in ABC. He already owned a VHF television station. ABC owned five. If he bought ABC, he would exceed the legal limit.

On July 9, ABC filed papers to block Hughes's purchase in United States District Court—and asked that he be compelled to appear in court. No member of the press had seen Hughes since 1958. ABC was trying to force his hand. They knew he would not want to appear.

Bautzer was roused at four in the morning by the ringing of his phone. One of Hughes's aides was calling from the penthouse of the Desert Inn in Las Vegas, where Hughes had taken up residence. The aide proceeded to read a memo from Hughes.

> I hate to awaken you, Gregson, but I don't like the way this thing is turning out at all. Up to now there has been no real issue about my being personally called at all. But at the hearing today or tomorrow, ABC will demand my appearance. This will bring into sharp focus all the old rumors of my death, disability, etc., etc. And thereafter if, for any reason, the deal fails to materialize, people will say that the reason was my unwillingness to appear.
>
> Now, Gregson, the minute this slant is put on things I am very likely to be sued for the losses that will no doubt be incurred by those individuals who bought stock when it was at its peak in loyal support of their confidence in me and then will be forced to take a loss if the deal fails to go through. You see, normally, it would be held that any such losses would be simply the risk of the speculator. But here we have a man who, in the public's concept, could win this fight if he would just try, but he is too content to lean back on his billion-dollar-ass and enjoy life (at least most people think I do).
>
> If I suffer a massive loss of face after two years of improving publicity, if I wind up sued by individuals who invested with me in my gamble, if my reputation as a successful businessman-financier-industrialist is shot to hell . . . if this is the result of my ABC attempt,

you may be sure that it will have been one of the saddest mistakes I have ever made, and I have made quite a few.

Now, Gregson, needless to say, this would be an awful disappointment to me. However, I did not muddle my way through ten years of the TWA lawsuits only to wind up in another one that could easily last another ten years. I don't like litigation, and there is no prize worth incurring more litigation.

Bautzer realized that he must do something. He filed papers with the court requesting that he be allowed to answer questions on the record instead of Hughes. On July 12, a federal judge ruled that Hughes did not have to appear; Bautzer could testify for him. ABC's action failed, and the offer remained open. Goldenson appealed, saying that Hughes had a history of antitrust litigation. He also quoted Elliot Hyman, the president of Warner Bros., who said that Hughes planned to use dummy corporations to acquire ABC stock. Bautzer had represented Hyman in his purchase of Warner Bros., and he could not have appreciated this move. Tongue planted firmly in cheek, Goldenson said he would be delighted to sit down and talk with Hughes.

July 15 was the deadline for ABC shareholders to respond to Hughes's purchase offer. By that date, Hughes had received 1.6 million shares of ABC stock. He was still 400,000 short. He had two choices. He could raise his offering price and extend the tender offer. Or he could keep the stock and sell it later. In either case he would have to abide by the outcome of proposed FCC hearings.

The scene at the Desert Inn was bizarre. Raymond Holliday, Hughes's adviser, and Robert Maheu, his chief aide, were talking to him from phones in adjoining suites, trying to reason with him. Holliday had not seen Hughes in years. Maheu, who was his chief of operations, had never seen him. On July 16, at 5:15 AM, Hughes sent Bautzer a message.

I am in a real predicament. Holliday and Maheu are absolutely twisting my arm off at the shoulder to persuade me to walk away from this tender. I am resistant to doing this for a number of reasons, the principal is that I feel some of the stockholders will be very disappointed if this happens. I am confident that dumping this much stock upon the market could cause a real break. Holliday and Maheu have as their major argument the claim that the Justice Department Antitrust Division will descend upon us and drive us crazy. You have often said several buyers were available. I don't really want a buyer. What I mainly want is somebody with whom I could trustee this stock in one way or another, just until we could have a few meetings with Justice and the FCC. In other words, I just don't want to have the stock transferred directly to me or Hughes Tool Company for fear this will be the signal for the Justice Department to light on us like a swarm of bees.

On July 16, 1968, the New York Stock Exchange halted trading on ABC stock, waiting for Hughes to declare his intentions. At noon, he announced that he was abandoning the ABC takeover. Hughes blamed his retreat on the "inordinate opposition" of ABC's management. It was more likely the mandates of the FCC that he feared. If hearings were held, he would be forced to attend. This was impossible. For a year Hughes had been secluded in his bedroom. He was not fit, either physically or mentally, to testify in court. He could, however, transmit orders and spend money. This he continued to do.

In the same year, Hughes asked Bautzer to negotiate the purchase of several casinos. This included the Paradise Island Casino in Nassau, the capital of the Commonwealth of the Bahamas. The five-hundred-room hotel was owned by the Mary Carter Paint Company. Hughes wanted to buy all the Carter hotels. Hughes questioned Bautzer in depth about all the details of the Paradise Island operation, including the projected earnings, and the costs of everything from security to water and road maintenance. But most of all he wanted to know about the rats. "When I was there last they had a very serious rat infestation which was publicized to the hilt in Florida," he told Bautzer. Hughes jokingly suggested that perhaps the rats had left the island when the name was changed from "Hog" Island to "Paradise" Island. The negotiations never resulted in a deal. Mary Carter took on a new name—Resorts International Inc. The company would go on to own successful resorts and casino properties.

Robert Maheu, who never had and never would meet Hughes face to face, once stated that Bautzer had not seen Hughes in person since 1956. Maheu was incorrect. A man named Maybe Tucker was Bautzer's chauffer from the late 1960s to the mid-'80s. He recalled several meetings between Bautzer and Hughes, some of which took place in the backseat of Bautzer's car. The final visit occurred at Bautzer's house in Palm Springs in 1969. Bautzer's son, Mark, was with them. After saying goodbye to Hughes, Bautzer sadly told Tucker and Mark that it was the last time they would ever see Hughes.

On April 5, 1976, Tucker was driving Bautzer through Bel Air. Bautzer was in the front seat with him. The radio was playing when there came a news bulletin that Howard Hughes had died. Bautzer made Tucker pull the car to the side of the road. According to Tucker, Bautzer wept like a child for ten minutes.

Following the billionaire's death, there was wild speculation as to the whereabouts of his last will and testament. "Over a period of time Mr. Hughes talked to me about various forms of bequests," Bautzer told the Los Angeles Times, "but he never asked me to draw up a will." Bautzer said that Hughes was a brilliant man who could have written a will without an attorney, and that he had most likely left a holographic will—that is, one written by hand. In his 1972 press conference Hughes had said that he planned to leave his money to the Howard Hughes Medical Institute in Miami. A large-scale investigation was launched to search for the will. Special Administrator

Richard C. Gano Jr. prepared a 274-page search report for the court claiming that two of Bautzer's former employees had seen a document that appeared to be a Hughes will. Bautzer testified in Los Angeles Superior Court that he had not prepared a will for Hughes. To the best of his knowledge, Hughes did not possess a will. Nevertheless, the court ordered that Bautzer search his files. Bautzer looked for someone he trusted to perform the task. Bautzer's longtime secretary Lea Sullivan had left him eleven years earlier when her second child was born, but Bautzer pressed her back into service.

While Sullivan agrees that Bautzer may not have drawn up a will for Hughes, she believes that one existed. She remembered talk of the document from her earlier time at the firm: "Hughes told Mr. Bautzer that he was sending his will over," recalled Sullivan. "Mr. Bautzer told me, 'We have to put it in the safe when it comes over.'" Sullivan was sure that it had been delivered. "If the Hughes office sent something over," said Sullivan, "then nine times out of ten, it went in the safe. The two women who worked in the accounting office, where the safe was, swore that there was a will sent over and that it was in that safe. I have no idea who took it. But it was in there."

When Bautzer asked Sullivan to find the will, he first sent her to a warehouse to look through all his old files. The building was very cold, so Bautzer hired movers to transport vast numbers of file cabinets to her home on Hutton Drive in Beverly Hills. "My dining room became the file room," recalled Sullivan. Television reporters huddled outside her house as she pored over files going back to the 1930s. She could not walk out the front door without having a microphone shoved at her. Sullivan thought it was futile looking for the will in the files, since she knew it had been kept in an envelope in the safe. Nevertheless, she searched every one.

The search for Hughes's will was intense, yet it turned up nothing more than a 1939 codicil. Gano told Judge Neil Lake that the only possibility of finding the will was an expanded search of Bautzer's files. Bautzer told the court that to search five thousand files in 235 drawers would take about ten weeks and cost approximately $17,000. In August 1977, Judge Lake called the memory of Bautzer's two former employees a "pretty thin thread" and halted the search.

If the will had gone into the safe in Bautzer's office on Canon Drive, there is one likely explanation for its disappearance. In the mid-1960s, Bautzer merged his small Beverly Hills firm with one run by the chairman of the California Democratic Party, Eugene Wyman. The new firm was big, with over a hundred employees, and Bautzer would no longer have complete control over the documents in the office. He could no longer guarantee the security of Hughes's secret papers. It is quite possible that at the time of the merger Bautzer returned the will to the Hughes office on Romaine Street with the rest of Hughes's sensitive documents. Sullivan recalled occasions when Hughes's men, "the Boys" as she called them, would come from his office to retrieve things from the safe. In the end, no will was ever located, and Hughes's money went to medical research.

Bautzer often said that Hughes was the shrewdest businessman he had ever represented and that Hughes deserved credit for building an empire. "Howard's success with Toolco has always been deprecated," said Bautzer. "They said he just lucked into it. He didn't. He worked endlessly, tinkering, calculating, jotting down dozens of ideas in an evening. He would leave a date to dash to the phone and talk to Houston—for hours. Once he interrupted a screening to cable a brainstorm to Toolco."

Charles Knapp, the former president of Financial Corporation of America and American Savings & Loan, was a client and friend of Bautzer's. Years after Hughes's death, Bautzer would reminisce about him over lunch with Knapp and his wife, Louise, at the Polo Lounge. Bautzer told the Knapps he had been asked several times to write a Hughes biography, but he refused. Publishers only wanted him to write bad things, not good. Bautzer's USC pal Richard S. Harris also witnessed how close he was to Hughes. "I sat in Greg's office many times when he would buzz his secretary and say 'Get Howard for me.' Thirty seconds later there would be a buzz on the intercom and Howard Hughes would be on the phone. Knowing the peculiarity of the man and his reluctance to talk to anyone, I thought their relationship was remarkable."

17

WHEN STARS
CALL IT QUITS

Howard Hughes occupied a great deal of Greg Bautzer's time in the 1950s, but the attorney had a lot of other work on his plate. By this time, when Bautzer negotiated a talent deal, he worked directly with the head of the studio, such as Harry Cohn at Columbia or Barney Balaban at Paramount. Darryl Zanuck at Fox and Jack Warner at Warner Bros. were close friends of Bautzer's, and business with them was often done during off-hours.

Bautzer used his relationships to do more than just negotiate deals for clients; he also used them to make new stars. Robert Wagner was one of the actors whose career Bautzer helped launch. In 2011, Wagner recalled the push Bautzer gave him: "I was just getting started, earning $75 a week at Fox doing screen tests and small parts. Dana [Wynter] and I worked on some films together, and when I met Greg he took a liking to me and decided to promote me. He would give me a call out of the blue and say, 'Drop by Joe Schenck's at six o'clock. We're going to be playing cards, and there are going to be some people there that I want you to meet.' When I got there, the house would be filled with all the heavyweights in the industry like Zanuck and

Charles Feldman. He would introduce me to each of them and say, 'This kid's got it. He's going to be a big star.' He created an atmosphere of success around me, and I loved him for it. When Natalie [Wood] and I got married, he started to represent her too. When her career took off he handled everything for us."

Motion picture pioneer Sam Goldwyn was still making movies, and Bautzer enjoyed doing business with him. Their wives were friends, and Goldwyn was always good for a laugh, intentional or not. English was Goldwyn's second or third language, and his mangling of it produced legendary "Goldwynisms" including "An oral contract isn't worth the paper it's printed on" and "Include me out." Bautzer experienced one of these malapropisms firsthand. He was in Goldwyn's office negotiating a deal for client Farley Granger, who was in Italy spending time with his platonic friend, the brassy actress Shelley Winters. Granger refused to speak to Goldwyn on the phone, letting Winters do the talking for him. As Bautzer sat on the couch, Goldwyn pled with Winters to let Granger come back to work on a picture. She kept teasing and refusing. Finally, when everything he tried failed, he slammed down the phone and said to Bautzer "That woman is a *cunt*—and I mean it in the unfriendly sense of the word."

Divorce cases were still the mainstay of Bautzer's law practice, and after the Bergman case, he hit another jackpot representing Nancy Barbato Sinatra in her breakup with Frank. In 1950, Sinatra's career was slipping. He had been a cultural phenomenon in the early 1940s, but the teenage bobby-soxers who screamed in ecstasy at his singing had grown up and moved on. To make things worse, he was having vocal problems. He had a wife of eleven years, Nancy, and three children. He also had a girlfriend, the oversexed, uninhibited Ava Gardner. After a year of romance with the star, he asked his wife for a divorce, but she refused. On February 5, 1950, in Houston, Sinatra made a scene when a photographer wanted to take a picture of him and Gardner eating spaghetti. Nancy saw the item in the papers and locked him out of their house. Then she hired Bautzer and had her day in court, the first of many.

"Unfortunately, my married life with Frank has become most unhappy," said Nancy. "I have requested my attorney to attempt to work out a property settlement, but I do not contemplate divorce proceedings in the foreseeable future." Nancy said she was not seeking an end to her marriage, simply control over part of Sinatra's income. "Mrs. Sinatra has no plans for divorce," Bautzer explained to the *Los Angeles Times*. "The separate maintenance suit is just her way of making Sinatra save his money. She'll put it away as a nest egg. Then, when nobody else wants him, she'll take him back, and they'll have something to live on."

On April 26, 1950, Bautzer and cocounsel Arnold Grant filed for separate maintenance. This would require Sinatra to pay Nancy alimony while they lived apart, even though they wouldn't be divorced. The complaint charged Sinatra with extreme cruelty and inflicting grievous mental suffering without provocation. Nancy claimed that Sinatra had earned $934,740 in 1949 and that the value of their community property was $750,000. Bautzer sought permanent alimony, saying that Sinatra had extreme wealth and was in a position to justify a high standard of living. He was seeking a "reasonable amount" for her and their three children: Nancy Jr., age nine; Frank Jr., age six; and Christina, age two. The court awarded her $2,750 a month temporary alimony. To put pressure on Sinatra, Bautzer obtained a restraining order forbidding MGM from paying him $85,000 it owed him for a lapsed contract. The company was one of several that were dumping him.

Bautzer tried to negotiate a property settlement of the Sinatras' community holdings, including an office building in Los Angeles, homes in Holmby Hills and Palm Springs, and the home Sinatra had purchased for his parents Marty and Dolly in Hoboken, New Jersey. By June, all Nancy and Sinatra could agree upon was conveying ownership of the Hoboken house to Sinatra's parents. Many friends thought Nancy was delaying the negotiations in the hope Sinatra would leave Gardner and return to her. "She's miserable about all his gallivanting," Bautzer told reporters, "but she's still very much in love with him." Nancy was hoping in vain; Sinatra was besotted with Gardner.

Eventually, Nancy realized that divorce was inevitable and changed her request from separate maintenance to terminating the marriage. The Sinatra court hearing was set for September but postponed by the attorneys' mutual agreement when a settlement appeared likely. Ultimately, Sinatra agreed to pay Nancy one-third of his gross income up to $150,000 and one-tenth of the gross above that figure until her death or remarriage, with payments never to fall below $1,000 a month. Nancy also got the Holmby Hills house, stock in the Sinatra Music Corporation, their 1950 gray Cadillac, and custody of the children. Sinatra got the Palm Springs house and a 1949 Cadillac convertible.

Even though Bautzer put Sinatra through the wringer in his divorce, they became friends. Twelve years later, Sinatra was back on top, more popular than ever, and spending his new wealth at the Hotel Las Brisas in Acapulco. Bautzer was there with Wynter, relaxing in a rented cottage. Sinatra needed a kitchen. He thought of Bautzer. "Hey, would you mind if I came down and cooked some Italian food?" he asked over the phone. "I'll send my man ahead of me."

"No, I don't mind," Bautzer replied. "You don't mind, Dana? Dana doesn't mind." It was a decision Wynter would come to regret.

Sinatra always brought an entourage to their place in Acapulco. It might include the Maharani of Baroda, playboy Porfirio Rubirosa, or actor Yul Brynner, his wife Doris, and son Rocky. One day Sinatra brought a man whom he introduced as Sam Mooney. The short, swarthy man never opened his mouth, but every time Bautzer and Wynter saw him, he was with a different young girl. These girls appeared to be only fourteen or fifteen, which Dana found disturbing.

One night Sinatra gave a dinner party at Teddy Stauffer's La Perla restaurant in Acapulco and invited the Bautzers. Wynter found herself seated between Sinatra and Mooney. When photographers showed up, Sinatra grew peremptory. "You can photograph from Dana past me down the table," he said, "but you can't photograph up the table." Dana was perplexed. Later that night she learned that Sinatra didn't want Sam Mooney in the picture. Sam "Mooney" was really Sam Giancana, head of the Chicago Mafia.

The next night Sinatra brought a group of people to the Bautzers' cottage in Acapulco. When Dana saw Giancana, she went to her room and closed the door. Bautzer came to look for her and found her in bed. He asked her to come back to the party. "No," she said. "Don't you know what this is? Sinatra is bringing hoodlums to our house. Somebody could be shot on our doorstep and he hasn't even the courtesy to say who this man is. I think it's appalling. I'm not coming back. The staff is there. You're there. You can cope with it if you want to."

One Christmas, she and Bautzer were at the airport in Mexico City. They spotted Giancana. He was tearing his hair in frustration. He could not board a flight to Chicago because the airlines were all overbooked. He rushed up to Bautzer. "For God's sake," said Giancana, "can't you get me a seat on a plane? I've got to get back. I'm stuck in this place. I don't know anybody." Wynter was pleased to see the criminal bereft of his power.

In the spring of 1965, Giancana was subpoenaed by a grand jury. To prevent him from invoking the Fifth Amendment, the government gave him immunity. He had to answer questions about the mob or be held in contempt. He decided contempt was better than testifying and was jailed for a year. After his release, he spent years hiding in Mexico, but was finally deported. Upon his return to the States, he became an FBI informant. In 1975 he was frying sausages in his Chicago kitchen when he was murdered execution-style.

Harvey Silbert, brother of Bautzer's former partner Bernard Silbert and later Bautzer's partner himself, did legal work for Sinatra. Bautzer may have tolerated Sinatra's mob connections to protect the firm. Though Wynter disliked the criminal atmosphere, she was grateful for one very important thing Sinatra did for her husband. Bautzer was watching a show in Las Vegas. Sinatra was sitting at a nearby table. Four men came in and sat directly behind Bautzer. One of them put his feet on the rungs of Bautzer's chair. Bautzer turned around and told the man to take his foot off. The man didn't. Bautzer pushed his chair back, stood up, and delivered his usual challenge. "Listen, you. Do you wanna come outside?" At that point, Sinatra shot from his seat and grabbed Bautzer by the arm.

"Greg," he said firmly, "we're late for the meeting. Come on. Hurry up." Bautzer didn't know what Sinatra was talking about. Sinatra gave Bautzer a steely-eyed stare and clenched his jaw. "Come on." He steered Bautzer outside the theater. Once out of earshot, he said, "Greg, don't you know who they are?" It turned out that Bautzer had been spoiling for a fight with the toughest Mafia guys in Vegas. He later admitted that Sinatra had saved his life. Bautzer really liked Sinatra. Both his wife and son remembered him playing Sinatra records constantly at home.

Another high-profile celebrity whose divorce Bautzer handled in the 1950s was Jeanne Crain. The case made headlines around the world, delivering lurid details of spousal abuse and infidelity for the times. The redheaded actress was universally popular and had given solid performances in many important films: *State Fair*, *Leave Her to Heaven*, and *Pinky*—she received an Academy Award nomination for the latter. She was married to Paul Brinkman, who acted briefly in the 1940s under the name Paul Brooks and was now manufacturing plastic aircraft parts. A devout Catholic, Crain had borne him four children. On March 29, 1956, she filed for divorce, represented initially by the distinguished lawyers Martin Gang and Milton A. Rudin. On May 16, she filed an amended complaint charging that Brinkman beat her, broke down her bedroom door, and raped her, almost in front of their children. Brinkman hired attorney Arthur Crowley to represent him. Crowley often represented celebrities, but not as many as Bautzer. Crain's attorneys filed motions to obtain a restraining order against Brinkman to keep him from molesting her. Crain said that her husband had threatened to kill her and take his own life. On June 14, Crowley filed a cross-complaint, accusing Crain of adultery with Homer Hoch Rhoads, a family friend. Rhoads owned an airline parts manufacturing business that sold supplies to the US Air Force. Motions were also filed to have Brinkman held in contempt of a prior restraining order and to issue a new restraining order, to have him turn over his guns to the court, to have his child visitation rights limited, and to forbid him from using jointly owned funds to employ detectives in connection with the case. Crowley threatened to take Crain's deposition and make her answer questions about her relationship with Rhoads.

Crain's motions for contempt and a new restraining order were scheduled to be heard in court on June 25, but before the hearing, Crain fired Gang and Rudin and hired Bautzer and his partner Gerald Lipsky. The switch was likely due to Crain's desire to hide the truth about her affair with Rhoads. Crain feared that revealing the truth about her affair with Rhoads would cause irreparable damage to her career, but lawyers are forbidden from assisting their clients in committing perjury. When Crain told Gang and Rudin that she was going to lie about her adultery, they undoubtedly told her that they could not continue to represent her. When Crain hired Bautzer, she was wiser and likely did not tell him the whole truth. Of course, Crain's choice of Bautzer as a replacement may also have had something to do with her dancing cheek to cheek with him at his wedding party the week before the switch.

Whatever the reason, Bautzer and Lipsky were not sufficiently prepared to argue the motions previously filed by Gang and Rudin and did not appear in court on the hearing date, so the motions were dropped. "We have just recently been substituted in this case," said Bautzer to the press. "We consider it a wiser strategy not to pursue these motions." On June 28, Crain gave a deposition at Crowley's office denying the infidelity accusations but admitting that she had been alone with Rhoads in his secretary's apartment. While Bautzer did not help her commit perjury, he found a way to guard her reputation by simply having her refuse to answer certain questions. She testified that Rhoads had been dressed the entire time she was with him and that they had done nothing more than talk about how her husband had helped Rhoads achieve sobriety. She admitted that she had visited Rhoads another time and kept both visits from her husband for several weeks. With Bautzer at her side, Crain refused to answer sixteen of Crowley's questions. Crain refused to say whether she ever told anyone that she loved Rhoads and she refused to answer questions about an alleged meeting with Rhoads at the intersection of Doheny and Hillcrest Drives, where a private detective reported that he saw Rhoads enter her car and embrace her. She also refused to answer questions about conversations with Rhoads's mother in which Crain said the woman was "acting like a cruel witch." When asked by the press for a description of what went on at the deposition, Bautzer demurred, saying only, "With four children involved in this case, I think it is advisable to make no comment."

Shortly after the deposition, Brinkman surprisingly withdrew the adultery charges, and an interlocutory (not final) divorce decree was granted in August. Brinkman got into a vicious public fight with Rhoads after Christmas, but on December 30, Crain and Brinkman reconciled. They went on to have three more children and remained married until Brinkman's death in 2003.

By the late 1950s, Bautzer wanted to stop handling divorces. His work for Hughes was thriving and he was tired of the typical acrimony. "Divorces are messy," he would later say. "It's a hand-holding business. In any divorce there are three sides. Hers. His. And the long view, standing off and looking at it all. But divorce clients want to be constantly reassured. They want you to hold their hands and keep telling them that they're right. All the way."

Yet when Rock Hudson came to him in 1957 and asked him to handle his divorce, Bautzer couldn't turn him down. The thirty-two-year-old actor was a box office sensation. According to the *Motion Picture Herald*, Hudson was Hollywood's top moneymaker. *Tarnished Angels*, *Written on the Wind*, and *Giant* had combined to put him on top. In 1955, when Hudson was still a Universal player on the way up, he had married Phyllis Gates. It was an odd match; she was not an actress but a secretary working for his agent, Henry Wilson. "I was very much in love," said Gates. "I thought Rock would be a wonderful husband. He was charming, his career was red-hot, and he was gorgeous. If I had heard things about his being homosexual, I just put them in the back of my mind. So what if it was true? We were having an affair and he asked me to marry him." Mere minutes after the Santa Barbara ceremony, Hudson called Hedda Hopper and Gates called Louella Parsons. Friends and family had to find out for themselves.

The honeymoon took place in Jamaica. Gates remembered a wonderful week and no problems. Hudson remembered a terrible week and a huge fight. Gates went to Kenya with Hudson in 1956 when he filmed *Something of Value* with Dana Wynter, but did not go to Italy with him in 1957 when he spent five months with Jennifer Jones and her husband David O. Selznick on *A Farewell to Arms*. Gates was hospitalized with hepatitis; when she got out, she began to feel neglected. She did not know that Hudson was having affairs with men on location.

There was talk that Universal had forced Hudson to marry Gates in order to kill an exposé in *Confidential* magazine, but most people who socialized with the couple thought them well adjusted. "Phyllis and Rock were at our house constantly," said their friend Roger Jones. "You get a feeling about people. They were happy together. They clicked."

Gates said Hudson changed after he returned from Italy and realized how popular he had become. He was suddenly in thrall to his own power. "He was out every night," recalled Gates. "During the day he was in a bad mood. You couldn't talk to him. You'd say, 'Would you like some coffee?' and he wouldn't answer. He would start an argument at the drop of a hat, then slam the door and not come back until the next morning." Gates became depressed, so she went to a psychiatrist, who suggested that Hudson also come in for a session. Hudson stopped going when the psychologist told him he had the emotional development of an eight-year-old. Hudson told Bautzer that his apartment on Crescent Heights Boulevard was bugged. Investigators found freshly cut wires, but no culprit.

In the divorce settlement, Gates was given alimony of $250 a week for ten years, plus a house on Warbler Place valued at $35,000; Hudson would continue to make mortgage payments. She also got 5 percent of Hudson's production company, 7 Pictures Corporation, and she got to keep a new Ford Thunderbird. For such a short marriage, the settlement was exorbitant. It smacked of a payoff.

Bautzer continued to represent Hudson in other matters. At Hudson's request he terminated the star's contract with Universal and got him a sizable block of stock in its parent company, the Music Corporation of America. Gates kept quiet for nearly thirty years. Only when Sara Davidson, Hudson's authorized biographer, approached her in the mid-1980s did she break her silence. Hudson was dying of AIDS.

Gates finally admitted her doubts about the reasons for the marriage. "I used to believe the marriage started with good intentions," she said, "but now I don't believe it was genuine. I'll bet you my marriage was arranged by Universal."

18

THE HEARST PROXY

For an incredible sixty years, William Randolph Hearst had been the most powerful publisher in the world. He was also a real estate mogul, an art collector, and a movie producer. It would be difficult to overstate his influence on culture, let alone history. It was monumental. In November 1950, he was eighty-seven and in failing health. He feared that once he was gone, his wife Millicent would deprive his mistress, silent movie star Marion Davies, of her portion of his estate. He had produced films for Davies for twenty years, but she was fifty-three and retired. He asked her nephew Charles Lederer to find a lawyer who could help without alerting anyone in the Hearst empire, specifically his five sons.

Lederer was a Hollywood fixture, having collaborated with his close friend the eminent playwright Ben Hecht on the screenplays for *His Girl Friday*, *Comrade X*, and *Kiss of Death*.* Lederer regularly played tennis and cards with Bautzer and told Hearst he was the man for the job. By this time Hearst was too infirm to spend time at La Cuesta Encantada, his palatial headquarters in San Simeon, Califor-

---

*Lederer would go on to write such other classics as *Gentleman Prefer Blondes*, *The Thing*, and the original *Ocean's 11*, among many others.

nia, so Bautzer met him at the Beverly Drive home he shared with Davies.

Hearst instructed Bautzer to draw up a trust agreement granting Davies control of his publishing empire. Hearst and Davies both signed it on November 5. "I want you to take care of Marion when I die," he told Bautzer. "I want her to feel that I'm still there looking after her. I think you'll be able to do that for her." Hearst then instructed his staff to deposit stock shares in Davies's name as a guarantee. He was too ill to see if his orders were being carried out.

Marion Davies was a unique entity in the history of Hollywood. Born Marion Douras to a middle-class Brooklyn family in 1897, she was groomed to attract a rich man. By age nineteen, the Ziegfeld Follies showgirl was doing just that. Fortunately for her, the man she attracted was genuinely taken with her. "Willie" Hearst was fifty-three and married, and Millicent would not grant him a divorce. So for the next thirty-five years, Hearst and Davies were an unmarried couple, but married in spirit and deed. Though nothing could be said publicly, there was the occasional innuendo. In 1934, when Hearst was criticizing "immoral" films, the *Los Angeles Times* published a rather pointed letter in response to his attack. "Wouldn't it absolutely clinch the cause of purity," suggested a reader, "if we could get Mr. Hearst to produce a picture portraying the true story of his upright life? It would make a wonderful theme in which to star Marion Davies." Davies tried to rationalize her status. "Love is not always created at the altar," she told Hearst. "Love doesn't need a wedding ring."

Hearst could not give Davies marriage, so he gave her stardom. Beginning with *Cecilia of the Pink Roses* in 1918, he produced a series of showcases for her and a snowstorm of publicity. Hearst columnist Louella Parsons was entrusted with the care of Davies's image and made sure that no morning paper was printed without a reminder that Davies was the country's most eligible bachelor girl. Davies repaid Hearst's devotion by being the perfect hostess of five mansions and by selling some of her jewelry in the late 1930s to get him through a fiscal crisis.

Hearst died on August 14, 1951. His will was filed for probate a few hours later and its contents made public. Upon reading the document, his empire was in an uproar. Millicent Hearst and her sons were incredulous that a voting trust agreement should make Marion Davies the sole voting trustee of the Hearst Corporation, the holding company of Hearst's publishing empire. Davies owned 30,000 shares, just 15 percent of the stock, but would have voting rights to 100,000 common shares and 170,000 shares (85 percent) of the preferred stock. She, therefore, would have power to choose all the officers and directors of the corporations. This was the posthumous, public confirmation of her illicit relationship with Hearst.

News of Hearst's bequest became a national sensation. *Time* magazine ran a feature story entitled "Hearst's Bombshell." On August 26, Hearst's son, Randolph Apperson Hearst, acting as an administrator of the estate, challenged not only the validity of his father's agreement but also its existence. "This so-called agreement," said Randolph, "was never executed, and, for this and many other reasons, it has no more effect than if it never existed." The stock shares that were supposed to have been deposited as a guarantee had not been; without them, the family was free to discount the agreement.

"The document will speak for itself when filed," said Bautzer. The signed agreement was soon found and papers were filed, but the Hearst family continued to challenge it. A battle was shaping up, the grieving mistress against the aggrieved widow. Davies did not relish the prospect of a down-and-dirty fight with Hearst's sons, most of whom had been cordial to her for many years. "I would do anything in the world to avoid hurting those boys," she said. "After all, they're half of W.R."

Even so, she wanted to honor Hearst's plans. "I'm not the fighting type," said Davies, "but I don't believe in disregarding W.R.'s wishes.

He had a reason for having the agreement drawn up. He thought I was the one who understood best what his policies and principles were and that I could see to it that his ideas were carried out." She asked Bautzer to help her find a solution to the conflict. "Gosh, I thought I'd have a peaceful time in my old age," said Davies. "Now look at the spot I'm in!"

After a month of talks, Bautzer negotiated a revised agreement with the Hearst heirs. Davies relinquished her voting rights but retained thirty thousand shares of stock. She was also granted the right to use the Hearst press to publicize her charities.

In October, Davies shocked the country when she married a family friend, Horace G. Brown Jr., at the El Rancho Hotel in Las Vegas. Brown was a former film extra and a retired merchant marine captain, and he resembled the Hearst of thirty years earlier. The marriage was based on little more than Davies's loneliness. In July 1952, she filed for divorce. Bernard Silbert represented her. Brown was aggravating, but he was also companionable, so Davies reconsidered and dropped her suit.

After Howard Hughes, Davies was Bautzer's second wealthiest client. Bautzer was honored by Hearst's request to serve as his surrogate and take care of Marion after his death. Bautzer intended to carry out Hearst's orders to the letter. Since her nephew Charles Lederer was one of his closest friends, Marion was almost like an aunt. Bautzer immediately started to investigate her property holdings. Hearst had placed real estate in her name, and Bautzer wanted to make sure she realized its full value. "I think we have an obligation as far as Marion is concerned," said Bautzer at a meeting with his law partners. "And I think that obligation is to increase the estate."

In addition to real estate, Davies also held a financial participation in Cosmopolitan Productions, which had produced fifty-four pictures for distribution by MGM. The company was originally set up by Hearst in the silent era to make pictures based on stories from his publications. It was called Cosmopolitan after his magazine of the same name. In the silent era, Cosmopolitan produced Davies's starring vehicles, but in the 1930s, it went on to produce such talking hits as *Young Mr. Lincoln*, starring Henry Fonda and directed by John Ford; *Ceiling Zero*, starring James Cagney and directed by Howard Hawks; and *The Story of Alexander Graham Bell*, starring Don Ameche and Henry Fonda. Now that television was paying substantial fees for movies, the library held considerable value. MGM controlled the distribution rights to the films but would not make a commitment to sell them to television. Bautzer put legal pressure on MGM to assure that the rights were licensed to television for appropriate fees and made certain Davies received her share of the profits.

Bautzer did more than simply manage Davies's assets. He handled her affairs as though he were her guardian, taking care of her every need. Davies grew to depend on him, calling him daily with her personal problems, both large and small. In 1953, she asked him to help her prepare for the New York wedding of John F. Kennedy and Jacqueline Bouvier. She knew that Millicent Hearst planned to attend. "Greg, I want to have a little black Rolls Royce," said Davies. "I want to buy one."

"Why, Marion?"

"Well, the widow is going to have a Rolls Royce and I want to have a Rolls Royce too."

Bautzer suggested she rent a limousine. Davies declined because she knew that New York license plates would give away the car as a rental. "But buying a Rolls, Marion. That will cost a lot."

"I don't care," said Davies.

"But for one day?"

"I'll probably stay several days."

"How about second hand?"

"OK," she said. "But only if it's in good shape."

Bautzer went about finding a used Rolls that he could have waiting for Davies at Grand Central Station on her arrival, but this was short notice. The only Rolls he could find was a small older model, one of the last handmade ones. It had a chauffeur's box in front, two seats in the back, and a hood that flipped up on either side to reveal the engine. In addition to being small and old, the car was dark green.

After traveling by train across the country, Davies and her entourage were greeted at Grand Central Station by Bautzer and an auto dealer. Then she saw the car. "Greg," she stammered, "this is not a black Rolls Royce. It's green." Bautzer responded that this was the best he could do if she wanted to purchase one. She took a long look at him. "That's the goddamnedest shade of black I've ever seen," she said haltingly, "but I'll take it."

When Bautzer and Wynter were married, Davies sent them the green Rolls with a big red bow tied to its hood and the pink slip in Wynter's name. The Bautzers used the Rolls for premieres and special events.

Davies was deeply fond of Bautzer. She would often say, "Greg has made me a rich woman." She wanted to reward him with a gift of land in her will. "No, thank you, Marion," said Bautzer. "That's very kind of you, but that is not correct and it can't be done." He explained that rules of professional responsibility bar a lawyer from being named as a beneficiary in a will he drafts. Davies was impressed by Bautzer's honesty and tried to get around the rule by giving him other gifts, but he would not accept them.

Bautzer also knew that if Davies left her money in the bank it would quickly disappear. She confessed her plight in a meeting with Bautzer. "Money lying in the bank is a terrible temptation to me and if I get touched for some I can't do anything about it," said Marion. "When I have it, my relatives can smell it." So he regularly presented Davies with investment ideas.

In July 1955, Bautzer negotiated Davies's purchase of the thirty-three-acre Palm Springs Desert Inn for $1.75 million. The property included frontage of 599 feet on Palm Canyon Drive, the main thoroughfare of the resort town. The Desert Inn was founded in 1909 by Mrs. Nellie Coffman. When Mrs. Coffman came to Palm Springs with her husband, Dr. Harry Clee Coffman, it had a total of fourteen residents. Guests were accommodated in a stable and tents. By the time of her death at age eighty-two in 1950, Mrs. Coffman had turned her property into a nationally known resort. Davies planned to continue in the grand tradition, keeping the hotel "open to all," a controversial stand against racism and anti-Semitism.

Davies also owned a row of brownstone apartments on Fifty-Seventh Street in New York City. On Bautzer's advice, she razed them and built an aluminum-sheathed high-rise. She named it the Douras Building in honor of her father, Barney Douras, who had once been a Manhattan judge. The property's monthly revenue shot from $20,000 to $120,000. Among her other properties were the Squibb Building on Fifth Avenue, acreage on the Miracle Mile in Los Angeles, and homes in Bel Air, Beverly Hills, and Santa Monica. All told, she was realizing half a million dollars yearly from her income property.

In 1955, *Time* magazine took note of Davies's growing real estate empire in an article titled "Tycoon Davies." The aging silent screen queen admitted that her increasing fortune was all due to her lawyers. "I do what they tell me. Greg has a great mind for real estate. He's smarter than I am," she told the reporter. Bautzer humbly deflected the compliment, saying, "She has a good sense of smell about a piece of land." Bautzer knew that it was always better to give the client credit regardless of the real story. He was paid for his services, and the client was entitled to the benefit.

Davies was known for her charities. In 1932, she had created the Marion Davies Foundation to provide care for children. In 1957, Bautzer helped her liquidate the foundation's assets. She had something special in mind. In January of 1958, two hundred dignitaries attended a ceremony at the Sheraton Town House in which Davies presented Edwin Pauley, chairman of the University of California Board of Regents, with a check for $1.5 million, at the time the largest individual monetary gift ever made to the University of California at Los Angeles. Her gift was earmarked for the construction of a new wing at the UCLA Medical Center. In it would be a children's clinic. President Eisenhower, Vice President Nixon, and California governor Edwin Knight sent telegrams extolling Davies. "Marion accompanies her check with her heart," said Bautzer when he presented it.

Davies died of cancer on September 22, 1961, at the age of sixty-four. Her funeral Mass was celebrated at the Immaculate Heart of Mary Church in Hollywood. Bautzer was an honorary pallbearer. He was fifty years old, but he could not fail to observe the irony that many of the mourners, though only in their sixties, were cut off from the Hollywood he knew because they were silent film "has-beens." The story of Marion Davies comprised a fortunate alliance, a giving nature, and a sunny sense of humor. She was universally loved and admired by the Hollywood community. In the sometimes-cynical film industry, Bautzer was lucky to have had such a friend and client.

19

JOSEPH SCHENCK
ENTERPRISES

In 1953, the Academy of Motion Picture Arts and Sciences chose to honor
Joseph M. Schenck with a special award, one given for "long and distinguished service to the motion picture industry." Schenck was one
of the original thirty-six founders of the Academy and had been head
of production at Twentieth Century-Fox for nine years. The award
was Hollywood's way of saying that despite a conviction for bribing
a union leader, he was respected and valued. But Schenck was not
content to rest on his laurels. In 1953, he and producer Mike Todd
founded the Magna Corporation and then partnered with Dr. Brian
O'Brien and the American Optical Company to create the widescreen
process called Todd-AO, which enhanced the quality of both cinema-
tography and projection.

By the mid-1950s, Schenck was no longer producing. When he
suffered a minor stroke in 1957, he went into semiretirement. His
brother Nick was still in New York, running Loew's Inc., the parent
company of MGM. Nick gave Joe an office in the Thalberg building
at MGM's studio in Culver City, California, even though Joe's principal business was by then real estate.

Bautzer felt affection and loyalty for Joe and thought it a shame that his mentor was no longer producing. Television was thriving and needed programming, and Bautzer thought Joe could supply it. Bautzer advised him to sell some of his real estate holdings and finance a new company. Of course, Bautzer had an ulterior motive. He wanted to become a producer himself and develop vehicles for his clients. For these reasons and more, Joseph Schenck Enterprises was born.

Schenck was no longer capable of handling the day-to-day details of a company, so Bautzer needed an administrator. He found that person almost by accident: Bernie Schwartz, the well-connected problem-solver who helped him negotiate the settlement between Gina Lollobrigida and Howard Hughes. After the nonlawyer Schwartz turned down a job in Bautzer's law firm, Bautzer made another offer. How would he like to run Joseph Schenck Enterprises? Schwartz packed up his wife and young son and headed for Hollywood.

The Schenck company's first television production was *One Step Beyond*, an anthology series sponsored by the aluminum manufacturer Alcoa. Each episode dramatized a paranormal phenomenon, and although the concept was obviously copied from the wildly popular *Twilight Zone*, it was sufficiently different to garner its own following.

Schwartz soon learned there was more to producing for Schenck and Bautzer than writing screenplays and hiring talent. One day Bautzer called Schwartz for a favor. "Howard has a new girl," he said. "Do you have anything for her?"

"Is she pretty?" asked Schwartz.

"Of course she's pretty. What a question! When did you ever see Howard Hughes go out with a girl who wasn't pretty? I'm telling you, this is driving me crazy. I'm in the middle of a half-billion dollar negotiation for a fleet of jets, but Howard refuses to discuss it until we get the girl a part."

"There's a part in an episode of *One Step Beyond*," said Schwartz, "but she probably wouldn't want it. It's not a big part."

Bautzer told Schwartz to see Hughes and tell him about the show. Schwartz drove to Hughes's home. The fabled eccentric was not impressed. The role she was being offered in *One Step Beyond* was too small. However, the girl might agree to appear if they rewrote the script to make her role more substantial. Schwartz wanted to please Bautzer, so he called his producer, director, and writers. They began a rewrite. The girl was sent an episode script and told to report to the makeup department at six o'clock Monday morning.

At two in the morning on Sunday, Bernie Schwartz's phone rang. "Am I disturbing you?" asked Hughes. He did not wait for a reply. "I don't like your script. I've been reading it. I don't like the actor you've cast as the leading man. I don't like the idea of this girl working with him. I've told her, and she's crying. Will you do me a favor? Pick her up at her apartment and bring her to my office. We'll both explain why she shouldn't do the show." That was that. After expending a weekend's worth of overtime, Schwartz had to find another actress for the script he specifically wrote for Hughes's girlfriend. Even worse, he now had to go out in the middle of the night and console her. Schwartz was not happy that Bautzer had gotten him into this mess. The actress's name is unknown, but like so many of Hughes's other kept women, she likely never achieved stardom.

Joseph Schenck Enterprises had originally been located at the MGM lot, but one day Nick Schenck ordered the curtains to be removed as a not-so-subtle way of indicating they weren't welcome any more. The company relocated. At first they rented rather shabby suites on Santa Monica Boulevard, across from Hollywood Memorial Park, but later they moved into an office at 190 North Canon Drive, one floor below Bautzer's own. Schwartz continued to run the company for many years, producing the well-received feature film *Journey to the Center of the Earth* in 1959. He went on to become an award-winning producer. His triumph was producing *Coal Miner's*

Daughter, a film that brought Sissy Spacek the 1980 Academy Award for Best Actress.

Schenck seldom visited the company that bore his name. As his strength waned in the late 1950s, he preferred to sit by the pool at his home on Carolwood Drive and later in his penthouse at the Beverly Hilton. Bautzer and Wynter looked after Schenck. As his health failed, that was literally all Wynter could do. She spent hours holding his hand, but he didn't recognize her.

About the same time, Bautzer ran into Marilyn Monroe at a party at David O. Selznick's home. Monroe had lived with Schenck in 1949 when he got her a contract at Twentieth Century-Fox. In the time since, she had written him many letters, which Schenck kept in a file cabinet in his office. When she overheard Bautzer say that Schenck was near death, she became hysterical, screaming that it could not be true—someone would have told her. She insisted that she see Schenck immediately. Bautzer grew angry, telling her that she should have visited Schenck when he could have enjoyed seeing her. Now it was too late.

Joseph M. Schenck died on October 22, 1961, at the age of seventy-three. The funeral was held at the Wilshire Boulevard Temple, and Bautzer was a pallbearer, along with Selznick, Samuel Goldwyn, Sol Lesser, Leo McCarey, Mervyn LeRoy, Harold Lloyd, Danny Thomas, and Irving Berlin. Bautzer delivered a eulogy but expressed himself most eloquently in an interview some years later: "Of all the people I have represented, the most powerful was Joseph M. Schenck. His was not the power of immense wealth, but, rather, the power of immense intelligence, perception, of humor and magnetism, and of what is rather rare in this industry today, integrity. He was genuinely sincere. Beyond that, he had charm. He loved people. He particularly loved women, and I am not prepared to knock that. Howard Hughes used women. Joe Schenck tried to help them. When he died, I became executor of his estate. There were probably twelve or fourteen women he had known—only a few carnally—for whom he provided in his will; in most instances it was for the rest of their lives."

On September 2, 1962, Bautzer lost his other mentor. Billy Wilkerson died of a heart attack at age seventy-two at his Bel Air home. Bautzer eulogized Wilkerson as a power player. "Billy used power for his personal gain for his paper and for his friends, but he was a brilliant man and a courageous one. He was what I would call a courageous desperado. I loved him."

20

THE BREAKUP

A few years into their marriage, Dana Wynter found herself embroiled, first in disagreements and then in arguments. When they were over, she could not remember how they had started. She sometimes felt confused, sometimes guilty. Bautzer was thoughtful and generous, and had that wonderful sense of humor. He was never petty or resentful of her spending. He could be delightful. This was when he was getting his way—and when he was sober. When he was vexed or imbibing, he was given to behavior that Wynter could not countenance. These breaches of decorum more than anything pointed out the differences in their backgrounds. Wynter believed that disagreements should be settled in a civil tone of voice and never in public. She was mortified when Bautzer argued in a restaurant, whether with her or someone else. She was brought up never to raise her voice, least of all in a public place.

Wynter hoped to change some aspects of his behavior. She thought that if she spoke to him calmly that he would hear her out. He would not. He took her constructive criticism as an attack. First his debater's mind would start working. Then he would find something that implied that she came from a better class than he. Once this reaction was triggered, there was no hope of an intelligent discussion.

Wynter tried putting her suggestions on paper. This was slightly more effective, but only if Bautzer read the note in private. He would then respond in a reasonable manner, and she would feel there was hope.

The behavior that Wynter found most insensitive, however, was his flirting. He would flirt with a woman not only in the same room with Wynter but right in front of her, almost under her nose. It embarrassed her, her friends, and even people who did not know them. Wynter wondered if Bautzer had ever been taught not to do these things. She was subjected to it at the party celebrating their return from their honeymoon, when Jeanne Crain threw herself at Bautzer on the dance floor and he did nothing to discourage her. Wynter burst into tears and left the party. When he got home, he confronted her. "What's the matter with you?" An argument ensued, and Wynter found it impossible to make him understand why she was offended.

Bautzer's relationship with his son, Mark, was also a source of concern. He had never been around children. When Mark was a toddler and afterwards, Bautzer was at a loss to relate to him. The debating champion could not shift gears. His child needed him to sit on the floor with him, to talk and draw, but Bautzer was incapable of this kind of interaction. He was not entirely inattentive, though. When he took two-and-a-half-year-old Mark to the Marineland amusement park in Palos Verdes, Hedda Hopper wrote that Mark was thrilled and wanted to return. "Well," said Bautzer, "why don't we take Eric, Jackie, or Wendy, or all three?"

"Let's take Wendy," said Mark, forgetting the boys. Hopper made a joke of Mark's interest in girls, saying "Like father, like son."

Perhaps Bautzer was spoiling Mark in an attempt to compensate for his parental shortcomings. "The day after I returned from a San Francisco meeting," said Bautzer, "I was called on the carpet by my son's nursery school and told that my three-year-old needs more discipline." But Bautzer wanted his son to enjoy special privileges and have the things he didn't have growing up. When Bautzer won a motor-cycle at a charity ball in New York, he told Hopper he would save it for Mark.

That was when Bautzer was sober. When Bautzer was drunk, he behaved very badly toward his son. When Mark would try to talk to him, his father would twist the boy's words and look for hidden meanings, as if he were cross-examining him on a witness stand. When Mark became confused and tongue-tied, Bautzer would take it as a sign of guilt. Usually Mark had done nothing to deserve the accusation. The lawyerly attack would have bewildered an adult, let alone a child who did not understand what his father was doing. "Greg didn't win thirty-one personal injury cases when he came home from the war by not knowing exactly how to manipulate emotions and reactions," said Wynter. Mark found these incidents hurtful until he grew old enough to realize that alcohol was talking and not his father.

There was one particularly bad episode when a drunken Bautzer locked himself in the nursery with Mark. Wynter tried to get him to open the door. "Get out of this house!" he shouted through the locked door. "Don't ever come back! You just get out!" Mark was no more than five at the time and fully believed that he would never see his mother again.

Waiting for Bautzer's return from work was a stressful ritual. The entire household was tense, wondering if he would be cheerful or angry, sober or drunk. For the few minutes after he arrived until his current state made itself known, everyone walked on eggshells. The anxiety was hard to bear, and Wynter was concerned that it was damaging Mark. The boy sometimes told her that he wished he had the kind of father other boys had. "My father never took me fishing," Mark recalled. "We never went camping or did things that other people did." Wynter told her son that his father had good qualities. He was a brilliant man who helped other people and loved to laugh.

His son inherited those qualities. Mark worked hard in school and brought home good grades. As he grew older, he learned to hold his own in arguments with his father, which few people could do. Despite Bautzer's inability to show it, he was proud of his son and loved him.

Bautzer did not love his in-laws. Dr. Wynter had divorced and remarried. When he brought his second wife to California for Christmas 1960, there was friction. At the time, Wynter was working on a Danny Kaye film called *On the Double* and had no time to make peace. The situation worsened. One night, fueled by alcohol, Bautzer began needling Dr. Wynter. The older man lost his temper and raised his fists. The gesture, coming from a small, usually reserved man, startled Bautzer. The strain began to tell on Wynter. She spent many a night sobbing. She consulted a specialist who warned her that she was on the verge of a nervous breakdown.

Wynter later said that nothing had prepared her for life with an alcoholic. She had never seen alcoholism. In Europe people tried to hide intoxication. She herself did not drink; she disliked the taste of alcohol. At first she thought that loving support could help Bautzer overcome his problem. It did not. He grew resentful of her concern, seeing her as an unwanted conscience. He thought she was counting his cocktails. The incidents became too ugly to ignore.

Wynter finally confronted him about his drinking. "Look," he told her, "I like it. That's why I drink. I was drinking with sailors in San Pedro when I was fourteen. I'm not going to give it up. I'm going to drink till the day I die."

The origins of Bautzer's alcoholism were a mystery to Wynter. Bautzer was a private individual. He did not talk about feelings. He did not talk about his childhood. She did not know that alcoholism ran in his family—that his uncle Paul had died of it. He never told anyone that his mother had remarried after his father's death when he was ten. Wynter suspected that he was fighting something. She felt there was insecurity beneath the bravado. Why else would alcohol affect him in that manner? "People do not carry on like that if they are easy in their skin," said Wynter years later.

Bautzer excused his drinking by saying that it did not affect his work. He claimed that it never gave him a hangover or prevented him from answering a complicated question after being awakened by a client in the middle of the night. Bautzer's tolerance for alcohol may have covered a multitude of sins, but Wynter was well aware that anger was not one of them. She witnessed his unwarranted confrontations with strangers. "Why don't you come outside for a fight?" he would say to some unsuspecting restaurant patron, someone who had not looked at him, much less provoked him. Wynter coped with these scenes as best she could. She said that she believed her husband was doing it to get attention and he knew that most of the time the person he accosted would not take him up on his offer. She said that she wished someone could film him trying to start a fight and then run the film for him when he was sober. Perhaps if he saw himself in that state he would stop drinking. His behavior made him look unattractive and gave others an advantage over him, which was something he had avoided all his life.

Bautzer would not admit to insecurities about his work, but Wynter knew that it put a tremendous strain on him, one that he sought to relieve with alcohol. He was constantly being approached by people with problems. He was expected to calm them, to reassure them, to fix their problems, as if the fees they were paying him entitled them to all of his time. He worked long, punishing hours on very little sleep. His briefcase sagged with documents that he had to review before his next workday. He was consumed by work. He could not even sleep without being assailed by duty. The telephone would jar him awake in the wee hours.

One night a call came from actor Robert Mitchum. "Greg!" he yelled into the phone. "Greg! I want you to sue the Beverly Hills Police Department!"

"Bob," said Bautzer groggily. "What is it? What happened?"

"A motorcycle cop just drove off with my license! Damned cops!" Bautzer went back to sleep and nothing more came of the drunken call.

On another occasion, Howard Hughes called in the middle of the night to seek his assistance with a problem he was having with his giant transport plane, the Hercules H-4. Commonly known as the "Spruce Goose" for its wooden structure, the plane was the largest ever built.

"Greg, you know the harbormaster wants that damned thing out of there and he said if it isn't moved out he's going to do something drastic."

"What sort of deadline did he give you?"

"In about six hours," said Hughes.

"For God's sake, Howard, couldn't you have given me just a few more hours than this? It's practically impossible!" For Bautzer little was impossible, and he managed to keep the harbormaster from harming the plane.*

Only once did Wynter see her husband lose patience with Hughes. Bautzer and Wynter were dining at the Bel-Air Hotel when they were told that there was a telephone call. The waiter brought the phone to the table. It soon became obvious that Hughes had crossed some sort of line. "Howard, that is not what you represented to the man," said Bautzer. "You know that perfectly well, and if you are now changing the story and you are reneging on that, I will have no part of it. All right. If you insist on standing on that, you can take your damned files back. I don't want any part of them. Yes. That's right. They'll be there in the morning." And with that, Bautzer slammed down the phone.

---

*Robert Maheu relates a similar story in his book *Next to Hughes*. According to Maheu, the government owned the plane and wanted to scrap it. Whether this is the same incident and whether it was Bautzer or Maheu who saved the plane is unclear.

By 1962, Wynter knew that her marriage was disintegrating. She had tried to change Bautzer and had failed. It was not just that he had bad habits. He had become his habits, and they made him unavailable to his family. His friends were a coterie of hard-drinking high rollers. One night, Bautzer went to a card game at the home of comedian Ernie Kovacs. When Wynter awoke in the morning, she was alone. "To hell with it," she said, and got into her car. She drove to San Francisco to find a lawyer, because she feared a Los Angeles lawyer would be subject to Bautzer's influence. She found a reputable lawyer and drove back to Los Angeles. She returned home to find her husband, for the first time ever, distressed and vulnerable. "Dana, don't leave me," he pleaded. "I need you." To see him like this was so unusual that she lost her resolve.

Later in the day a box of long-stemmed red roses were delivered. The card read: "To Mrs. Bautzer from Ernie Kovacs. It's my fault. I'm the one you should be cross with. Anyway, I'll be around a little later to explain everything." When Kovacs arrived to apologize, he looked at the flowers. He said there was some mistake. They weren't right. "But Dana, I ordered long, long-stemmed roses."

Winter was touched. "Surely the stems are long enough," she said. "They're lovely."

"No," he said. "I'm really cross with the florist." An hour after Kovacs left, another box arrived. It contained three dozen stems without blossoms—and a bottle of glue.

Wynter confided her problems to a friend. She was advised that the situation would not improve and was certainly affecting Mark. One evening in 1965, without warning or fuss, Wynter spoke to her husband. "Greg, I'm sorry," she said quietly. "I'm going to leave, and that's the way it is." Bautzer was startled. He did not know what to say. There was no drama. Wynter did not want to sue for large sums of alimony. She only wanted adequate support for Mark and a house for them to live in.

Because her requests were modest, Wynter expected the separation agreement to be amicable. But she was taking on the best celebrity divorce lawyer in Hollywood. He earned his living by fighting. She was astonished when her husband offered only ten years of child support, until Mark's sixteenth birthday. She found a lawyer through the Bar Association. He insisted that they examine her husband's finances, but she refused. "Mrs. Bautzer, if I may say something," he began. "Either you are a very nice woman or you are an extremely stupid one."

Although Wynter's refusal to investigate Bautzer's finances cost her most of her leverage, her lawyer convinced Bautzer that his offer would be a public embarrassment. Bautzer saw the light and agreed to $90,000 for the purchase of a home in Mandeville Canyon for Wynter and Mark, $2,000 per month tax-free alimony, and Mark's schooling and medical expenses. After signing the separation agreement, Wynter took her son with her to Europe and began work on a television series, *The Man Who Never Was*.

Wynter did not realize until years later, when Mark found a private investigator's report hidden in their Palm Springs home, that Bautzer had suspected her of infidelity. The document contained descriptions of her actions and phone conversations over a four-year period in the early 1960s, but it contained nothing incriminating or even unusual. When Wynter learned about it she became extremely upset. Just because Bautzer had witnessed rampant adultery among his colleagues and clients, he had no reason to suspect her.

Bautzer tried to be a good ex-husband, though. He never disparaged his ex-wife to son Mark. He saw Mark regularly and celebrated Christmas with them. Bautzer expended a lot of effort. He meticulously planned the event, carefully selecting gifts. Unfortunately, the champagne cork would pop and he would start drinking. Before long he would be upset over some trifle and storm out of the house.

Despite the separation, Bautzer never stopped caring for Wynter and Mark. When she needed something, he provided it. He repaired landslide damage to her house, even though it was not his responsibility. When property taxes in Mandeville Canyon became too much for Wynter and she had trouble selling the house, Bautzer bought it from her and rented it out so that she could buy a house in Benedict Canyon. When it was time to close escrow he made sure that the papers were signed even though he was in the hospital. When Wynter expressed a love of Ireland, he helped her finance the construction of a house there.

Although the couple separated in 1965, they did not legally divorce until 1981. Bautzer and Wynter remained cordial. His calls would come out of the blue. He would tell her amusing stories and make her laugh. They felt like old friends. At these times, she could enjoy his kindness and generosity without having to deal with his dark side. Sometimes they attended social functions together, such as the 1970 premiere of *Airport*, in which Wynter starred.

Wynter acted primarily on television through the early 1980s, appearing on such classic shows as *Marcus Welby, M.D.*, *Hawaii Five-O*, *Ironside*, *McMillan & Wife*, *Fantasy Island*, *The Rockford Files*, *Hart to Hart*, and *Magnum P.I.* When Mark entered college, she moved to Ireland and became a journalist, contributing to *Cosmopolitan* and *Country Living*. She was a lifetime member of the National Union of Journalists in England and the Foreign Press Association. She never remarried. At the time of her death in 2011, she was living in Ojai, California, with son Mark.

VI

KINGMAKER

21

INVENTING ROBERT EVANS

The rise to power of Paramount Pictures production chief Robert Evans is one of the most famous in motion picture history, but the true story has been hidden for decades. Evans started out in the fashion business, running clothier Evan-Picone with his brother. His life took an unlikely turn in the mid-1950s when he was spotted on a business trip at the Beverly Hills Hotel by retired actress Norma Shearer, the acknowledged Queen of Hollywood. She thought Evans should play her late husband, MGM cofounder Irving Thalberg, in a new film. *The Man of a Thousand Faces* would tell how Thalberg helped make Lon Chaney a star. Even with Shearer's sponsorship, Evans had an uphill climb as an actor. When he was cast as a bullfighter in Twentieth Century-Fox's 1957 adaptation of *The Sun Also Rises*, his limited abilities caused his fellow cast members to go on strike. Ava Gardner, among others, wanted him fired. Studio head Darryl F. Zanuck came to the set, watched him perform, and made a pronouncement: "The kid stays in the picture."

In order to understand the circumstances that led to Robert Evans taking the reins of Paramount, it is necessary to appreciate the club-like society of power brokers that existed in Hollywood at the time and the special relationship between Greg Bautzer and the notoriously mysterious lawyer Sidney Korshak. Romanoff's restaurant at 140 South Rodeo Drive in Beverly Hills was a Hollywood institution where the powerful dined and conducted business in high style. Its founder was Mike Romanoff, another self-invented legend. The former pants-presser claimed to be a descendent of the tsars, which was all the qualification he needed to run a restaurant. As the golden age of movies waned, so did the glamour of formal dining. Romanoff was not going to serve dinner to women wearing Capri pants, so on New Year's Eve 1962, he closed his restaurant.

But some Hollywood denizens were unwilling to let it go. Kurt Niklas had been its headwaiter and maître d' for thirteen years. Director Billy Wilder urged him to open his own version of the restaurant, and Romanoff was willing to help him. If Niklas could find backers, Romanoff would provide his liquor license and furnishings. "I went to see Billy," said Niklas. "Within twenty-four hours he had checks in the mail for ninety thousand dollars." In reality, funding didn't happen nearly that fast, but the story has become folklore. Investors included the agent Irving "Swifty" Lazar; actors Tony Curtis, Jack Lemmon, and Dean Martin; producers Otto Preminger, Sam Spiegel, and Jack Warner; and two attorneys—Sidney Korshak and Greg Bautzer.

The new restaurant would be less formal than Romanoff's but equally elitist. "Let's not call it any fancy name," said Wilder. "The future is in simple things." He suggested naming it "the Bistro" and giving it the demimonde ambience of his film *Irma La Douce*. The Bistro opened on November 1, 1963, at 246 North Canon Drive. Bautzer sat at table number three, which was to the left of the entrance, in a corner. It was the place to see and be seen, and it was the only table with a telephone. It became known as the "lawyer's table." When Bautzer was not using it, Korshak was.

Sidney Korshak thought of the Bistro as his office. Hailing from Chicago, he had no law offices in Los Angeles; in fact, he was not licensed to practice law in California. He was a labor union lawyer with connections to the Chicago mob. Bautzer told *Variety* editor Thomas M. Pryor that Korshak had gotten his start as a driver for Al Capone. His power derived from his ability to act as a go-between for respectable businessmen, such as Universal topper Lew Wasserman, and underworld figures who controlled the unions. A call from Korshak could start a strike or stop one. Korshak's other function was investing mob revenue in legitimate businesses.

Although Korshak and Bautzer hadn't really been acquainted when they both worked on Howard Hughes's abortive RKO sale in 1952, they had since developed a strong working relationship. It was unusual for Korshak to be interviewed, but his regard for Bautzer took precedence over his need for anonymity, so he met with publicist Henry Rogers in 1988 shortly after Bautzer's death, when Rogers was planning a biography of Bautzer. As cofounder of the giant public relations firm Rogers & Cowan, Rogers was among the close-knit circle of power elite to which Bautzer and Korshak belonged. He was a pioneer in the field of independent publicity for movie stars. Before Rogers, stars relied on the studios to handle their publicity. Rogers changed all that when his client Joan Crawford won her Oscar for *Mildred Pierce*. Rogers had fabricated a story that Las Vegas gamblers favored Crawford to win. It wasn't true, but it was printed in scores of papers across the country, and Crawford believed it made the difference. Soon, other stars hired Rogers to work his magic for their careers. Korshak had known Rogers for decades and trusted him as a fellow member of their exclusive group.

"I liked Greg Bautzer," Korshak told Rogers. "Greg was an excellent lawyer. He was very bright. He was a name-dropper, but his clientele and his personal relationships entitled him to be a name-dropper."

Unfortunately, his only failing as a man was his drinking. That was a problem he was never able to solve."

Korshak went on to recount his first meeting with Bautzer: "My wife Bernice and I lived in Chicago at the time, but we were vacationing at the Racquet Club in Palm Springs. Bernice was on the court playing tennis with Dinah Shore. I was sitting in the bar, watching Mel Clark, a gambler I knew from Chicago, play gin rummy with three men. I didn't know them and Clark didn't bother to introduce me. I looked at Clark's hand. He was sitting with gin but evidently didn't know it. He just kept playing. Someone else called gin. I couldn't stand it. I said to Clark: 'You stupid son of a bitch, you've had gin for the last five minutes and never called it.'

"Suddenly there was a roar from one of the players. This six-foot-four giant stood up and started to yell at me. His yelling mounted in intensity until he invited me to step outside. That was OK with me. I walked outside and waited for what was to be the fight of the century. Suddenly the giant stormed out, holding up his hands in apology. 'Hey, I don't want to fight with you,' said he. 'You're Sidney Korshak. I've always wanted to meet you. I'm Greg Bautzer.' We both started to laugh, shook hands, and Greg remained a friend of mine from that day until the day he died."

In truth, Bautzer and Korshak were more business associates than friends. Bautzer had access to the inner workings of the industry, to the plans and projects of actors, producers, and executives, not to mention inside information about their private lives. He helped Korshak and received help in return. When Bautzer had to deal with a problem that involved unsavory characters, Korshak would make a backroom power play. One such maneuver involved actress Susan Hayward and the scandal magazine *Confidential*. Hayward was brilliant and high-strung, given to screaming matches with her husband, Jess Barker. On April 26, 1955, while Bautzer was representing her in a child-custody battle, Hayward tried to kill herself. *Confidential* was planning a major exposé. Bautzer asked Korshak for assistance. Within days, Bob Harrison, publisher of *Confidential*, changed his plans. "In accordance with your request," he wrote Korshak on November 29, "we are dropping the Susan Hayward story from the upcoming issue of *Confidential*. Love and kisses, Bob."

Although Korshak was willing to help Bautzer, he held a long-standing grudge against Bautzer's number-one client, Howard Hughes. Korshak's friends had forfeited $1.25 million walking away from the RKO purchase after Hughes publicly exposed their underworld backgrounds. Korshak never forgave Hughes.

According to Wynter, Bautzer would not represent gangsters. However, he did invest in shady ventures if Korshak requested it. The Acapulco Towers in the eponymous resort city were built in 1968 by gambling kingpin Moe Morton and Beverly Hills real estate developer Jules Berman. Morton put up $100,000 and Berman put up $400,000. Morton hinted to associates that he was the "bagman" for Las Vegas gangsters and had access to funds skimmed from Vegas. According to the Illinois Bureau of Investigation, gangsters Meyer Lansky and Sam Giancana "were around the edges of the transaction." Morton also bribed Mexican officials to get a waiver of the statute prohibiting non-Mexicans from owning land there. When Berman discovered evidence of bribes, he threw Morton bodily out of the hotel.

Morton turned to Korshak for investors. Korshak rang up various Hollywood friends, painted the picture of a private time-share, and started collecting. Among those who plunked down $50,000 were Bautzer and his law partner Eugene Wyman, actress Donna Reed, Twentieth Century-Fox executive William Goetz, and City National Bank founder Al Hart.

The hotel was off the beaten path, intentionally so. Even though it was patronized by Acapulco resident Merle Oberon and her husband, Italian industrialist Bruno Pagliai, and stars Tony Curtis, Cyd Charisse, and Kirk Douglas, the facility was empty part of the year. This made it suitable as a hideout for underworld figures such as Meyer Lansky and Sam Giancana.

The first high-rise on the Las Vegas Strip was the Riviera Hotel and Casino, which opened in 1955. Bautzer was connected to it through his law partner Harvey Silbert, brother of Bernard Silbert and a friend of Korshak. Harvey Silbert had entered into a partnership with the three Gensburg brothers, manufacturers of toys and games, to form the Gensbro Hotel Company and lease the land on which the Riviera was built. The nine-story hotel had three hundred rooms and the largest showroom in Vegas, the Clover Room, which seated seven hundred. Liberace was a featured act, earning an unheard-of $50,000 per week. Dean Martin, who was also a part owner of the Riviera, had his own lounge, Dino's Den, where Engelbert Humperdinck launched his singing career. Korshak told friends that he hired most of the entertainers at the casino, and he had the power to forgive debts—such as the $43,000 that a young man named Robert Evans racked up at the craps table one night.

Evans knew Korshak from the 1950s, when the two met at the Racquet Club in Palm Springs. He loved to sit at Korshak's knee soaking up gangland tales. Korshak liked Evans so much he virtually adopted Evans as a son. Evans later said in his biography that he and Korshak spoke almost daily. Korshak talked up Evans and introduced him to Bautzer. Evans loved Bautzer's showbiz stories as much as he did Korshak's gangster lore. "Bob Evans used to hang around, and I never understood why Greg had faith in him," said Dana Wynter. Perhaps Bautzer saw in Evans a version of his younger self: a well-dressed up-and-comer who made appearances at the right parties, escorting a beautiful girl, and flattering the rich and powerful. Then again, maybe Bautzer is the one who taught him how to do it. Whatever the reason, Bautzer took Korshak's lead and started promoting Evans also. He took Evans on as a client and helped him start a fledgling career as a producer, optioning books to adapt for the screen.

In his 1994 autobiography, *The Kid Stays in the Picture*, Evans recounted his ascent to the summit of Paramount Pictures. According to him, it started when Charles Bluhdorn, the head of Paramount's parent company, Gulf & Western, read an article by Peter Bart in the *New York Times*. "I Like It. I Want It. Let's Sew It Up" described Evans's aggressive producing style. Bluhdorn, a bombastic Austrian who had started at the bottom and relied on street smarts, read the article and decided he wanted Evans to work for him. Evans got a call from his lawyer. "Pack your bags, Bob," said Bautzer. "We're going to New York."

"I've got plans, Greg."

"Break 'em. Charlie Bluhdorn just bought Paramount. He wants to meet you. He read that article about you in Sunday's *New York Times*." The meeting went well. Bluhdorn first hired Evans to head production in Europe, then quickly promoted him to head the entire studio.

The true story isn't as simple as Evans tells it. "Don't you believe it," said Wynter. "It was Greg. He forced him on Bluhdorn. After Greg got him that job, I remember the whole town was falling down laughing." The reality is that Bautzer had been working on Evans's career for a while. He had previously secured Evans a three-picture producing deal at Twentieth Century-Fox that resulted in the Frank Sinatra vehicle *The Detective*. According to Wynter, Bautzer had also done work for Bluhdorn at Gulf & Western.

Super-agent-turned-producer Michael I. Levy, who represented such stars as Elizabeth Taylor and Richard Burton, handled Evans before he started at Paramount. He concurs with Wynter's view. "Bautzer set up the first meeting for Bobby Evans with Bluhdorn and pushed it through. He arranged for certain people to call Bluhdorn about Bobby and say wonderful things."

Albert S. Ruddy would later produce *The Godfather* for Evans. He was privy to the machinations that put Evans on top and confirms that they were not accomplished by a mere newspaper article. "Greg Bautzer's the guy that set Bobby Evans up with Charlie Bluhdorn," said Ruddy in 2011. "Bobby was a charming guy. He looked good, with a great tan, and he was down at the Racquet Club all the time hanging around with Greg. [Bautzer] gave Bluhdorn a line of bullshit about how this kid knew everyone in Hollywood."

It was Bautzer who knew everyone. Bluhdorn, on the other hand, was new to Hollywood. Bautzer mesmerized him with personal tales of Crawford, Gable, and Lamour. "I mean, Charlie was starstruck," said Wynter. "And naive. And kind of innocent in that area. And he wanted a studio. He wanted 'the business.' You know, show business. And Greg got it for him. And he also got Bob Evans his spot." Ruddy agrees. "Charlie Bluhdorn knew Greg's connections," he said "Greg was known as 'the Kingmaker.' He was handling Howard Hughes, Kirk Kerkorian, everybody. Charlie was smart. If you're going into the movie business, you go to Greg Bautzer."

For his part, Evans has neglected Bautzer's involvement in his ascent to the throne, sometimes giving credit instead to Korshak and implying that the mob got him his job as head of Paramount. The razzle-dazzle story has the cloak-and-dagger allure of one of Evans's own movies, but it is pure fiction. Ruddy laughs at the notion: "Bob is still trying to hang on to that whole thing that Sidney Korshak and the mob ran everything and got him his job. That's such bullshit."

Pundits didn't think Evans had the experience necessary to head a studio. The *New York Times* labeled it "Bluhdorn's Folly," and *Hollywood Close-Up* crudely referred to it as "Bluhdorn's Blowjob." *Life* magazine pulled no punches as it summarized the opinion in the industry. "Robert Evans is an outrage. He has no more right to be where he is than a burglar. He has no credentials, none of the requirements for membership. Robert Evans has never produced a film, doesn't know about movies, and so why should he be a boss of Paramount with control of over twenty-five pictures a year, costing $100,000,000, influencing the cultural intake of millions of Americans? He is too good-looking, too rich, too young, too lucky and too damned charming."

Backing Evans turned out to be one of Bautzer's greatest moves. Despite the industry's initial skepticism, Evans moved Paramount from a last-place studio to first with *The Odd Couple, True Grit, Love Story, Rosemary's Baby, The Godfather,* and *Chinatown,* all of which were blockbusters and Academy Award winners. While Evans has been accused of taking more credit for creative aspects of these pictures than he deserves, no one has ever denied that he is the person responsible for selecting and promoting the projects at the studio. He often had to fight Charles Bluhdorn to get them made. In that regard, his significance to the success of Paramount and the style of motion pictures produced in the 1970s cannot be overstated.

Evans never did things in a small way. In 1980, the Drug Enforcement Agency arrested him and his brother Charles as they tried to purchase five ounces of pure pharmaceutical cocaine. For some reason Evans failed to call Korshak to get him out of a jam. Bautzer was shocked. "You didn't bring in Korshak?" he asked. "I'm not hearing right. Do you know who his closest friend is? A top guy at the DEA. They go back more than thirty years. Went to college together, schmuck." He sighed in disbelief. "And you're the guy who made Paramount number one."

22

KIRK KERKORIAN
BUYS MGM

Greg Bautzer had worked in small law firms since he opened shop on Hollywood Boulevard in 1936. A small firm allowed him both freedom and power. He could set his hours and choose his clients. When it came to billing practices and his expense account, he could do as he pleased. He didn't have to answer to a management committee. The disadvantage was that he lacked the manpower to handle really big corporate financing and mergers. He could advise Howard Hughes on such business deals, but other firms with more lawyers were always required in order to verify the other company's corporate assets. Those bigger firms earned bigger fees from all the work they put into the transaction. Simply put, there was a limit to how much his small firm could handle, and thus a limit to how much money he could make.

Sidney Korshak had an idea to help his friend make a transition to a larger, more lucrative firm. Eugene Wyman was a young lawyer from the same city as Korshak—Chicago. Wyman had been recently named chairman of the California Democratic Party. He was thirty-five and a master fundraiser. He had started his firm in 1952 with partner Marvin Finell, concentrating on humble insurance-defense litigation. Wyman and Finell's partnership was born out of necessity; in those days, big law firms wouldn't hire Jewish attorneys. Well-respected litigator Frank Rothman joined the firm a short time later. He described their "we try harder" approach to getting business: "There was a dedication to the practice, born of fear we wouldn't succeed. If we were going to get AT&T as a client, we had to take it away from a big firm that had represented it for a long time."

Korshak brought Bautzer and Wyman together, and they agreed to merge their two firms. Wyman's was larger, but Bautzer's clientele immediately increased the firm's cachet. In 1968, Bautzer's law school friend Thomas Kuchel completed his third term in the US Senate and joined the firm, bringing even more political muscle. After the merger, their business increased so dramatically that both Wyman and Bautzer offered Korshak a finder's fee, but he refused. He was happy to see Bautzer in a new setting, the firm of Wyman, Bautzer, Rothman, Finell & Kuchel, with offices in the United California Bank Building at 9601 Wilshire Boulevard in Beverly Hills. "Greg evidently needed the back-up of a large organization," recalled Korshak. "Once he and Wyman teamed up, new business started to roll in."

The firm underwent a further metamorphosis when Bautzer signed Las Vegas casino owner and financier Kirk Kerkorian as a client. Tall and athletic, with wavy dark hair, Kerkorian was the son of Armenian immigrants, a grammar-school dropout who converted a fascination with flying into tycoon status. His early life reads like fiction: As a teenager, he belonged to Los Angeles street gangs. However, he took responsibility seriously, and to help support his impoverished parents, who had lost the family farm, he worked at any job he could find: golf caddie, steam cleaner, car refurbisher, furnace installer, bouncer in a bowling alley bar. At his older brother's suggestion, he decided to try boxing, and was successful enough to win the Pacific amateur welterweight championship, earning him the ring name "Rifle Right Kerkorian."

After taking a flight in a Piper Cub airplane with a friend, Ker-korian fell in love with flying. He began the airline career that would make him rich by taking lessons from the famed female flier Pancho Barnes at her Happy Bottom Riding Club in the Mojave Desert. He paid for lessons by milking her cows and cleaning her barn. Located near Edwards Air Force Base, Pancho Barnes's club hosted many of the twentieth century's greatest test pilots and would go on to fame as the backdrop for the novel and motion picture *The Right Stuff*. With the coming of World War II, Kerkorian went to Canada with a recommendation from Barnes and enlisted in the Royal Air Force, delivering Mosquito bombers to Scotland. After the war, he broke speed records to deliver used warplanes on dangerous flying routes, pocketing enormous fees. In 1947, he established a charter airline to fly gamblers to Las Vegas; it made him rich. In 1968, he sold his airline to the Transamerica Corporation for stock worth $104 million and then purchased the Flamingo Hotel and Casino, the same one for which Bautzer had purchased the land on behalf of Billy Wilkerson twenty years earlier. In 1969, Kerkorian and architect Martin Stern built the International Hotel, which, with fifteen hundred rooms, was the largest in the world, and with both Barbra Streisand and Elvis Presley performing, a Las Vegas phenomenon. Kerkorian next set his sights on a motion picture studio.

While Korshak told Henry Rogers that he brought Kerkorian and Bautzer together, it is more likely that international jeweler Bobby Altman introduced them. Both Kerkorian and Bautzer were close friends of Altman. Michael I. Levy supports the Altman connection. "During the 1970s when I got to know Greg, I used to go to Cannes all the time. He introduced me to one of his best friends, Bobby Alt-man, who was the jeweler for the Middle East. When he would go to Cannes, he would have this bag filled with diamonds as big as your thumbnail. Bobby Altman was also Kirk Kerkorian's best friend. We became really close. We talked once a week. Bobby Altman put Ker-korian together with Greg."

Intensely private, modest, and reserved, Kerkorian warmed to Bautzer. "I like to talk with Greg," said Kerkorian, "whether it's about business, politics, or just about anything. We hit it off." Bautzer entertained the super-trader with stories of the stars he had known, and the magnate had to admire any lawyer who had the bravery to tell Bugsy Siegel to "sit down and shut up." Kerkorian flew Bautzer to Monte Carlo, Cap d'Antibes, and Paris. They shared an interest in tennis, flying, and women. They were both self-made men who knew what it took to achieve success. Attorney Ernest Del, one of present-day Hollywood's foremost deal makers, got his start working with Bautzer and saw the friendship firsthand. "Kirk Kerkorian worshiped Greg for two reasons: First, he was Howard Hughes's lawyer. Second, he enjoyed living Greg's lifestyle. Kerkorian was a shy guy. Greg knew the moves, and Kirk appreciated it. Greg would make the dates and reservations, and show him how to have a good time."

Bautzer was a natural choice for the type of work Kerkorian had in mind: he wanted to buy Metro-Goldwyn-Mayer. Bautzer had just represented Elliot Hyman in his 1967 purchase of Warner Bros. for Hyman's Seven Arts Ltd. The deal was a harbinger of things to come in the industry—a time when the studio ownership would change frequently. The studio system was fading, and had been since 1948, when the Paramount Consent Decree forced film companies to divest themselves of their theaters. The vertical integration begun by Adolph Zukor in the 1920s had finally run afoul of antitrust laws. As the studios surrendered their exhibition arms, they were weakened further by recalcitrant talent. When stars like James Stewart and Burt Lancaster refused to sign seven-year contracts and then formed their own production companies, deal-making agents and lawyers like Lew Wasserman and Greg Bautzer assumed the power previously held by moguls like Louis B. Mayer. Then came television. Americans were buying seven million TVs a year and motion picture attendance dwindled. By 1949, studio revenues had plunged from $87.3 million to $48.5 million. The major studios tried competing with the small screen and independent producers, but it was a losing battle. At MGM, when ticket sales dropped, Nick Schenck fired Mayer and looked to younger talent. By the late 1960s, the family-owned studio system had been replaced by corporate-owned entities. MGM struggled to keep its doors open. It was prime for the picking.

When Bautzer first called MGM about a possible takeover, the board of directors assumed he was acting on behalf of Howard Hughes. The prospect of being owned by the billionaire who had wrecked RKO was not a cheery one. But when the company learned that the interested party was Kerkorian, there was no sigh of relief. On July 22, 1969, he made a tender offer of $35 a share for 1.74 million shares of MGM stock. If successful, Kerkorian would own 30 percent of the company. "This offer is inadequate and not in the best interest of shareholders," said MGM board chairman Edgar F. Bronfman, who was also patriarch of the Seagram's liquor empire. MGM sued Kerkorian in US district court, asserting that his European financing violated the Securities and Exchange Act, which required collateral of five times the amount of loan. "It seems to me," said Bautzer, "that MGM is going to extremes to preclude the rights of its shareholders to determine if they want $35 for a share of stock, stock that was selling at $27 the day the tender offer was made. If stockholders have faith in the MGM management to turn the company around, they should hold onto their stock. If they don't, they should take their cash and take a walk." Meanwhile, Bautzer's partner, Jerald S. Schutzbank, who had previously served as California Commissioner of Corporations, hired former US Supreme Court justice Arthur Goldberg to prepare arguments on Kerkorian's behalf. Goldberg's court papers argued that the tender offer would be harmful to no one but MGM management, who might find themselves out of a job.

Kerkorian's offer was set to expire on midnight on Friday, August 8, 1969. At four that afternoon, federal judge Charles H. Tenney denied MGM's request to prevent the tender offer, ruling that SEC regulations did not regulate foreign lending institutions. The offer went through, but its tally would take several days. "We're looking for the time to sit down with MGM management to discuss the future of the company," said Bautzer. "Mr. Kerkorian's concern is for the stockholders of MGM. Incidentally, he will now be one—a big one." On August 12, Kerkorian was declared the winner with 1.325 million shares.

He now owned a large percentage of the stock, but he was not entirely in control. Bronfman still owned 16 percent of the company's stock. Time Inc. owned 5 percent. Interests sympathetic to MGM had purchased another 100,000 shares. Kerkorian was ahead, with 22 percent, but his margin was slim.

MGM management held out hope of independence as they waited for a call from Kerkorian. The two sides communicated through statements to the press. "Kerkorian hasn't been in touch with us at all," said a spokesman. "We don't know what he has in mind." Bautzer replied, "We're willing to sit down with MGM management and we are hopeful of such a meeting, but we have not had any session with anyone at MGM as yet." In reality, neither side wanted to talk to the other. On September 10, Kerkorian made an offer for 620,000 more shares of MGM common stock at $42 per share. The $26.6 million offer would expire on September 23. When that day arrived, he gained 33 percent of the company, and with it unchallenged control of MGM.

Kerkorian's first order of business was new management. He knew airlines and casinos, but not filmmaking. He needed a studio head who could inspire confidence in stockholders. Kerkorian met with MGM's current president, Louis F. "Bo" Polk, whom Bronfman had hired less than a year prior. Polk was a conservative executive given to quoting statistics. Kerkorian nixed him and turned to Herb Jaffe, a former literary agent who was running production at United Artists—and who also happened to be Kerkorian's tennis partner. Jaffe had been warned about the challenge of reviving MGM and declined the job. When the *Los Angeles Times* asked Bautzer to comment, he refused.

Bautzer had a replacement for Jaffe waiting in the wings, a client for whom he had been trying to find a job for more than three years: James T. Aubrey, the former president of CBS Television whom Bautzer had tried to include in Howard Hughes's takeover plans for ABC. During his five years at CBS, the blue-eyed Ivy Leaguer had created a network that dominated the airwaves and arguably popular culture. In the 1963–64 season, for example, CBS had all twelve of the top daytime serials and twelve of the top fifteen primetime series. These included proletarian fare like *Gilligan's Island*, *The Beverly Hillbillies*, *Green Acres*, and *The Munsters*; and critical successes like *The Smothers Brothers Comedy Hour* and *The Wild, Wild West*. Aubrey ruled with absolute authority, reporting only to founder and chairman William S. Paley. "He was it," said *Hillbillies* producer Martin Ransohoff. "People thought Aubrey had a divining rod in the middle of his desk." Yet the Princeton graduate despised his audience. "The American public is something I fly over," he once said. He kept his distaste to himself. Lucille Ball called him the "smartest one up there." *Life* magazine called him "the world's No. 1 purveyor of entertainment." John Houseman, who had coproduced *Citizen Kane*, called him the "Smiling Cobra" for his spitfire temper.

Paley fired Aubrey without warning on February 27, 1965. Rumors flew about why. Aubrey had been accused of unethical conduct. He let a friend, actor Keefe Brasselle, produce three series without first shooting pilot episodes, and the series were disastrous flops. Aubrey had also been needlessly dismissive, even cruel, to talent he considered expendable, in particular to the beloved veteran comedian Jack Benny, whom he shoved out the door with a remark about his age and obsolescence. Moreover, Aubrey had abused corporate privileges, and worse, mixed business and personal expenses—some very personal expenses. "I don't pretend to be any saint," said Aubrey. "If anyone wants to indict me for liking pretty girls, I guess I'm guilty." Bautzer liked pretty girls, too, but not five at a time. "Aubrey was the fourth president of CBS as Caligula was the fourth of the twelve Caesars," wrote journalist Murray Kempton. "Each carried the logic of his imperial authority as far as it could go." Author Jacqueline Susann based the amoral hero of her novel *The Love Machine* on Aubrey. That was fiction; the facts were epic. "No man made bigger profits—or more enemies," said the *Washington Post*.

In August 1965, Hedda Hopper speculated on gossip that Aubrey and Bautzer were going to start a motion picture company together. Bautzer declined to comment. He and Aubrey were well matched, given their penchant for both outdoor and indoor sports, and their overweening self-confidence. However, no film venture occurred. Then in 1968 came Hughes's attempt to take over ABC; when Hughes pulled out, Aubrey's hopes of running the network were dashed.

Kerkorian questioned Aubrey's credentials. It was true that Aubrey lacked experience in feature film production, but Bautzer argued that this was a plus, not a minus. It meant he owed no favors to agents or producers. Aubrey knew product and could deal with talent. He was first, last, and always concerned with the bottom line, which was all Kerkorian cared about. "Jim Aubrey has a real good sense of smell about what the American public wants to buy for entertainment," Bautzer told *Time* magazine, recycling one of his oft-used expressions to compliment a client's abilities. He arranged a meeting between Aubrey and Kerkorian.

Kerkorian was self-made. Aubrey was Ivy League. He was surprised that Kerkorian wanted to engage him without the formality of a contract, but he adjusted to the Las Vegas mode. "I don't want a contract," Aubrey told Kerkorian. "If I do a good job on this, the contract will take care of itself. If you don't like the way I'm doing it, you can say 'Get lost, Jim' without any obligations." On that basis, and with Bautzer's endorsement, Kerkorian hired Aubrey. His salary would be $208,000 per year plus an option to buy 17,500 shares of MGM preferred. Kerkorian expounded his business philosophy: "Clear out the nonproductive items, keep the productive ones, and you have a successful business."

Bautzer's management of the MGM takeover earned him the recognition of the *New York Times*. The story included a picture of him in mid-laugh, dressed in a dark suit, sitting in a rented Park Avenue penthouse. At fifty-eight, he had changed his hair. It was now completely white, no longer curly, but still thick, parted on the side and combed forward. He looked like a mature movie star, slightly weathered but still striking. He explained why he would not join MGM's board. "I think that a lawyer is better able to serve a company if he's not a director," he said. "There is a place for the lawyer who can use his legal knowledge to be an architect—in the corporate sense. That's what I hope to do." The article noted Bautzer's celebrity status and history of dating starlets, but also praised his legal talent. "Greg is extremely difficult on behalf of his clients" said an unnamed industry source. "You don't keep people like Hughes and Kerkorian as clients if you can't deliver."

Even before Kerkorian bought MGM, the company had been selling off parcels of real estate to raise cash. But the company he purchased was in worse shape than he had imagined. MGM had posted losses of $35 million, was $80 million in debt, and faced write-offs of $75 million because of box-office failures. Kerkorian told Aubrey to slash costs. Drastic measures were necessary to keep the company afloat. The cobra bared his fangs, terminated thirty-five hundred employees—half the studio's work force—and canceled twelve projects. In fact, Kerkorian authorized Aubrey to sell everything but the film library. "We sold off acreage, European movie houses, whatever we could," said Aubrey. "Nostalgia runs strong out here, so we were criticized for selling Judy Garland's red shoes. To us, they have no value. No intrinsic value whatever." What was not sold became landfill near the San Diego Freeway—furnishings, corporate records, music scores, screen tests, and outtakes. "Jim Aubrey took everything that wasn't nailed down," said former executive Sam Marx. "And a lot that was."

Aubrey's slash-and-burn policy was not redeemed by creative projects. The films he produced were not successful, and the filmmakers he encountered came away bleeding. Four-time Oscar-winning director Fred Zinnemann had *Man's Fate* canceled and was then presented with a bill for $3.5 million. Michelangelo Antonioni also lost a project. Sam Peckinpah fought with Aubrey over the editing of *Pat Garrett and Billy the Kid*. The good news was that Aubrey's austerity program had reduced MGM's bank debt from $80 million to $22.5 million. The bad news was that its product was mediocre. And there were still bills to pay. The $72 million in European loans was due in 1970, and the stock market had been falling. Kerkorian attempted to raise money in a secondary public offering of his International Leisure stock, but the SEC blocked the registration, because he had not filed financial statements relating to the Flamingo Hotel purchase. Kerkorian claimed that the sellers had withheld financial information. He was forced to sell half his ownership in International Leisure.

While Kerkorian went back to purchasing cruise ships and casinos, Aubrey brought in TV producer Dan Melnick, who then scored hits with Michael Crichton's *Westworld* and the thriller *Slither*. But when Melnick pitched Steven Spielberg's *Jaws*, Aubrey turned it down. In 1973, MGM's owner was not much interested in the movies MGM made. He had another use in mind for the MGM brand. "The studio that brought you *Ben-Hur* and *The Wizard of Oz* will now bring you crap," began a pungent sentence in *Fortune* magazine. The four-letter word did not refer to the execrable quality of MGM's films but to the game of chance. Kerkorian was building the largest casino and hotel in the world, the MGM Grand. The studio from which he had acquired the hotel's name would have to get by on six films a year.

But Aubrey himself would soon feel the squeeze. The turning point came in October 1973, when Kerkorian sold MGM's domestic theatrical distribution arm to Arthur Krim at United Artists. Then, after a cursory glance at the Bistro's menu, Kerkorian signed a deal for $20 million at the restaurant and sold all of MGM's foreign holdings to the Cinema International Corporation, a distribution arm jointly owned by Universal and Paramount. "For propriety's sake," wrote Joyce Haber in the *Los Angeles Times*, "let's not call it a liquidation, but what was once a major-major is now a mini-minor."

The news hit Aubrey like a blast of cold air. He told his own associates that if he were an ordinary stockholder, he would file a lawsuit. He then wrote an open letter to Kerkorian, telling him what he thought of the transactions. Kerkorian did not take it well. He consulted with Bautzer, who agreed that his former friend and client had committed grievous transgressions by making the disagreement public. Aubrey owed everything to Kerkorian and Bautzer. Now he was biting the hands that fed him. Of course, there were some who thought that the self-indulgent Aubrey had long since gone out on a limb. His nightlife was notorious. But for all his nocturnal peccadilloes, he had never evinced disrespect for his boss—not, that is, until now. He received an invitation from Bautzer, who had very definite feelings about disloyalty.

On October 30, Aubrey sat in Bautzer's office, sipping a drink. Without warning, Bautzer looked him in the eye and delivered the axe. "Kirk wants you out," said Bautzer. "It's over."

Aubrey stared at him, then remembered that he had no contract. He asked what kind of settlement Kerkorian was planning. "Kirk doesn't believe in contracts," said Bautzer. "And he doesn't believe in settlements, either." Aubrey was shocked. He thought he deserved a parting gift. In order to save face, Aubrey gave *Time* magazine a self-serving statement. "The job I agreed to undertake has been accomplished." It was his last major job in the entertainment industry.

Kirk Kerkorian can hardly be blamed for his inability to return MGM to its former stature. It is easy to see Kerkorian's lack of experience in the business as the cause, but reviving MGM's former glory was an almost impossible task. The studio was drowning in debt, and revenues were dwindling industry-wide. Bautzer's choice of Aubrey to run the company was likely no worse than many other options. While Aubrey's talent in television failed to translate to motion pictures, Aubrey had no emotional ties to the business and was willing to do unpopular things to protect the bottom line. It is doubtful any other executive would have been so fiscally responsible. True, a fresh creative genius might have found new projects, like Evans did for Paramount, but lightning seldom strikes twice. Bautzer had gambled and won with Evans. He had lost with Aubrey. By the late 1960s, selecting motion picture projects had become a very high-risk business. Studios were revolving doors, where production heads changed every two or three years. Hardly any succeeded long term. Kerkorian and Bautzer did the best they could. It's difficult to say someone else would have done better.

Bautzer continued to advise Kerkorian into the 1970s. In this capacity, he dealt with Frank Rosenfelt, the new president of MGM. Their connection went back to the days when Bautzer carried orders from Hughes to Rosenfelt, who was then RKO studio counsel. In 1980, when Rosenfelt urged Kerkorian to replace production chief Richard Shepherd with David Begelman, Bautzer was incredulous. Begelman had been removed from the post of production chief at Columbia Pictures after a major scandal. He had embezzled tens of thousands of dollars. "You can't go out and hire a convicted felon," Bautzer argued at the top of his voice in a meeting with Kerkorian and other MGM executives. "This man would be in jail today if he hadn't hired himself a helluva smart lawyer." Begelman's attorney, Frank Rothman, was in the room; he also happened to be Bautzer's law partner.

"I feel very strongly on this Begelman issue," Rosenfelt continued. "If I don't get Begelman as my production chief, I don't think I want to remain as president of MGM."

The Begelman scandal had begun in 1977 with a letter from the Internal Revenue Service to actor Cliff Robertson claiming that he owed tax on a $10,000 payment from Columbia. Robertson had received no such payment. The cashed check was located. Robertson's endorsement had evidently been forged. A criminal investigation led to Begelman. There were more forgeries, in all a total of $75,000. Rumor had it that Begelman needed the money to cover gambling debts. "On Fridays there was this poker game upstairs at Ma Maison," recalled producer Andre Morgan. "David wasn't a very good gambler. It was this floating poker game that took him down."

Bautzer was a regular at the card game. It is likely he knew even more about Begelman than was already publicly known. Bautzer was furious. How could a publicly held company hire a man who was a thief and a liar? Kerkorian sided with Rosenfelt. "If you feel that strongly about it, Frank," he said, "then I think we should go with Begelman." Bautzer stood up and stormed out. He was eventually vindicated: all Begelman's projects flopped except for one, Steven Spielberg's *Poltergeist*.

In May 1981, Kerkorian purchased United Artists from the Transamerica Corporation for $380 million. The purchase was widely viewed as a way of regaining the MGM distribution arm that he had rashly sold in 1973. The company became known as MGM/UA Entertainment. In February 1982, Bautzer's partner Frank Rothman was installed as head of MGM/UA. Rosenfelt and Begelman continued in their posts but had to report to Rothman. He was an odd choice for a studio head. "Things are as exciting as they can be. It's certainly a challenge," Rothman said in all honesty, since he was primarily a litigator, not a transactional entertainment attorney. One of his first jobs was firing Begelman. In 1986, Kerkorian sold MGM/UA to television magnate Ted Turner. But Turner couldn't afford to keep it, and after just seventy-four days, he sold United Artists and the MGM trademark back to Kerkorian, retaining only the MGM film library.

Bautzer and Frank Rosenfelt may not have been the best of friends, but MGM's president was impressed by the scope of Bautzer's influence. "He seemed to know everyone in the world," said Rosenfelt, "and on a personal level, not a superficial one. He could go anywhere, see anyone. I remember there was a time when we were talking a merger deal with CBS. 'If we keep on talking like this,' Greg told me, 'nothing will ever happen. Let's go see Bill Paley.' I replied: 'Will he see us?" and Greg said, not in a boastful tone, 'Of course he'll see us.'"

The next thing Rosenfelt knew, he, Kirk Kerkorian, and Bautzer were in CBS founder William Paley's New York apartment. "We didn't make a deal," said Rosenfelt, "but when we got home and told our story, no one believed us. Bill Paley never had business meetings in his home. When he condescended to have a meeting with you, it was in his office in the 'Black Rock' on Fifty-Second Street—never in his home."

Bautzer's relationship with Kerkorian was also on a personal level. Mark Bautzer saw Kerkorian live vicariously through Bautzer. "Kirk's a low-key guy and he's a very gentle soul," said Mark. "He just wanted to do his deals and go home. I think he wanted to be able to cut loose, but he was bound by his idea of his position in town. He couldn't cut loose like my dad did. That's why they used to spend every summer together. They would go to Monte Carlo every summer for two or three weeks." The trip was made in Kerkorian's private DC-9. Even Bautzer was impressed. "Talk about comfort!" he said. "The inside is like a living room. He has a telephone that rings up in the air and he can talk to anyone, anywhere. Now that's the only way to fly!" When Bautzer called his son, Mark couldn't believe that a jet would have a phone. But he believed in the rapport between his father and the mogul. "Kirk was into my father's energy and into the fact that when he walked into a room you could feel his presence. There would be a buzz."

23

THE BIG FIRM

With all the business Howard Hughes and Kirk Kerkorian provided, Wyman-Bautzer, as it was called by everyone, quickly became one of the city's largest and most prestigious firms. Lucrative clients such as Campbell Soup and Bank of America sought their services. Young attorneys joined the firm who would one day go on to be some of the most successful lawyers in Los Angeles: Ernest Del, Patricia Glaser, Terry Christensen, Louis "Skip" Miller, and Andrew White. Stanton "Larry" Stein, now one of today's top entertainment litigators, joined the firm directly after earning his law degree from USC. "It was remarkable. There was no firm that could compete with what they were offering. The attraction was the political power, the Hollywood connections. Their clients were remarkable. Gene was a political guy. Kuchel was a political guy. Rothman was a great trial lawyer. Finell was a great corporate lawyer/business lawyer. But the entire entertainment practice was a result of Greg. No one else."

Wyman-Bautzer grew to forty partners and nearly one hundred associates. By the early 1970s, the firm needed bigger offices. They moved from the United California Bank Building in Beverly Hills to Century City, the new center of power in Los Angeles. Twentieth Century-Fox had sold its backlot to real estate developers. Where

Chicago had once burned and India had been flooded, steel and glass towers now stood. Wyman-Bautzer occupied three floors of the brand-new Century Plaza Towers, located at 2049 Century Park East. As Frank Rothman put it, "We were flying high."

In 1973, the firm suffered a major blow when Gene Wyman suffered a fatal heart attack while riding in an elevator with his chauffeur at the firm's office building. Wyman was just forty-seven, practically the same age Bautzer's father was when he died. Frank Rothman replaced Wyman as managing partner. In tribute, the partners decided to continue using Wyman's name on the firm.

By this time, Bautzer was an institution in Los Angeles. He was among the power elite, a socialite and fundraiser, serving as chairman for the local chapter of the American Heart Association and soliciting the money to build the Los Angeles Music Center. (The fact that the Music Center was the pet project of Dorothy Chandler, wife of the publisher of the *Los Angeles Times*, had more than a little to do with his motivation. Courting favors from the press had always been a priority.) "It was a different time in Hollywood." recalled Andre Morgan. "Before the total conglomeratization happened, Hollywood was a small club. If you wanted to do a deal at Universal, you had to know Lew Wasserman, who used to eat at the Bistro. If you wanted to get anything done at Paramount, it came down to what Charlie Bluhdorn wanted. And who was the guy who could get through to Lew or Charlie at any time?—Greg Bautzer."

Attorney Ernest Del was a Bautzer protégé in the 1970s and saw the power he wielded. "Greg was on the phone a lot with Lew Wasserman and Sidney Korshak solving the problems of Hollywood. There was nothing illegal or nefarious about it that I could tell. They were the behind-the-scenes guys who knew everybody, and if there was an industry-wide problem, they were the ones who figured out how to solve it."

In 1975, restaurateur Patrick Terrail opened Ma Maison in a small house at Melrose Avenue and King's Road in West Hollywood.

Bautzer added the trendy new place to his routine. "I owned a piece of the restaurant," said Michael I. Levy. "Every Friday, Greg would have lunch there. He had a special table in the corner near the door. Everyone who came in or out had to stop and say hello." While lunching with his boss at Ma Maison, Del learned things they don't teach in law school. According to him, Bautzer would take clients to Ma Maison because it was where the most important people ate when they were in Los Angeles. "Clients would be sitting there with him and Jackie Onassis or Henry Kissinger would walk in the door. That really impressed the clients." But it wasn't just where you took a client that impressed them; it was how you presented yourself. "He taught me how to stand out from the pack as a lawyer. How to impress a client," said Del. "He taught me how to talk to the maître d', where to sit in a restaurant, how to give the waiter your order, what wine to order. Little things that have nothing to do with the practice of law, but which impress the client and make them want to sign with you over other lawyers." Most important, he instructed Del to tip upon arrival to get good service. "What good does it do to tip when you're leaving?" Bautzer would say.

"I learned a lot from Bautzer," said Levy. "He had an unbelievable ability to listen. Not just to hear you, but to listen. He wasn't thinking what he was going to say next." Bautzer also displayed a phenomenal ability to impress clients with his intelligence. "He could answer a question immediately on any subject," said Levy. "His retention was amazing. His memory for minutiae. I believe he researched everybody before they met him. That's how he impressed."

As Bautzer entered his midsixties, he continued to handle scandalous legal matters that got his name in the newspapers. In 1976, Bautzer represented tennis player Renee Richards, who had undergone sex reassignment surgery a year earlier at age forty. The United States Tennis Association (USTA) was barring the transgender woman from playing in the women's competition at the US Open. "We have examined the decision," said Bautzer. "We find it discriminatory. It isn't whether Renee wins purses that counts. She only asks the right to be recognized as a woman. She surely has that right. If they want to take that discriminatory action, they're going to be faced with appropriate action, and it could go all the way to the Supreme Court." Renee won her case and was allowed to compete professionally as a woman. In 1977, she reached the doubles final at the US Open with teammate Betty Ann Stuart, losing a close match to Martina Navratilova and Betty Stöve. She went on to coach Navratilova to two Wimbledon wins, and was inducted into the USTA Eastern Tennis Hall of Fame in 2000.

Bautzer got himself into hot water representing Albert S. Ruddy and Andre Morgan in a matter that nearly broke up the law firm. The producing partners wanted Burt Reynolds to star in a movie they were making called *Cannonball Run*. Unfortunately, Reynolds was under an exclusive agreement with Paramount Pictures in which he had committed to do three pictures, and he still had one more left, a middling comedy titled *Paternity*. By this time, Robert Evans was out, and Barry Diller, Michael Eisner, and Jeffrey Katzenberg were running Paramount. Ruddy and Morgan managed to get a copy of Reynolds's contract and discovered a loophole. Under the terms of the contract, Paramount had to notify Reynolds of the start date of his next picture. He was only exclusive to Paramount commencing on the date they set for the start of the picture. As luck would have it, there was just enough time left before Reynolds's next Paramount picture to allow him to shoot *Cannonball Run*. Ruddy and Morgan offered Reynolds an unbelievable $5 million for five weeks' work on the film.

When the executives at Paramount heard that Reynolds was doing *Cannonball Run* before their picture, they went ballistic and ordered their lawyer, Frank Rothman, to sue the producers. The problem was, Bautzer and Rothman were law partners. Law firms are forbidden from suing their own clients without consent, so Rothman asked Ruddy and Morgan to sign a letter allowing him to sue them. "That takes balls," Morgan said of the request. "That takes big balls. Are we really going to sign a letter so that Frank Rothman can represent Paramount to sue Greg Bautzer's client?" Ruddy and Morgan refused to sign.

Everyone turned to Bautzer to fix it, and he turned to Paramount's owner, Charlie Bluhdorn. Bautzer came up with the idea of having Paramount distribute *Cannonball Run*—that way everyone would be happy. "Listen, I've spoken to Charlie," Greg told Ruddy and Morgan, "Charlie says he has no problem. You go in and sort it out with the boys [at Paramount]. You make a fair deal for you and you make a fair deal for Charlie, and this can all go away." Diller and Eisner left the deal-making to Katzenberg. Unfortunately, Katzenberg's idea of making a "fair deal" was not the same as Ruddy's and Morgan's. Katzenberg met Morgan at the Paramount lot to negotiate. It did not go well. "I'm going to do you a favor. We're going to buy you out on this movie," said Katzenberg. Morgan was confused. He wasn't looking to be bought out, and he told Katzenberg this. "You don't understand," replied Katzenberg. "We own Burt Reynolds. I'm going to let you make this movie providing you give us all rights. We'll give you 30 percent of the profit."

Paramount owning the picture made no sense to Morgan. He knew how much money the picture would generate. It would earn at least $15 million just from selling the broadcast rights to ABC television. He and Ruddy had already secured production funding and in addition to Reynolds had cast Dean Martin, Sammy Davis Jr., Roger Moore, Farrah Fawcett, and Jackie Chan. Morgan felt they were entitled to the lion's share of profits. Paramount was doing nothing other than relinquishing a potential lawsuit that Ruddy and Morgan thought they could win. The producing partners were willing to let Paramount distribute the picture and take a small distribution fee in exchange for fronting advertising costs, but allowing Paramount to own the picture outright was out of the question. Katzenberg didn't see it the same way. He also believed that he could win a lawsuit, based on the exclusivity clause in Reynolds's contract, and that as a result, he was holding all the aces.

The problem would not go away. A summit was held in Rothman's office with Bautzer, Ruddy, and Morgan. Rothman was livid, literally huffing and puffing on his pipe. He started by lecturing Ruddy and Morgan on how much money Paramount paid him as a monthly retainer. "I personally drafted the extension of Burt's deal," said Rothman. "It's airtight. And I've given my word to Michael Eisner and Barry Diller that there's no way out of it. Now you explain to me how the fuck this law firm gets in this kind of a fucking mess!"

Everyone was tense in the room except Bautzer, who spoke up in his clients' defense. "Now, Frank, I've spoken to Charlie, and, you know, we've been representing the boys for the last nine months, and I've got to tell you, they haven't really done anything that's out of the ordinary." Rothman's eyes bulged with anger. Andre Morgan still laughs about what happened next. "When he heard this, Frank Rothman literally bit through the stem of his pipe. The first thing you hear is a 'snap' and the next thing you see is a piece of pipe flying across the room." Everyone in the room was sweating bullets, but Bautzer was laughing. He knew it was all a sideshow that would somehow work itself out. The meeting ended with Bautzer telling everyone he would speak to Bluhdorn and find a solution.

As it turned out, this was one that Bautzer couldn't resolve. Unlike the days when Robert Evans was running Paramount, Bluhdorn could not intercede on Bautzer's behalf with Diller, Eisner, and Katzenberg. They were too strong willed. But Bautzer also knew that Paramount would not interfere in the making of *Cannonball Run*. Before a court grants a motion for a preliminary injunction, it requires the plaintiff to post a bond to reimburse the defendant if the action turns out to be a mistake. If Paramount tried to stop production on *Cannonball Run* and turned out to be wrong about its interpretation of Reynolds's contract, it would be opening itself up to millions of dollars of liability. Bautzer told Ruddy and Morgan privately, "Listen, for the sake of the law firm, I can't be seen to be doing anything, because this thing has turned into such a giant mess. If you want my advice, go make the movie. This will never come to trial."

Of course, Bautzer was right. Burt Reynolds met with Diller and threatened physical violence if Paramount interfered in his ability to make an easy $5 million. *Cannonball Run* got made and was a huge success, giving rise to an equally successful sequel. For the sake of their friends at Wyman-Bautzer who were going to lose their jobs, Ruddy and Morgan eventually signed the conflict waiver, allowing Paramount to sue the producers and the film's distributor, Twentieth Century-Fox. Before the case came to trial, Eisner and Katzenberg left Paramount to run Disney, and Diller left to run Fox. Amazingly, when Diller joined Fox, he found himself on the same side of the lawsuit as Ruddy and Morgan. He declared that the case had merit and paid $1 million to settle the very same lawsuit that he had brought against Fox. Ruddy and Morgan never paid a dime.

Years later, Morgan realized Bautzer's wisdom in telling him to go make the movie and not worry about a lawsuit. Bautzer knew that in time it would all work itself out. "Because to Greg, it was still all about relationships; it was all about people. He had seen them come, he had seen them rise, he had seen them fall, and he had seen some of them come back again. He understood it was all on the wheel. Keep the relationships, keep the dialogue, and never make it personal. And if you want to talk about lessons learned from that, it's 'We can fight in the day, but we can still drink together in the evening.' There was a certain honor among thieves in those days. You get along, I'll get along. I'll win this one, you'll win that one. We're not going to kill each other. It's a small town."

Someone else who benefited from Bautzer's wisdom was rising litigation protégé Patricia Glaser, who joined the firm in 1973 after graduating from Rutgers University Law School. She thrived under Bautzer's philosophy of absolute devotion and loyalty to the client. Partner Allan Goldman described their symbiotic relationship: "She was the one on whom he relied the most as someone who understood him and would be loyal to his clients."

It was Glaser to whom Bautzer turned when tragedy stuck at Kirk Kerkorian's MGM Grand Hotel and Casino. On November 21, 1980, a massive fire broke out at the hotel, caused by an electrical ground fault inside a wall. Eighty-five people were killed, most through smoke inhalation. It is still the worst disaster in Nevada history. Bautzer called on Glaser to handle the volumes of legal work required. She tenaciously defended Kerkorian in the legal battles that ensued, suing the insurance companies who "stiffed" Kerkorian and obtaining a $76 million settlement. While the matter was a catastrophe for all it touched, it was a financial boon for the firm, earning tremendous fees from the mountain of legal work. Bautzer received the largest share, some say as high as 15 percent of the firm's total profit. As for Glaser, she soon became one of the top female lawyers in Los Angeles.

Bautzer continued to shake up the motion picture business when he represented producer Mitsuhara Ishii in the making of the 1982 Korean war film *Inchon!* The film, which starred Jacqueline Bisset, Ben Gazarra, and Laurence Olivier, received unfavorable publicity when it became known that it was funded by the Reverend Sun Myung Moon of the controversial Unification Church. At the time, Moon was on trial for tax evasion; he would eventually be sentenced to eighteen months in prison. Greg was quoted as saying, "I don't care whether it's a Unification Church project or Christian Science project. The film shows America in the best possible light. It's one hundred percent factual in showing the magnificence of the American fighting forces."

Greg employed his Washington connections for the production after the government turned down the producer's request for five thousand US troops as extras in South Korea, which they needed for a scene. Greg made some calls, and shortly thereafter the Pentagon contacted the production, saying that the troop request had been reconsidered and approved.* When Ishii could not find a studio to distribute the picture, Bautzer arranged a "rent-a-system" deal at MGM, by which Ishii advanced the advertising budget and the studio deducted a fee before remitting the remaining proceeds back to Ishii.

As he entered his seventies, Bautzer worked less. Afternoons were reserved for playing cards, not legal battles. Still, in 1985, Bautzer renewed his reputation as the master of scandal when he represented Farrah Fawcett. She was being sued by an actress who claimed that Fawcett had her blackballed after a rumored affair with actor Lee Majors, Fawcett's husband. "Farrah never knew this lady and never met this lady, and she would like to leave it that way," said Bautzer. "These are totally unfounded claims." The court granted Fawcett's motion to toss out the suit for failing to properly state an actionable claim.

In 1986, Bautzer represented televangelist Gene Scott in a lawsuit seeking to void his pending purchase of the Church of the Open Door on Hope Street in downtown Los Angeles. Bautzer's association with Scott was strange. Although Scott had been a minister for decades, he was a controversial figure. Scott hated the "televangelist" label, but he had raised millions through television appearances, in which he preached Bible interpretation while writing illegible and overlapping notes on a chalkboard. White-haired, bearded, and sporting aviator sunglasses, he never failed to remind viewers that he held a doctoral degree from Stanford University. For unknown reasons,

---

*Bautzer most likely called his good friend and tennis partner General Alexander Haig, who was President Reagan's secretary of state.

he would also show viewers videos of his wife's dancing show horses. Sometimes, he would simply appear on television sitting in a folding lawn chair, refusing to preach until he received a certain amount of money in phoned contributions.

The basis for Scott's case seemed to be Scott's inability or unwillingness to go through with the deal he made to buy the church. A woman named Lehua May Garcia allegedly uncovered a long-forgotten deed that dedicated the church to "the promulgation of the eternal trusts of God's Holy Word." The deed pledged that the buildings could not be used as a monument to any man but only to God. She interpreted this to mean that the church could not be sold to a televangelist. On behalf of Scott's Wescott Christian Center, Bautzer filed a lawsuit, seeking to rescind the sale. According to Bautzer, Scott believed his purchase might have been illegal, and on that basis, he refused to pay the purchase price. Claiming a contract was illegal was a similar tactic to the one Bautzer had employed decades earlier against actress Jean Simmons on behalf of Howard Hughes. Observers contended that the entire suit was a ploy to stave off pending foreclosure, and Garcia was later revealed to be in Scott's employ. The suit was rendered pointless when the city revealed that the church had suffered irreparable earthquake damage, which killed the deal.

For those who knew Bautzer over the years, it seemed that he represented Scott merely to keep his name in the headlines in the twilight of his career. Scott was hardly on the level of clients like Hughes, Kerkorian, or Davies. It was embarrassing to other members of the law firm, who thought it beneath their dignity. Still, Bautzer professed a friendship with Scott and refused any criticism for taking him on as a client.

Although the Scott case was an unusual fit for Bautzer, he did have other clients who were not celebrities or multimillionaires. Unbeknownst to the public or to his star clients, he did work pro bono. Willie Brown, a former state assemblyman and mayor of San

Francisco, discovered this one night when leaving a restaurant with Bautzer. A parking valet asked Bautzer a question about something other than his car. Brown was curious about their connection. Bautzer reluctantly admitted that he was representing the young man. "They're all my friends," he said, trying to downplay his philanthropy.

Bautzer sometimes "forgot" to bill friends for legal services. Herbert Maass, a friend and client for over thirty years, told of the time Bautzer refused to charge him for his divorce. "You're such a good friend of mine," said Bautzer, "that if I telephoned you in the middle of the night, told you that I was in jail and asked you to come down and bail me out for $50,000, I know you would do it. And I would do that for you. You know that, don't you?" Maass had to agree. Bautzer never billed actress Jayne Mansfield. Some inferred that he received another form of payment. He denied it, saying he didn't find her attractive.

Bautzer still represented friends and clients from his early days. "I met a lot of his older clients, many of whom were his former girlfriends," said Ernest Del. "If he was tied up and couldn't take them to dinner, he would ask me to have dinner with them as his surrogate. I took out Ginger Rogers, Rosemary Clooney, and James Mason's ex-wife, Pamela Mason. They would swoon and get a starry look in their eye as they talked about him. They were never sore that he had broken up with them. They were still in love." Del thinks he knows the secret to Bautzer's magic. "He had the romance, the elegance, the champagne, the diamonds, but he also had the 'bad boy' quality. The women went nuts for it. If he had been just one or the other, it wouldn't have been the same."

For years Bautzer had cultivated the image of the most generous man in town. At Christmas, Bautzer bought costly gifts for friends and coworkers. Jean Parker, who worked for both Bautzer and Joe Schenck, once received a porcelain jewelry box from Tiffany's. She assumed that his secretary bought multiple pieces of the same item, but she eventually learned that he took the time to go to stores and select individual gifts himself. His thoughtfulness was extraordinary. Billy Wilder's wife Audrey had dated Bautzer years before she met Wilder. Bautzer sent her mother a bouquet of flowers on Mother's Day for ten years after they stopped dating. Giving gifts had won him clients, friends, and lovers. The element of surprise and the appropriateness of the gift usually achieved the desired result. The gifts grew more costly, even extravagant—and, of course, they imposed an obligation on the recipient.

But as Bautzer aged and times changed, bestowing baubles began to look manipulative, grandiose, or just plain silly. The most deadly word in Los Angeles is "yesterday." Bautzer's gestures were becoming dated. One time in the 1970s, Bautzer and a colleague went to pick up a client at the airport. Maybe Tucker, Bautzer's chauffeur, held the car door open. "What a lovely watch," said the client.

"Tucker, give him your watch."

"But Mr. Bautzer—"

"Just take off the watch and give it to the gentleman."

The client was embarrassed. Bautzer forced him to take it. The next day Bautzer bought Tucker another watch.

"I once made the mistake of admiring the tie Greg was wearing," recalled a colleague. "In what seemed to be a fraction of a second, he had untied his tie, torn my tie off, put his on me, and then spent the rest of the day tie-less, telling everyone he had given me his tie because I liked it. I didn't like it that much."

Bautzer's aggressive approach to his work was also becoming old-fashioned. There was a well-known refrain among Los Angeles legal circles: "In a fight, there's no one I'd rather have by my side than Greg Bautzer." Herbert Maass witnessed his combative style. "There was a time when his temper—or feigned temper—worked to his advantage and mine," said Maass. "With my divorce came a custody battle involving our six children. Bautzer called Mr. Stroock, of the

New York law firm of Stroock, Stroock & Lavan, and used a string of four-letter words that Mr. Stroock had never heard in such volume before, proceeded to call him a lot of names which included more four-letter words, and finally said, 'Mr. Stroock, we'll see you in court.'" The suit was settled in two days. It was an act, a tactic he used to make the other side uncomfortable. "The opposing team would settle because they didn't want to contend with his screaming," said his son, Mark.

Attorney Bobby Schwartz, son of producer Bernie Schwartz, learned one of Bautzer's tricks of the trade when he was just a law student: "I started seeing an eye doctor in Century City when I was in law school in the early 1980s. Sometime after 1984, I was getting my glasses from the technician in the office, and I was discussing what I did, etc. The guy asked if I knew Greg Bautzer. I said I did. He said that every year Greg would come in for his eye exam and order a dozen pairs of eyeglasses. 'A dozen?' I asked. 'A dozen,' he said with a big smile. He said that Greg liked to use them as props to snap in half in court or in a meeting to scare the person on the other side and make sure he—or the judge—knew how angry Greg had become about the issue."

But in the 1980s, practicing law became less about personality and more about caution. Malpractice was a new concept, and a worrisome one. One way to avoid it was research, but this became a process in itself—first researching and then writing long, technical legal briefs. It was tedious and expensive. It certainly was not glamorous, whereas Bautzer still carried the glamour of old Hollywood.

There was little glamour to be found elsewhere at Wyman-Bautzer. His law partners were accomplished, but they were not stars. They were not legends; he was. Old-fashioned or not, he was the rainmaker, the partner who brought the big clients such as Hughes and Kerkorian. When Bautzer was dealing with legends like himself, he had no patience for legal minutiae.

Ernest Del thought Bautzer was above the rest. "Greg was brilliant. Right up to his last day, he had the sharpest mind of anyone I ever knew. He didn't get hung up on complicated legal issues, but rather what was practical. Often lawyers are answering the wrong questions. They're lost in technical legal battles. He saw the big picture. He taught me that it was important to understand what the client wants you to accomplish and if you can do it, do it."

"He didn't want to hear about administrative problems," recalled one of his colleagues. "He cut people off when they started." Bautzer did not suffer fools gladly, and he made sure his partners and associates were perpetually conscious of his top-dog standing. With so many years of experience, he had little patience for young partners' transgressions. They would quake in their boots as they walked down the hall to his office and would leave his office after a meeting like children coming out of the principal's office. Another colleague witnessed a number of these meetings. "I would be in Greg's office when he gave someone a tongue-lashing. He would then turn and wink at me, after making sure, of course, that they were leaving."

Near the end of his career, Bautzer sensed the shift in the legal profession. Although his share of the firm's profits was 15 percent, he thought that money was corrupting the practice of law. At a certain point, he could no longer contain his feelings. The firm was throwing a Christmas party at the Hillcrest Country Club. "Anyone who had anything to say could step up to the microphone and say it," recalled Lori Weintraub Ferrer, a lawyer at the firm who went on to become a studio executive. "The speeches were usually humorous and festive, conducive to the holiday spirit. Greg walked in, and it was obvious that he had been drinking." Bautzer grabbed the microphone and a hush came over the room. He looked out at the partners in the firm.

"He told them that they no longer cared for their clients in the great tradition of the legal profession," said Weintraub Ferrer. "They cared only about billable hours. They were in a rat race to see how many hours they could bill their clients every month. Billing was more important than doing a credible job. An angry rumble went around the room. When he finished, no one applauded. Evidently, everyone was angry with him. Either they didn't believe him, or he came too close to telling them the truth, which they didn't want to hear."

24

THE LOVE OF HER LIFE

Greg Bautzer continued to play the role of the glamorous bachelor well into his sixties. For exercise he walked around the Franklin Canyon reservoir or played a game of early-morning tennis, after which he would walk to the Beverly Hills Hotel and have breakfast in the Polo Lounge. Bautzer continued to impress women, too. He had not lost his sex appeal.

For a young agent like Michael Levy, seeing Bautzer operate was an eye opener: "I was with him many times when he was with women. He listened to them and he responded. They loved him for it. And you would not believe how women are attracted to power. He would go into the Racquet Club, and women—young women, married women, movie actresses—would come over and sit at the table. Natalie Wood came running across the room to hug and kiss him. I knew she was a client, but it was a different kind of hugging and kissing. And he was a fabulous dancer. He would walk up to a woman—it didn't matter who she was with—and he would ask her to dance. You would watch these two people and you knew that from the time he took her to the dance floor to the time he sat her back in the chair he had captivated her. Because he was a total gentleman."

Though still legally married to Dana Wynter, they were separated and free to see others. In the late 1960s, *Silver Screen* magazine had linked Bautzer with actress Diahann Carroll in a lengthy tabloid article entitled "How a White Millionaire Won Diahann." A talented and beautiful actress, Carroll was the first African American woman to star in a television series based entirely on her character; every week between 1968 and 1971, *Julia* followed the story of a widowed nurse struggling to raise a young child. The magazine article intimated that the couple had become involved after Carroll's relationship with actor Sidney Poitier ended. At the time, interracial dating was still unusual. Neither Bautzer nor Carroll ever confirmed the relationship, but they were frequently spotted together in Los Angeles and Las Vegas. Bautzer also dated model Nancy Cuffman. She accompanied him to events like Swifty Lazar's September 1969 Oscar party, and they mingled with stars like Lucille Ball, Jack Benny, Kirk Douglas, John Huston, and Gene Kelly. The lissome lass and the silver-haired attorney made a striking couple, but that was the extent of it. After a short while they drifted apart.

In 1972, Bautzer started dating the woman who would become his fourth and final wife. Niki Schenck Dantine was a long-legged beauty with flowing red hair. She was Hollywood royalty. Her father was Nick Schenck, chairman of Loew's, which owned MGM in its glory years. Her mother was Pansy Wilcox, a classical singer who performed each week on the WHN radio station in New York City. At the time Niki and Bautzer became involved, she was thirty-eight and separated from actor Helmut Dantine, with whom she had three children. Niki had first seen Bautzer when she was a teenager. She watched him play tennis on her uncle Joe's court and fell in love. In the years since, she had continued to watch him. After she separated from Dantine, their paths crossed.

Bautzer's first recorded date with Niki was on New Year's Eve 1972 at the wedding of actor Laurence Harvey and model Pauline

Stone. It took place at the home of novelist Harold Robbins, and Bautzer reportedly tried to push Niki into a small boat in the pool. For the next few years, Bautzer and Niki were seen at various events: Tony Martin's opening at the Century Plaza Hotel; the fifth annual pre–Academy Award dinner at the Bistro; and at a benefit for autistic children by SHARE (Share Happily And Reap Endlessly), which was Niki's favorite charity. In May 1974, they attended the premiere of *That's Entertainment*, and Bautzer watched his Hollywood life flash before his eyes in two hours of MGM film clips: Joan Crawford, Ginger Rogers, Clark Gable, and so many others he had known. The film presented them as quaint relics of the studio's glorious past.

Bautzer was not a relic; he still had the energy of a twenty-one-year-old and was more powerful in the industry than he had ever been. But something was eating at him. In 1975, former talent agent Dick Dorso opened a men's shop on Camden Drive and renewed his friendship with Bautzer, who patronized the store and brought in customers. "He was a loyal friend," said Dorso. "But he had deteriorated. He was drinking heavily and seemed to be set on self-destruction." Dana Wynter occasionally talked to him. "Greg, aren't you happy?" she asked. "You've got everything. You've got success, you've got your health, you've got money, and you've got looks. Why aren't you happy?"

In 1979, Bautzer had a heart attack and was placed in intensive care. Niki took care of him. "No one ever received the tender care that Niki gave him," recalled Herbert Maass. "When he got out of the hospital, Niki insisted that he stop drinking. So did the doctors." So did numerous friends. "Once in a while I would get up the courage to talk to him about his drinking," said Dorso. "I would always start by saying: 'We who love you want you to stop drinking.' He would sit there, nodding in agreement." Bautzer did make token efforts to quit both drinking and smoking. "He tried to quit when he had his first heart attack," said son Mark. "Then he recovered, so he thought, 'Well, I kicked the heart attack, so I can get back on the booze.'"

Bautzer's friends, now gravely concerned, intervened. This impressed him, and he vowed to give up hard liquor. From then on he would only drink wine. Surely that could not hurt. "But he just doubled up on the wine," said Mark. "He would drink two bottles of wine. You wouldn't be able to tell he was drunk. But he'd have just one more glass, and that would put him over the edge."

Bautzer's relationship with Niki was serious, but the couple decided not to consider marriage until after their children were grown. Bautzer was also still legally married to Dana Wynter, whom he would not divorce until 1981. Niki encouraged him to live with his son in a home on Summit Ridge Drive in order to heal their relationship and be a positive influence on Mark's life. Now past seventy, Bautzer was sporting a mustache and big dark glasses. He could no longer pretend that he was the dashing swain of years gone by. "He didn't want to age," said Mark. "He was scared to death of death. That was obvious. It somehow belittled his virility. . . . He was actively at war with the aging process."

In 1983, Bautzer entered the hospital and underwent triple bypass surgery. Niki stayed by his side the whole time. By 1984, he and Niki had been together more than ten years. He wanted to take care of her and protect her—and so they decided to marry. The wedding took place in early October aboard Kirk Kerkorian's jet over international waters between Marbella and London. Guests included Bobby Altman, Baron von Thyssen, and Frank Rothman. Judge Marianna Pfaelzer, a former Bautzer law partner, officiated the vows. Judge Pfaelzer later hosted a party at her home so that another judge could perform a second wedding ceremony to avoid any doubt about the validity of the airborne one.

Upon returning to Los Angeles, Bautzer was intent on giving up drinking and tried to limit himself to one glass of wine a day. Bautzer still did the things he loved. He continued to represent clients like Kirk Kerkorian and Gene Scott. Columnist James Bacon noticed the atypical glass of wine one day at the Bistro. "I'm an alcoholic," Bautzer told him. "That's why I drink white wine." But his battle with the bottle was not entirely successful. It was an open secret that he found ways to have more than just one glass. He conspired with restaurateur Wolfgang Puck and maître d' Bernard Erpicum to bring him a glass of wine whenever he went to the men's room at Spago restaurant. At the new Bistro Gardens restaurant, he used another method. "Bring me a cappuccino," he said to the waiter as Niki watched him out of the corner of her eye. "But no booze in it." The beverage was delivered. He tasted it and pronounced it safe to drink. One time, he grimaced after tasting it. "This cappuccino has booze in it," he said to the waiter. "I said no booze." The waiter—who was new—hurried back to the bartender, who explained to him that "No booze" was code for "Put two shots of Scotch in it." The bartender spiked the cappuccino and sent it back. Still, it was undeniable that he drank less when he was hiding his intake, and the limitations he maintained had a positive effect on his health. Eventually, he managed to stop drinking altogether.

Bautzer never stopped battling, though. In 1987, he was visiting the Bel-Air Hotel. While walking across a small bridge, he encountered a younger man coming from the other direction. The man saw that Bautzer was weaving so he stepped to the left to let him pass. Bautzer took umbrage at this and also stepped to the left. The man moved to the right. So did Bautzer. "You got a beef with me, Dad?" said Bautzer in a threatening tone of voice. "What's your beef, Dad?" The man was not interested in continuing the conversation. He put his hands under Bautzer's arms, picked him up, and dumped him in a bed of ferns. After the man left, Bautzer dusted himself off and told his son that he had been mugged. Mark investigated. "My dad was mugged," he told a valet. "Aren't you guys looking out for him?"

"Mugged?" said the valet, laughing. "Your dad was talking when he should have been listening!"

Near the end of his life, Bautzer seemed to gain more control. One of the last social engagements he attended was at the Palos Verdes home of William Keischnick, CEO of Arco. When Bautzer arrived, some guests were apprehensive. "I hope he behaves himself," said Roz Rogers, wife of Henry Rogers. To everyone's relief, Bautzer did behave himself, charming all who were present.

"It's obvious that all he needed was the right woman in his life," remarked Roz at the end of the evening. "As you can see, Niki is the right woman."

October 26, 1987, was a Monday morning. Bautzer was getting ready to go to the office. Niki was helping him. While he was dressing, he suffered a fatal heart attack. He was seventy-six. The *Los Angeles Times* reported tributes from the city's most prominent legal figures. "He was a hell of a guy," said Frank Rothman. "If you ever needed a friend to back you up in a fight, there was a guy you wanted." Many recalled how Bautzer loved his work. "He had an enthusiasm for the practice of law at an age when most people aren't alive," said attorney Howard Weitzman, who had joined Bautzer's firm the previous year. "He was a trial lawyer through and through." Judge Barbara Lee Burke told a story about Bautzer's recent appearance in her courtroom. "He was so courtly and so charming," said Burke. "We had a squeaky door. During a break one day he went out and got a can of oil to fix it. After the trial he called me up and invited me out to lunch. We got to be friends. He was such an exceptional person. A magical person. This strong, tough man. But also so kindly."

Services were held at Beverly Hills Presbyterian Church on Thursday, October 29. Eulogies were given by Reverend Gene Scott, Thomas Kuchel, Paul MacNamara, and Willie Brown. Scott spoke of how he and Bautzer had had conversations about theology, which Scott thought guaranteed his entrance into Heaven. Brown spoke of how Bautzer befriended people from all walks of life. Kuchel touched upon Bautzer's early days at USC and, as a friend of sixty years, opined that Bautzer's pluses far outweighed his minuses. MacNamara joked that Bautzer had gotten into a fight three weeks earlier on Melrose Avenue.

Bautzer's body was interred in a crypt at Westwood Memorial Park, hardly one mile from his office in Century City. The list of pallbearers was impressive. It included Alexander Haig, Kirk Kerkorian, Sidney Korshak, Jerry Perenchio, Cubby Broccoli, Patty Glaser, and Lew Wasserman. Honorary pallbearers included such august names as Army Archerd, Tom Bradley, David Brown, Governor Pat Brown, Sammy Cahn, Arthur Cohn, Warren Cowan, Kirk Douglas, Freddie Fields, Beldon Katleman, Tony Martin, Jean Negulesco, Frank Sinatra, Jack Valenti, and Richard Zanuck. On his tomb Niki placed the sentiment As Long As Memory Lives, So Will My Love.

In his last will and testament, Bautzer made provisions for a party to be thrown for his friends. On January 5, 1988, Bobby Altman, Mark Bautzer, and Niki Bautzer hosted a huge party at the Bistro. Two hundred and fifty friends attended. Among them were Kirk Douglas, Sidney Poitier, Lew Wasserman, Milton Berle, Swifty Lazar, and Sherry Lansing. Blowup photos showing Bautzer throughout his years in Hollywood were displayed as if he were a movie star. To those who knew him, he was that—and much more.

EPILOGUE

Within a year after Bautzer's death, the firm he cofounded hit the rocks. The seeds for its destruction had been planted years earlier in the power vacuum that had been created when managing partner Frank Rothman left to run MGM/UA for Kerkorian. Stephen Silbert, son of Bernard Silbert, took the reins, but soon Rothman asked Silbert to be his right-hand man, and Silbert left also. Top-flight litigator Terry Christensen established an executive committee consisting of four partners. He was said to run the firm with an iron hand, and the Christensen years were considered to be some of the best years, but he too was enticed to work for Kerkorian's Tracinda holding company. When these top lawyers departed, so did some of the top clients.

The downfall started in earnest the year before Bautzer's death, when Christensen brought in star criminal attorney Howard Weitzman as a partner. Weitzman had recently represented automaker John DeLorean on cocaine charges. The remaining partners hoped Weitzman could develop a white-collar criminal defense department to handle insider trading cases, which appeared to be a growth area. Corporate attorney Ronald L. Fein and four other partners from Jones, Day, Reavis & Pogue joined the firm. They claimed to have A-list Fortune 500 companies as clients and everyone thought they would be big rainmakers. According to partner Skip Miller, the new partners spent lavishly and failed to produce sufficient business to justify their extravagance. Partner Jay Rakow, who had joined the firm in 1980, complained about Fein's spending habits. "There was some resentment that Ron was champagne taste on a beer budget."

When Christensen tried to return to the firm in 1988, the new partners feared he would take control. They voted against his rejoining, and a civil war ensued. Many of the talented young partners departed to form Christensen, White, Miller, Fink & Jacobs. Litigation followed, with the old partners accusing the defectors of stealing clients. Both firms asked Niki Bautzer for permission to use Bautzer's name as the first name of their firm. His fame carried significant advertising clout. In the end, Niki declined to let either side use her husband's name.

"This was a law firm I was so proud of," lamented Miller in a lengthy *Los Angeles* magazine article. "We attained things we weren't supposed to be able to attain. We won cases other people said couldn't be won—antitrusts, takeovers, very tough litigation. . . . We were, I thought, more resourceful, smarter, more aggressive than these other more famous, more well known law firms."

Everyone agreed that Bautzer's death was not the cause of the firm's demise. But when asked, Patty Glaser said that had he lived, he might have figured out a way to keep it together. Glaser went on to lead her own firm, which now boasts more than eighty lawyers. She continues to represent Kirk Kerkorian and is one of the most successful female lawyers in the country. She has always given credit to Bautzer for her start. "He was wonderful to me. I would probably walk in front of a train for him." In many ways, Glaser has carried on Bautzer's style of loyalty and devotion to a client. "If there's a declaration of war, I am going to be your worst enemy," she once said. "It's not because I am smarter than you are. I don't see myself that way. But I'm sure very dogged and very determined, and if you attack my client, I will do what I have to do—obviously appropriately, legally, and ethically—to protect my client's interests."

Law partner Terry Christensen apparently took loyalty and devotion to a client a bit too far when he represented Kirk Kerkorian in a divorce from then-wife Lisa Bonder. Christensen had been a close confidant of Bautzer, one of the only lawyers Bautzer would take with him to meet with Howard Hughes in person near the end of the billionaire's life. In 2008, Christensen was accused of engaging in illegal wiretapping of Bonder's phone. Christensen had hired private detective Anthony Pellicano in order to get evidence against her. Patty Glaser personally defended Christensen at trial even though she had never tried a criminal case. Kerkorian testified in defense of his longtime lawyer, describing Christensen as "excellent, honest, and a true friend." The court found Christensen guilty of conspiracy to commit wiretapping and sentenced him to three years in prison. At the time of this writing, Pellicano is serving a fifteen-year sentence in federal prison for wiretapping and other crimes. Christensen's conviction is on appeal and he remains free until it is decided.

In 1989, Kerkorian sold MGM/UA to Pathé Communications, led by Giancarlo Parretti, an Italian publishing magnate. A short time later, Parretti lost control of Pathé, and the company defaulted on the loans used to purchase the company. After the studio passed through the hands of creditors and subsequent owners, Kerkorian bought it again in 1998. Deeply in debt from a leveraged acquisition of PolyGram Filmed Entertainment, Kerkorian sold the studio for a third and final time in 2004 to a consortium of investors led by Sony Corporation of America, Texas Pacific Group, Providence Equity Partners, and other investors. The reported sale price was $5 billion, earning Kerkorian an enormous profit.

Twenty-five years after Bautzer's death, his influence continues to be felt. Today, there remain scores of lawyers practicing law who worked with him at Wyman-Bautzer. Multitudes of clients remember the work he did for them. Those who knew him as a friend miss his larger-than-life personality. And there are still more than a few women who long for his embrace. Though he may not have been the first lawyer to concentrate on representing entertainment clients, he was certainly one of the earliest to turn it into a profession, and he was the most powerful entertainment lawyer the industry has ever known.

In the end, Bautzer's legacy is the way he created a public image in order to advertise his services and the swashbuckling way he practiced law. He planned his life as if it were a movie. He wrote the script, cast himself as the star, and directed it himself. Years later he admitted that the $5,000 he borrowed to finance his wardrobe was what got his career off the ground. "I would never have achieved the prominence I did and achieved the success I did as a lawyer," he said, "if I had not borrowed $5,000 and used it in the way I did." Of course, Bautzer had special talents that also helped him achieve success. His charisma was almost magical. "Greg would walk into a dimly lit restaurant and stand in the doorway for thirty seconds," recalled his friend Paul MacNamara. "In that time, half the women in the room would be freshening their lipstick and straightening the seams in their stockings. Many of them hadn't turned around to look. They just felt something." He did not merely use personality to seduce; he used it to forge friendships and create alliances. Acquaintances basked in his glow, but, more important, they felt valued, because a charming and gracious gentleman was doing his best to value them.

Bautzer's partners and associates such as Bentley Ryan, Bernard Silbert, Arnold Grant, Gerald Lipsky, Jerald Schutzbank, Woody Irwin, and many others deserve to share the credit for his early success. They toiled in his shadow and aided his ascent, but didn't share the limelight. "I've been asked many times if I wasn't a little jealous of Greg, who was always out in front and I was always in the background," said Irwin. "There was never any jealousy on my part, or any of the other associates and partners, because we knew that Greg was a star unto himself in the movie business and a certain degree of his fame and notoriety rubbed off on us. There was something about Greg that always brought us the controversial cases and we always seemed to be in the newspapers."

The cumulative effect of Bautzer's influence on Hollywood is impossible to gauge. No one knows the number of actors, directors, writers, and others whom he helped. He played a major role in the lives of Howard Hughes, Lana Turner, Joan Crawford, Dorothy Lamour, Ginger Rogers, Kirk Kerkorian, and many others. Would there have been a *Coal Miner's Daughter* if he had not made Bernard Schwartz the head of Joseph Schenck Enterprises? Would there have been a *Godfather*, *Love Story*, *True Grit*, *Rosemary's Baby*, or *Chinatown* if Bautzer had not gotten Robert Evans his job at Paramount?

Bautzer was more than admired by his peers; he was esteemed. In the early 1980s, actor Warren Beatty befriended Bautzer. By then, Beatty had inherited Bautzer's title as the most eligible bachelor in filmdom. Bautzer's son, Mark, joined the two notorious rakes for lunch one day at the Bistro. Beatty was seeking advice for a planned Hughes biopic. When Bautzer left the table briefly, Beatty confided, "You know, Mark, your father was my idol all through my childhood." Two-time Oscar winning producer Albert S. Ruddy confirmed that the sentiment was common. "He was everyone's idol," said Ruddy. "We all wanted to be Greg Bautzer."

ACKNOWLEDGMENTS

In researching this book, I made many new friends and received the generous assistance of strangers. With much humility, I gratefully acknowledge their contributions.

First is the late Dana Wynter, Bautzer's third wife and mother of his only child, Mark. Dana had tremendous admiration for her ex-husband's achievements and believed that he deserved to have his place in history recorded. Even though they were separated in the mid-1960s and divorced in the 1980s, Dana defended her ex-husband's honor for the rest of her life, sending letters to editors whenever she thought his reputation had been maligned in print. Sadly, she passed away from heart failure in May 2011. Although she was ailing during the last three months of her life, she shared her memories and insights with me on almost a daily basis. For a brief time, we enjoyed an unexpected friendship.

A big thanks is also owed to the late Henry Rogers for donating his papers to Brigham Young University. Rogers, who was cofounder of the world-famous public relations firm Rogers & Cowan, started his own biography of Bautzer shortly after Bautzer's death but abandoned the project due to research difficulties. Rogers's memories of conversations with Bautzer and interviews with his contemporaries, some of whom have since passed away, were a godsend. These include:

Mark Bautzer, Louis Blau, Dick Dorso, Arthur Groman, Richard S. Harris, Woody Irwin, Kirk Kerkorian, Sidney Korshak, Herbert Maass, Ann Miller, Frank Rosenfelt, Bernard Silbert, Lori Weintraub Ferrer, and Dana Wynter.

Lea Sullivan was Bautzer's personal secretary from the early 1950s through the mid-1960s. At Dana Wynter's request, Lea consented to be interviewed for the first time about her beloved boss and his most important client, Howard Hughes. Lea has known many of the most famous celebrities of the twentieth century and is a living witness to history, although she is too modest to brag about it.

Attorney Robert Schwartz gave me the final push to write this biography the day he told me that Bautzer was responsible for starting his father's career in Hollywood. This book was conceived in Bobby's office at O'Melveny & Myers.

Jean Parker, Joseph Schenck's personal assistant and Bautzer's confidential employee, furnished great insights into the Schenck-Bautzer relationship and the unusual services that Bautzer provided for Hughes. Parker revealed for the first time that she kept the accounting books and wrote the checks that Bautzer signed for Hughes's harem of kept women.

A legendary Hollywood historian, the late Charles Higham, deserves the credit for uncovering FBI documents revealing Bautzer's involvement with the suspected Nazi spy Hilde Kruger. He came upon the FBI papers while researching his book *Errol Flynn: The Untold Story*. Higham shared his knowledge with me over a long lunch at Musso & Franks.

Bautzer's distant cousin David Stielow contacted Mark Bautzer and Dana Wynter to discuss the Bautzer family tree during the time that Dana was helping me. It was an incredible coincidence. David provided valuable information about Bautzer's relatives, including a copy of uncle Paul Bautzer's autopsy report, which revealed the family's history of alcoholism.

In addition to those mentioned above, the following people were interviewed and made important contributions: Dan Cavalier, Arlene Dahl, Ernest Del, Bernard Erpicum, John Fahey, Fred Kroll, Michael I. Levy, Pia Lindström, Charles McDougal, Louis "Skip" Miller, Andre Morgan, Bob Newhart, Wolfgang Puck, Albert S. Ruddy, Stanton "Larry" Stein, Richard van Treuren, Robert Wagner, Lori Weintraub Ferrer, Andrew White, and Ken Ziffren.

I also wish to express my appreciation to those who helped me locate documents and photographs: Special collection curator James V. D'Arc of Brigham Young University provided access to the papers of Henry Rogers and over the course of four years has become a good friend. Curator Ned Comstock of the University of Southern California allowed me to review Charles Higham's papers and found several newspaper articles for me about Bautzer. Special collections archivist Octovio Olivera of the University of California Los Angeles found photo negatives of Bautzer in court from the *Los Angeles Times* Collection. Curator Dace Taube of the University of Southern California uncovered photos of Bautzer's college years from the *Los Angeles Examiner* files. Harriet Dallinger, widow of the renowned Hollywood photojournalist Nat Dallinger, and their children Timothy Dallinger and Antionette Dallinger Griffin provided nearly thirty phenomenal photo negatives documenting Bautzer's life over the course of three decades. Bob Walsh, stepson of Hollywood Brown Derby owner Bob Cobb, and Brown Derby historian Mark Willems, provided several wonderful photographs and photo negatives along with terrific stories over lunch at Chez Jay. William R. Wilkerson III provided an excellent photo of Bautzer with his father, Billy Wilkerson, and insight into their relationship. San Pedro Historical Society Docents Anne Hansford and Al Bitonio helped research information on Bautzer's parents and his childhood.

In addition, I thank the people who aided and encouraged me. Lions Gate Entertainment general counsel Wayne Levin, the best boss in the world. The late Steve Rothenberg, president of Lions Gate Theatrical Releasing, a good friend and fellow biography fan. Early readers Bob and Tina Gale and Robin Voris, each of whom gave me honest and valuable criticism. Writers Linda Perigo and Mark A. Vieira, who both gave me writing advice. Jeffrey Goldman and Paddy Callistro, who provided publishing advice. My publisher Cynthia Sherry, senior editor Yuval Taylor, and project editor Devon Freeny, each of whom helped make this into a much better book than I could have written on my own. Also, Mary Kravenas at Chicago Review Press and Jen Wisnowski at IPG, who worked so hard on marketing and promotion.

And finally and most important, I thank my wife, Selene, who helped me in more ways than I could possibly list. Without her, this book would not exist.

Appendix A

BAUTZER'S CLIENTS

Bautzer represented hundreds if not thousands of clients in his fifty-year career. The following is a short list of his known clients.

Buddy Adler	Robert Evans
Nicky Arnstein	Farrah Fawcett
James T. Aubrey Jr.	Clark Gable
Jack Benny	John Garfield
Ingrid Bergman	Judy Garland
Freeman Bernstein	Paulette Goddard
Charles Bluhdorn	Farley Granger
Cyd Charisse	Susan Hayward
Jeanne Crain	William Randolph Hearst
Broderick Crawford	Katherine Hepburn
Henry Crown	Rock Hudson
Arlene Dahl	Howard Hughes
Marion Davies	Elliot Hyman
Laraine Day	Gene Kelly
Marlene Dietrich	Kirk Kerkorian
Kirk Douglas	Carole Landis

Mario Lanza
Charles Lederer
Michael I. Levy
Sophia Loren
Tony Martin
Zeppo Marx
Robert Mitchum
Andre Morgan
Merle Oberon
Laurence Olivier
Patti Page
George Raft
Renee Richards
Hal Roach
Mickey Rooney

Albert S. Ruddy
Joseph Schenck
Reverend Gene Scott
Ann Sheridan
Nancy Barbato Sinatra
Ray Stark
Franchot Tone
Robert Wagner
Jerry Wald
Walter Wanger
Jack Warner
William R. Wilkerson
Natalie Wood
Darryl Zanuck

Appendix B

BAUTZER'S LEADING LADIES

Bautzer dated scores of women. The following is a short list of his more famous romantic interests.

Wendy Barrie
Mari Blanchard
Carol Bruce
Joan Caulfield
Marguerite Chapman
Rosemary Clooney
Buff Cobb*
Joan Crawford
Nancy Cuffman
Niki Schenck Dantine*
Marlene Dietrich
Ava Gardner
Greer Garson
Paulette Goddard
Rita Hayworth

Sonja Henie
Marion Jahns*
Isabel Jewell
Evelyn Keyes
Susan Kohner
Dorothy Lamour**
Carole Landis
Peggy Lee
Mary Maguire
Pamela Mason (Mrs. James
    Mason)
Marilyn Maxwell
Merle Oberon
Barbara Payton
Ella Raines

Jane Randolph
Ginger Rogers
Ann Sheridan
Simone Simon
Ann Sothern
Claire Trevor

Lana Turner **
Jane Wyman
Dana Wynter*
Audrey Young (Mrs. Billy
  Wilder)

* MARRIED
** ENGAGED

NOTES

PROLOGUE

"If you were going into . . ." Ruddy, interview by the author.
The New York Times ran . . . Sloane, "Lawyer Keeps Late Hours with Clients."
In the same month . . . Buhrman, "Hello Greg? . . . This Is Howard Hughes," 38.
"a rinky dink sort . . ." Ibid.
"Greg was so immaculately dressed . . ." Morgan, interview by the author.
"Rudolph Valentino would . . ." Erpicum, interview by the author.
"He was the most important . . ." Puck, interview by the author.
"There were two rows . . ." Morgan, interview by the author.
"He was the most powerful . . ." Erpicum, interview by the author.
"The first time . . ." Ruddy, interview by the author.
Bautzer couldn't stand to lose . . . Levy, interview by the author.
"Greg had a loyalty . . ." Harris, interview by Rogers.
"I was usually very depressed . . ." Maass, interview by Rogers.

1. DEBATE CHAMP

"our popular young businessmen" . . . Out of Town Society, *Los Angeles Times*, August 11, 1901.
"a fighting editor" . . . Edward F. Bautzer's obituary, *St. Louis Globe Dispatch.*
"I fought several duels . . ." "Clayton Editor Invites Rival to Mortal Combat," *St. Louis Republic.*
"Did you stop to think . . ." "San Pedro Postmaster Is Not Believer in Hoodoos," *Los Angeles Times.*
"It's time to go" . . . Young, police report, May 25, 1910.
His death certificate . . . Missouri State Board of Health, certificate of death for Paul Garfield Bautzer.

295

"*I want to be a lawyer*" . . . Wynter, interviews by the author.
"*one of San Pedro's* . . ." "Group C Boasts All Boys," *Los Angeles Times*.
the nickname "Lincoln" . . . San Pedro High School, *Black and Gold*.
"*We are living* . . ." "Second Prize Oration," *Los Angeles Times*.
"*Herbert Wenig took three shots* . . ." "Orators Want to Honor State," *Los Angeles Times*.
"*Isn't she beautiful?*" . . . Buhrman, "Hello Greg? . . . This Is Howard Hughes," 39.
"*Resolved, that modern advertising* . . ." Groman, interview by Rogers.
"*Only Greg would think* . . ." Blau, interview by Rogers.
"*He was a hotshot* . . ." Harris, interview by Rogers.
"*I am the greatest* . . ." Wynter, interview by Rogers.

2. "PRESTO! A CELEBRITY"

"*I evaluated myself* . . ." Notes in Henry C. Rogers Papers.
"*I needed to become known*" . . . Ibid.
"*I decided to borrow* . . ." Ibid.; also Niklas, *The Corner Table*, 80.
"*Greg had a flair* . . ." MacNamara, "Gone with the Winds," 26.
"*Greg was ambitious* . . ." Silbert, interview by Rogers.
"*I took any case* . . ." LeBlanc, "Superstar Lawyer."
"*under the wing*" *of* . . . King, From Waikiki, May 30, 1937.
"*Friends say it's* . . ." Chatterbox, *Los Angeles Times*, March 28, 1937.
"*I met beautiful women* . . ." Notes in Henry C. Rogers Papers.
"*Presto, I was* . . ." Ibid.
"*If you are guilty* . . ." Snow, "Counsel for the Indefensible," 72.
"*Jerry Giesler was a hero* . . ." LeBlanc, "Superstar Lawyer."
Giesler then took . . . "Montague Shifts Fight," *Los Angeles Times*.
a Los Angeles Times columnist named them . . . Around and About in Hollywood, *Los Angeles Times*, November 11, 1937.
the press labeled him . . . "Hollywood Playboy Faces Court Today in Check Case," *Los Angeles Times*.
"*The investigation which authorities* . . ." Ibid.

3. THE SWEATER GIRL

"*Every day, in every* . . ." In re: Marriage of McKim.
"*lushly lustrous*" . . . Hopper, Hedda Hopper's Hollywood, August 15, 1939.
"*a figure worthy of* . . ." Hopper, Hedda Hopper's Hollywood, August 20, 1938.
"*She always looks like* . . ." Fidler, Jimmie Fidler in Hollywood, June 4, 1940.
Turner was once onstage . . . Fidler, Jimmie Fidler in Hollywood, November 25, 1940.
"*with a new titian-haired beauty* . . ." Beau Peep Whispers, *Los Angeles Times*, February 13, 1938.
"*He was tall and husky*" . . . Turner, *Lana: The Lady, the Legend, the Truth*, 43.
"*We went dancing* . . ." Ibid., 44.
"*I was scared*" . . . Ibid.
"*My only regret is* . . ." Buhrman, "Hello Greg? . . . This Is Howard Hughes," 39.

One day, Judy Turner cut . . . Wayne, *The Golden Girls of MGM*, 165.

"She was so nervous . . ." Ibid., 166.

"This young lady has . . ." Ibid.

"I did feel passion . . ." Turner, *Lana: The Lady, the Legend, the Truth*, 44.

"Lana Turner gets fresh flowers . . ." Hopper, Hedda Hopper's Hollywood, June 14, 1939.

"Greg Bautzer, Lana Turner's best boyfriend . . ." Kendall, Around and About in Hollywood, February 13, 1939.

When Bautzer returned to Los Angeles . . . Diehl, "Zhivago Scripter Writes His Rites."

"I didn't sleep with him . . ." Turner, *Lana: The Lady, the Legend, the Truth*, 44.

a "sexual merry-go-round" . . . Higham and Moseley, *Princess Merle*, 103.

One day, Turner received . . . Turner, *Lana: The Lady, the Legend, the Truth*, 45.

"Lana Turner is a full-fledged . . ." Hopper, Hedda Hopper's Hollywood, September 15, 1939.

"The film business reeks . . ." Turner, *Lana: The Lady, the Legend, the Truth*, 48.

"That Shaw is the most . . ." Wallace, "The Loves of Lana Turner," 37.

"If Lana Turner would forget . . ." Hopper, Hedda Hopper's Hollywood, June 14, 1939.

"Suppose I were to . . ." Turner, *Lana: The Lady, the Legend, the Truth*, 50.

"I've lost her" . . . Ibid., 51.

"MGM means more . . ." Ibid., 55.

Jimmie Fidler reported that . . . Fidler, Jimmie Fidler in Hollywood, June 21, 1940

"Get your things . . ." Turner, *Lana: The Lady, the Legend, the Truth*, 61.

"Let me put it . . ." Ibid., 5.

4. TWO GODFATHERS

"Billy Wilkerson couldn't topple . . ." Zack, "A Conversation with Greg Bautzer," 39.

"Billy brought Paris . . ." Wilkerson, *The Man Who Invented Las Vegas*, 10.

"Billy's real mistress . . ." "Restaurants: Hollywood Institution," *Time*.

"You don't gamble unless . . ." Behlmer, *Henry Hathaway*, 46.

"I have tried industriously . . ." "Nicky Arnstein Explains," *Los Angeles Times*.

Legend has it . . . Levy, interview by the author.

"attorneys Gregson Bautzer and . . ." "Arnstein Suit Settled," *Los Angeles Times*.

"When Joe Schenck put his . . ." Buhrman, "Hello Greg? . . . This Is Howard Hughes," 38.

"all an agent could demand . . ." Zack, "A Conversation with Greg Bautzer," 40.

fronting for Lucky Luciano . . . Russo, *Supermob*, 126.

5. THE SARONG GIRL

"Bautzer was a real . . ." Lamour and McInnes, *My Side of the Road*, 101.

"You've won many . . ." Fidler, Jimmie Fidler in Hollywood, May 9, 1940.

"Dottie, as she is known . . ." Parsons, "Dorothy Lamour Makes Friends Everywhere."

"Greg Bautzer stopped by . . ." Lamour and McInnes, *My Side of the Road*, 102.

"Where would I be without . . ." Fidler, Jimmie Fidler in Hollywood, May 15, 1940.

Their farewell embraces . . . Fidler, Jimmie Fidler in Hollywood, October 16, 1940.

"The Cat and the Canary was . . ." Hope and Thomas, *The Road to Hollywood*, 31.

a playboy described as . . . "Carole Landis Asks Divorce," *Los Angeles Times.*

an "ugly and surly" demeanor . . . "Carole Landis Charges Mate Blocked Career," *Los Angeles Times.*

"I no longer care . . ." Ibid.

Bautzer and Lamour were in a restaurant . . . Hopper, Hedda Hopper's Hollywood, June 13, 1941.

"Greg and I had lots . . ." Lamour and McInnes, *My Side of the Road*, 117.

"I had just taken a company . . ." LeBlanc, "Superstar Lawyer."

"I knew that Greg was not . . ." Lamour and McInnes, *My Side of the Road*, 117.

6. THE SPY WHO LOVED HIM

"She was one of a bevy . . ." McGregor, letter to Freddie [Unknown].

Getty was a Nazi sympathizer . . . Angell, FBI memorandum, May 27, 1941.

"William R. (Billie) [sic] Wilkerson advised . . ." Findlay, FBI memorandum.

"Mr. Wilkerson stated that while Miss Kruger . . ." Ibid.

He decided the best way . . . Higham, interview by the author.

They found no evidence . . . Angell, FBI memorandum, February 20, 1941.

Kruger was later involved . . . Ailshie, "Activities of Katherina Mathilde Kruger (Hilda Kruger)."

Kruger escaped arrest . . . Office of Chief of Naval Operations, "American Republics—Totalitarian Penetration In—Social Forces."

J. Edgar Hoover was certainly . . . Hoover, letter to Adolf A. Berle Jr., March 19, 1947.

7. LIEUTENANT COMMANDER, USN

On February 2, 1942 . . . US Navy personnel file of Lt. Comdr. Bautzer.

The application process . . . Sickel, memorandum to Chief of the Bureau of Navigation.

He wrote a request . . . Bautzer, application for transfer to flight training (LTA).

"This officer will be sent . . ." US Navy personnel file of Lt. Comdr. Bautzer.

According to a law school buddy . . . Gardner, Robert Gardner's Verdicts, August 30, 2005.

"Is Bautzer there . . ." Cavalier, interview by the author.

"Greg seemed to be a loner . . ." Fahey, interview by the author.

Years later, naval blimp historian . . . Van Treuren, "Georgia Draw."

"Borden Chase, who wrote . . ." Mannix, letter to Bautzer.

"Not until I . . ." Bautzer, letter to Admiral Rosendahl, July 14, 1945.

"The day I was married . . ." Bautzer, letter to Jean Rosendahl.

The "man who made millions laugh" . . . "Irvin Cobb's Ashes Laid to Rest in Kentucky," *Los Angeles Times.*

"If we are proceeding . . ." Bautzer, letter to Admiral Rosendahl, April 6, 1944.

"He was always in . . ." McDougall, interview by the author.

"Bautzer was a lot older . . ." Kroll, interview by the author.

"I was talking to an officer . . ." Bautzer, letter to Admiral Rosendahl, March 7, 1944.

"I do hope their statements . . ." Admiral Rosendahl, letter to Bautzer.

Bautzer "got heavy" . . . "Attorney Bautzer Held on Drunk Charge," *Los Angeles Times.*

8. TOE TO TOE WITH BUGSY SIEGEL

"The first thing I know . . ." Buhrman, "Hello Greg? . . . This Is Howard Hughes," 38.
"Be on the other side . . ." Wilkerson, *The Man Who Invented Las Vegas*, 26.
"When I feel the table . . ." Ibid., 33.
"I watched Billy . . ." Ibid., 24.
"Take that number . . ." Ibid., 39.
"So there I was . . ." Buhrman, "Hello Greg? . . . This Is Howard Hughes," 38.
"It was Billy's decision . . ." Wilkerson, *The Man Who Invented Las Vegas*, 74.
"A real gentleman . . ." Ibid., 75.
"His face would darken . . ." Ibid., 70.
"Why would anyone want . . ." Ibid.
"Billy was sticking to . . ." Ibid., 79.
"Billy was in a difficult . . ." Ibid., 88.
"I'm the one who makes . . ." Ibid., 90.
"You're gonna have to . . ." Ibid., 93.
"I have something very unflattering . . ." Wynter, interviews by the author.
"Forty-eight percent . . ." Wilkerson, *The Man Who Invented Las Vegas*, 98.
"If your partner were . . ." Ibid., 107.
"There was every chance . . ." Ibid., 109.
"Siegel was not the right . . ." Ibid., 113.

9. LOVER DEAREST

"The rest of the world . . ." Thomas, *Joan Crawford*, 151.
"Look, Joan . . ." Guiles, *Joan Crawford: The Last Word*, 143.
"She liked men who gave . . ." Considine, *Bette & Joan*, 221.
Greg *"treated her like . . ."* Guiles, *Joan Crawford: The Last Word*, 143.
"To be Joan Crawford's boyfriend . . ." Thomas, *Joan Crawford*, 153.
"Crawford expected her escort . . ." Guiles, *Joan Crawford: The Last Word*, 143.
"A night with Joan . . ." Considine, *Bette & Joan*, 223.
"It would surprise no one . . ." Hopper, Hedda Hopper's Hollywood, May 15, 1946.
"Joan Crawford has reached . . ." Hopper, Hedda Hopper's Hollywood, October 9, 1946.
"I wish I could be . . ." Guiles, *Joan Crawford: The Last Word*, 150.
"That son of a bitch . . ." Ibid., 151.
"I've been trying . . ." Ibid., 150.
"There was a decided hush . . ." Ibid., 149.
"First they ordered . . ." Niklas, interview by Rogers; and Lansky, "O, Happy Days!"
"simply made for each . . ." Bret, *Joan Crawford: Hollywood Martyr*, 171.
"Greg was the most ferocious . . ." Dorso, interview by Rogers.
"She was predatory . . ." Considine, *Bette & Joan*, 221.
"Is it a sin . . ." Hopper, Looking at Hollywood, February 10, 1947.
"She was drunk with . . ." Kashner and Schoenberger. *A Talent for Genius*, 296.
"Those parties were all . . ." Turner, *Lana: The Lady, the Legend, the Truth*, 45.
"Greg woke up at seven . . ." Considine, *Bette & Joan*, 222.

"Crawford liked to be treated . . ." Ibid., 205.

"She put them there" . . . Bret, *Joan Crawford: Hollywood Martyr*, 171.

Crawford recalled the details . . . Guiles, *Joan Crawford: The Last Word*, 151.

"You know," said Goddard . . . Hopper, "Niven Sees Himself as Star of Classics."

"I felt like Alice . . ." Dahl, interview by the author.

"These two battle . . ." Considine, *Bette & Joan*, 205.

Bautzer's tennis chum . . . Dorso, interview by Rogers.

Johnny Dugan also witnessed . . . Notes in Henry C. Rogers Papers.

"part of the Communist . . ." Kotsilibas-Davis and Loy. *Myrna Loy: Being and Becoming*, 205.

"One or two may . . ." Ibid., 206.

"No, I'm sorry" . . . Ibid., 207.

"mail order divorce" . . . "Court's Ability to Restrain Mexico Divorce to be Tested," *Los Angeles Times*.

"I have not yet talked . . ." "Paulette Will Seek Divorce from Meredith," *Los Angeles Times*.

"I lived at . . ." Greg Bautzer, interview in "Joan Crawford," *The Hollywood Greats*.

Crawford biographies maintain . . . MacNamara, "Gone with the Winds," 34

Reflecting on his long affair . . . Greg Bautzer, interview in "Joan Crawford," *The Hollywood Greats*.

"Joan leaned across . . ." Ibid.

"If anyone was abused . . ." The Ear, *Washington Post*, November 8, 1981.

10. DIVORCE OF THE CENTURY

Get Me Giesler! . . . Giesler, *The Jerry Giesler Story*, 261.

"David said he'd . . ." Kobal, *People Will Talk*, 460.

Bergman was offering . . . "Ingrid Bergman Business Manager Quits," *Los Angeles Times*.

"You shouldn't talk . . ." Spoto, *Notorious*, 156.

Bergman was "horrified" . . . Bergman and Burgess, *Ingrid Bergman: My Story*, 262.

"I do not think he would . . ." "Ingrid Bergman Business Manager Quits," *Los Angeles Times*.

the rumor of her pregnancy was . . . "Hollywood Sees Hoax in Reports of Bergman Baby," *Los Angeles Times*.

"I saw her less . . ." Ibid.

"We've just turned over . . ." "Dr. Lindstrom Given Bergman Property Plan," *Los Angeles Times*.

"They have been guilty . . ." "Stromboli Ban Urged by Bishop," *Los Angeles Times*.

"under a friendly arrangement" . . . "Ingrid Bergman Orders Suit for Divorce Filed in Mexico," *Los Angeles Times*.

"Dr. Lindström is not holding" . . . Ibid.

"We know that Miss Bergman . . ." "Ingrid Will Return for Custody Fight," *Los Angeles Times*.

"a horrible example . . ." Falsani, *Sin Boldly*, 139.

"moral turpitude" . . . "Turpitude Ban No Bar to Ingrid," *Los Angeles Times*.

"We have not been advised . . ." Ibid.

"We still want to know . . ." "Court Fight Still Looms over Ingrid's Daughter," *Los Angeles Times*.
In his 1962 autobiography . . . Giesler, *The Jerry Giesler Story*, 261.

11. CHANGE PARTNERS AND DANCE

"Hollywood's greatest escape . . ." Hopper, "Law Student Mari Blanchard Has Case."
"Greg Bautzer, who's usually . . ." Hopper, "Columnist Discounts Hendrix Tiff."
"Ginger Rogers is the most . . ." Hopper, "Astaire Way of Life Aims at Happiness."
"Greg was Bachelor Number One . . ." Rogers, *Ginger*, 416.
"as nervous as a cat . . ." Hopper, "Jessel Preparing Scripts for Haver."
"Greg Bautzer almost came out . . ." Brent, Carrousel, November 23, 1949.
The writer printed . . . Burns, "Love Comes Last," 52.
"The guy has something . . ." Townsend, "Torch Song," 88.
"like a couple of school kids . . ." Hopper, "Subversive Elements Detected in Pictures."
"Our dates would go . . ." Rogers, *Ginger*, 420.
"If they were getting along" . . . Adamson, "Ann Savage."
"It's a little premature . . ." "Ginger Rogers Dodges on French Romance," *Los Angeles Times*.
Bautzer went to her home . . . Rogers, *Ginger*, 418.
"Greg liked to get . . ." Ibid., 417.
Lee considered Bautzer . . . Lee, *Miss Peggy Lee*, 158.
"I am so sorry" . . . Ibid., 151.
"What a fool I was!" . . . Ibid., 158.
Hedda Hopper asked Blanchard . . . Hopper, "Law Student Mari Blanchard Has Case."
"When I needed . . ." Dahl, interview by the author.

12. THE BERGMAN SEQUEL

"My mother rejected . . ." Lindström, interview by the author.
"There were dozens of reporters" . . . Ibid.
The first to testify was . . . "Judge Testifies for Ingrid," *Los Angeles Times*.
"I have seldom seen . . ." Ibid.
"My impression of him . . ." Lindström, interview by the author.
Bautzer's examination was reported . . . "Pia's Answer," *Time*; also "Ingrid's Daughter Spurns Italy Visit," *Los Angeles Times*.
Pia had delivered her testimony . . . "Ingrid's Daughter Spurns Italy Visit," *Los Angeles Times*.
"I felt ashamed . . ." Lindström, interview by the author.
"She said she had to take . . ." "Ingrid Bergman Gives Birth to Twin Daughters," *Los Angeles Times*.
"I told her it is impossible . . ." "Ingrid's Daughter Spurns Italy Visit," *Los Angeles Times*.
Pacht offered into evidence . . . Ibid.
Judge Lillie issued her ruling . . . "Visit to Ingrid by Pia Barred by Court Action," *Los Angeles Times*.

"All I can say now . . ." "Ingrid Plans Visit to Pia in July or Early August," *Los Angeles Times.*
"I had no communication . . ." Lindström, interview by the author.
"I've gone from saint . . ." O'Neil, *Movie Awards*, 189.
The next time Pia . . . Lindström, interview by the author.

13. BATTLING BOGIE

"Watch out for him" . . . MacNamara, "Gone with the Winds," 29.
"Greg wasn't a staggering . . ." Ibid., 31.
"Bogie thought of himself . . ." Hyams, *Bogie*, 123.
"Bigwigs have been known . . ." Ibid.
"I'm going to beat you . . ." Ibid., 126.
"And who should come in . . ." Hamilton and Stadiem, *Don't Mind If I Do*, 164.
"His looks were enough . . ." MacNamara, "Gone with the Winds," 31.
Bautzer was reported to be "stardusty" . . . Screen Gossip, *Toledo Blade*, July 1, 1947.
he was "cruising the glitter spots" . . . Kilgallen, "Grant, Selznick Mystery Combination."
"He was suave . . ." Miller, interview by Rogers.
"The only thing funny . . ." Crowther, review of *The Groom Wore Spurs.*

14. AN ELEGANT WIFE

"We were on the second . . ." Sullivan, interview by the author.
"You see that girl . . ." Wynter, interview by Rogers; and Wynter, interviews by the author.
"Greg Bautzer came stag . . ." Wilkerson and Borie, *Hollywood Legends*, 276.
"You know," said Zanuck . . . Wynter, interview by Rogers; and Wynter, interviews by the author.
"You know, Miss Wynter" . . . Ibid.
"There's somebody new . . ." Ibid.
"I'll be there" . . . Ibid.
"He was an original" . . . Ibid.
"Let's go to Mexico" . . . Ibid.
"nerves of a burglar" . . . Ibid.
"How can you not . . ." Ibid.
"I hope I'm that lucky" . . . "Bautzer Sidesteps Story He Will Wed Actress," *Los Angeles Times.*
"Greg intended to go . . ." Undated clipping in Henry C. Rogers Papers.
"The moon was high . . ." Wynter, interview by Rogers; and Wynter, interviews by the author.
On June 10, 1956 . . . Ibid.
They needed to alert . . . Wynter, interview by Rogers; and Wynter, interviews by the author.
A few weeks after . . . Ibid.
"My record was just . . ." Newhart, *I Shouldn't Even Be Doing This*, 79; and Newhart, interview by the author.
Another swell party . . . Wynter, *Other People Other Places*, 23.
"The games were too . . ." Wynter, interview by Rogers; and Wynter, interviews by the author.

"Let me tell you . . ." Dorso, interview by Rogers.
"I couldn't bear . . ." Wynter, interview by Rogers; and Wynter, interviews by the author.
"this kind of showing off" . . . Ibid.
the Reagans cornered Bautzer . . . Wynter, interview by Rogers; and Wynter, interviews by the author.
A short time later . . . Day in Sacramento, *Los Angeles Times*, February 6, 1963.

15. THE RICHEST CLIENT IN THE WORLD

when Bautzer and Di Cicco arrived . . . Notes in Henry C. Rogers Papers.
But the story Bautzer told . . . Mark Bautzer, interview by Rogers.
Just after midnight . . . "Actors' Agent Attempts Death," *Los Angeles Times*.
Regardless of how . . . "Settlement Seen as Near in Suit Against Hughes," *Los Angeles Times*.
"When Howard Hughes . . ." Buhrman, "Hello Greg? . . . This Is Howard Hughes," 39.
He said that he wanted out . . . Russo, *Supermob*, 128.
"RKO's contract list . . ." Jewell and Harbin, *The RKO Story*, 244.
"the financial feat . . ." Russo, *Supermob*, 129.
One actress to sign . . . Hopper, Hedda Hopper, September 17, 1954.
Then, in 1955, someone recommended . . . Robert Schwartz, interview by the author.
"Mr. Bautzer worked clear through . . ." Sullivan, interview by the author.
"I want no divided responsibility . . ." Barlett and Steele, *Empire*, 256.
Hughes had a change of heart . . . Ibid., 257.
"Other than being his lawyer . . ." Sullivan, interview by the author.

16. BILLIONAIRE SECRETS

"There are only three things . . ." Notes in Henry C. Rogers Papers.
"The stress of working . . ." Sullivan, interview by the author.
"That guy is driving me . . ." Notes in Henry C. Rogers Papers.
Lea Sullivan remembered . . . Sullivan, interview by the author.
One night when Sullivan . . . Sullivan, interview by the author.
Hughes would personally fly . . . Wynter, interviews by the author.
the Bautzers were in Acapulco . . . Ibid.
"Have you asked her?" . . . Higham, *Howard Hughes*, 156.
Black Gold Productions . . . Parker, interview by the author.
He found his targets . . . Anderson, "Hughes Courtships Were Much Like Corporate Business."
Tony Curtis recalled . . . Curtis and Golenbock, *American Prince*, 127.
"A playboy who became . . ." "Howard Hughes," *Life*.
"From the looks . . ." "Welcome Home, Howard!," University of Nevada.
Bautzer heard of Stuart's weakness . . . Stuart, interview by the author.
"You're not going to . . ." Higham, *Howard Hughes*, 212.
Publisher Robert Loomis . . . Higham, *Howard Hughes*, 213.
"Irving may have had . . ." Haber, "Hughes Alive, Well . . . but Don't Quote Me."
"I don't know him . . ." "Principal Points Made in Interview," *Los Angeles Times*.

he was writing an exposé . . . Haber, "Joe and Elke and Life in a Doll's House."
"I'm not saying that . . ." Ibid.
"I estimated the Hughes book . . ." Ibid.
"I have no desire . . ." Hack, *Howard Hughes*, 305.
Goldenson told stockholders . . . Ibid.
"Mr. Hughes would like . . ." Barlett and Steele, *Empire*, 337.
"I hate to awaken you . . ." Drosnin, *Citizen Hughes*, 147.
"I am in a real predicament . . . Barlett and Steele, *Empire*, 338.
Hughes blamed his retreat on . . . Ibid., 339.
"When I was there last . . ." Ibid., 334.
Robert Maheu, who never . . . Maheu and Hack, *Next to Hughes*, 95.
A man named Maybe Tucker was . . . Tucker, interview by Rogers.
Bautzer wept like a child . . . Ibid.
"Over a period of time . . ." "Where Hughes's Billions Go," *Los Angeles Times*.
"Hughes told Mr. Bautzer . . ." Sullivan, interview by the author.
"My dining room became . . ." Ibid.
Judge Lake called the memory . . . Luther, "Fees of $600,000 Denied by Judge."
"Howard's success with Toolco . . ." Brown and Broeske, *Howard Hughes*, 127.
Bautzer would reminisce . . . Notes in Henry C. Rogers Papers.
"I sat in Greg's office . . ." Harris, interview by Rogers.

17. WHEN STARS CALL IT QUITS

"I was just getting started . . ." Wagner, interview by the author.
Bautzer experienced one of these . . . Wynter, interviews by the author.
"Unfortunately, my married life . . ." Kelley, *His Way*, 145.
"Mrs. Sinatra has no plans . . ." Kelley, *His Way*, 151.
a "reasonable amount" . . . "Mrs. Sinatra's Suit Against Mate Delayed," *Los Angeles Times*.
"She's miserable about . . ." Kelley, *His Way*, 153.
"Hey, would you mind . . ." Wynter, interview by Rogers; and Wynter, interviews by the author.
"You can photograph from Dana . . ." Ibid.
"No," she said . . . Ibid.
They spotted Giancana . . . Ibid.
she was grateful for one . . . Ibid.
"We have just recently . . ." "Jeanne Crain Drops Her Demands for Protection," *Los Angeles Times*
She testified that Rhoads . . . "Jeanne Crain Denies Misconduct Charges." *Los Angeles Times*.
"With four children involved . . ." "Crain Divorce Case Smolders in Law Offices." *Los Angeles Times*.
"Divorces are messy . . ." LeBlanc, "Superstar Lawyer."
"I was very much in love" . . . Hudson and Davidson, *Rock Hudson*, 96.
"Phyllis and Rock were at our . . ." Ibid., 97.
"He was out every night" . . . Ibid., 103.
"I used to believe . . ." Ibid., 98.

18. THE HEARST PROXY

"I want you to take care . . ." Wynter, interview by Rogers; and Wynter, interviews by the author.

"Wouldn't it absolutely clinch . . ." "Hearst and Purity," *Los Angeles Times.*

"Love is not always . . ." Davies and Marx, *The Times We Had*, 30.

"This so-called agreement" . . . "Hearst-Davies Pact Legality Attacked," *Los Angeles Times.*

"The document will speak for . . ." "Hearst's Bombshell," *Time.*

"I would do anything . . ." Ibid.

"I think we have . . ." Typed meeting minutes in Marion Davies Papers.

"Greg, I want to have . . ." Gindick, "Mystique."

Davies was deeply fond . . . Wynter, interviews by the author.

"Money lying in . . ." Typed meeting minutes in Marion Davies Papers.

Time magazine took note . . . "Tycoon Davies," *Time.*

"Marion accompanies her . . ." "Marion Davies Presents $1,500,000 to UCLA," *Los Angeles Times.*

19. JOSEPH SCHENCK ENTERPRISES

One day Bautzer called Schwartz . . . Bernard Schwartz, interview by Rogers.

At first they rented . . . Parker, interview by the author.

In the time since . . . Ibid.

When she overheard . . . Wynter, interview by Rogers; and Wynter, interviews by the author.

"Of all the people . . ." Zack, "A Conversation with Greg Bautzer," 39.

"Billy used power . . ." Ibid., 40.

20. THE BREAKUP

The behavior that Wynter . . . Wynter, interview by Rogers; and Wynter, interviews by the author.

When he took two-and-a-half-year-old . . . Hopper, Entertainment, December 6, 1962.

"The day after I returned . . ." Hopper, Entertainment, December 13, 1963.

"Greg didn't win thirty-one . . ." Wynter, interview by Rogers; and Wynter, interviews by the author.

There was one particularly bad . . . Ibid.

"My father never took me . . ." Mark Bautzer, interview by Rogers.

"Look," he told her . . . Wynter, interview by Rogers; and Wynter, interviews by the author.

"People do not carry on . . ." Ibid.

"Why don't you come . . ." Hopper, Hedda Hopper, August 20, 1962.

One night a call came . . . Wynter, interviews by the author.

On another occasion, Howard Hughes . . . Wynter, interview by Rogers; and Wynter, interviews by the author.

Only once did Wynter . . . Ibid.

One night, Bautzer went . . . Ibid.

"To Mrs. Bautzer . . ." Ibid.
"Greg, I'm sorry . . ." Ibid.
"Mrs. Bautzer, if I may . . ." Ibid.

21. INVENTING ROBERT EVANS

"I went to see Billy . . ." Russo, *Supermob*, 280.
"Let's not call it . . ." Loper, "The Bistro's Secret of Success."
"I liked Greg Bautzer . . ." Korshak, interview by Rogers.
"My wife Bernice . . ." Ibid.
"In accordance with . . ." Russo, *Supermob*, 126.
The Acapulco Towers . . . Ibid., 339.
Korshak told friends . . . Ibid., 213.
"Bob Evans used to . . ." Wynter, interview by Rogers; and Wynter, interviews by the author.
Evans got a call . . . Evans, *The Kid Stays in the Picture*, 111.
"Don't you believe it" . . . Russo, *Supermob*, 322.
"Bautzer set up . . ." Levy, interview by the author.
"Greg Bautzer's the guy . . ." Ruddy, interview by the author.
"I mean, Charlie was . . ." Wynter, interview by Rogers; and Wynter, interviews by the author.
"Charlie Bluhdorn knew . . ." Ruddy, interview by the author.
"Bob is still trying . . ." Ibid.
Pundits didn't think . . . Evans, *The Kid Stays in the Picture*, 119.
"Robert Evans is an outrage . . ." Russo, *Supermob*, 322.
"You didn't bring in . . ." Russo, *Supermob*, 477.

22. KIRK KERKORIAN BUYS MGM

Sidney Korshak had an idea . . . Korshak, interview by Rogers.
"There was a dedication . . ." Neumeyer, "The Case of the Battling Barristers," 60.
"Greg evidently needed . . ." Korshak, interview by Rogers.
"During the 1970s . . ." Levy, interview by the author.
"I like to talk . . ." MacNamara, "Gone with the Winds," 30.
"Kirk Kerkorian worshiped . . ." Del, interview by the author.
"This offer is inadequate . . ." Wood, "MGM Will Oppose $35 Million Offer."
"It seems to me" . . . Dallos, "Kerkorian Violated Securities Laws."
"We're looking for the time . . ." Dallos, "Kerkorian Beats MGM Attempt to Halt Tender."
The two sides communicated . . . Dallos, "Kerkorian Reports 1,325,000 Shares."
"He was it" . . . Rosenfield, "Aubrey: A Lion in Winter."
"The American public . . ." Morrow, "Goodbye to Our Mary."
the "smartest one up there" . . . Rosenfield, "Aubrey: A Lion in Winter."
"The world's No. 1 . . ." Oulahan and Lambert, "The Tyrant's Fall That Rocked the TV World."
the "Smiling Cobra" . . . "Lion and the Cobra," *Time.*
"I don't pretend . . ." "The Return of Smiling Jim," *Time.*
"Aubrey was the fourth . . ." Rosenfield, "Aubrey: A Lion in Winter."

"*No man made bigger profits . . .*" Ibid.
"*Jim Aubrey has a real . . .*" "The Return of Smiling Jim," *Time.*
"*I don't want a contract*" . . . Ibid.
"*Clear out the nonproductive . . .*" Ibid.
"*I think that a lawyer . . .*" Sloane, "Lawyer Keeps Late Hours with Clients."
"*Greg is extremely difficult . . .*" Ibid.
"*We sold off acreage . . .*" Rosenfield, "Aubrey: A Lion in Winter."
"*Jim Aubrey took everything . . .*" Marx, "Speaks for Ghosts."
"*The studio that brought you . . .*" Cook, *Lost Illusions*, 303.
"*For propriety's sake*" . . . Haber, "$20 Million Deal Sealed at Bistro."
On October 30, Aubrey . . . Bart, *Fade Out*, 59.
"*The job I agreed . . .*" "Lion and the Cobra," *Time.*
"*You can't go out . . .*" Bart, *Fade Out*, 173.
"*On Fridays there was . . .*" Morgan, interview by the author.
"*If you feel that strongly . . .*" Bart, *Fade Out*, 173.
"*Things are as exciting . . .*" "Attorney for Kerkorian to Run MGM, UA," *Los Angeles Times.*
"*He seemed to know . . .*" Rosenfelt, interview by Rogers.
"*Kirk's a low-key . . .*" Mark Bautzer, interview by Rogers.
"*Talk about comfort!*" . . . LeBlanc, "Superstar Lawyer."
"*Kirk was into my father's . . .*" Mark Bautzer, interview by Rogers.

23. THE BIG FIRM

"*It was remarkable . . .*" Stein, interview by the author.
"*We were flying . . .*" Neumeyer, "The Case of the Battling Barristers," 62.
"*It was a different time . . .*" Morgan, interview by the author.
"*Greg was on the phone . . .*" Del, interview by the author.
"*I owned a piece . . .*" Levy, interview by the author.
"*Clients would be sitting . . .*" Del, interview by the author.
"*I learned a lot . . .*" Levy, interview by the author.
"*We have examined . . .*" Amdur, "U.S. Open Won't Recognize Test Taken by Dr. Richards."
Bautzer got himself into hot water . . . Morgan, interview by the author.
"*That takes balls . . .*" Ibid.
"*Listen, I've spoken . . .*" Ibid.
"*I'm going to do . . .*" Ibid.
"*I personally drafted . . .*" Ibid.
"*Now, Frank, I've . . .*" Ibid.
"*Listen, for the sake of . . .*" Ibid.
"*Because to Greg, it was still . . .*" Ibid.
"*She was the one . . .*" Osborne, "Heavy Hitter, Natural Born Killer."
She tenaciously defended Kerkorian . . . Ibid.
"*I don't care whether it's . . .*" Pollock, "Inchon! Shooting for the Moonies."
Greg made some calls . . . Beckerman, interview by Rogers.
"*Farrah never knew . . .*" "Writer Quits, but Show Must Go On," *Atlanta Journal.*
A woman named Lehua May Garcia . . . Murphy, "Suit Citing Forgotten Deed Could Scuttle Sale."
"*They're all my friends*" . . . Willie Brown eulogy for Bautzer in Henry C. Rogers Papers.

"*You're such a good friend . . .*" Maass, interview by Rogers.
"*I met a lot of his . . .*" Del, interview by the author.
One time in the 1970s . . . Notes in Henry C. Rogers Papers.
"*I once made the mistake . . .*" Ibid.
"*There was a time when . . .*" Maass, interview by Rogers.
"*The opposing team would settle . . .*" Mark Bautzer, interview by Rogers.
"*I started seeing an eye doctor . . .*" Robert Schwartz, interview by the author.
"*Greg was brilliant . . .*" Del, interview by the author.
"*He didn't want to hear about . . .*" Notes in Henry C. Rogers Papers.
"*I would be in Greg's office . . .*" Ibid.
"*Anyone who had anything . . .*" Weintraub Ferrer, interview by Rogers; and Weintraub
     Ferrer, interview by the author.

24. THE LOVE OF HER LIFE

"*I was with him . . .*" Levy, interview by the author.
Silver Screen Magazine had linked . . . Moran, "How a White Millionaire Won Diahann."
Bautzer's first recorded date . . . Haber, "Harvey Rite at Robbin's Gala (Almost)."
"*He was a loyal friend*" . . . Dorso, interview by Rogers.
"*Greg, aren't you*" . . . Wynter, interview by Rogers; and Wynter, interviews by the author.
"*No one ever received . . .*" Maass, interview by Rogers.
"*Once in a while . . .*" Dorso, interview by Rogers.
"*He tried to quit . . .*" Mark Bautzer, interview by Rogers.
"*He didn't want to age*" . . . Ibid.
"*I'm an alcoholic*" . . . Notes in Henry C. Rogers Papers.
He conspired with restaurateur . . . Puck, interview by the author; and Erpicum, interview by
     the author.
"*Bring me a cappuccino*" . . . Notes in Henry C. Rogers Papers.
In 1987, he was visiting . . . Mark Bautzer, interview by Rogers.
"*I hope he behaves . . .*" Notes in Henry C. Rogers Papers.
"*He was a hell of a guy*" . . . Overend, "Greg Bautzer, Attorney to the Stars, Dies."
"*He had an enthusiasm . . .*" Ibid.
"*He was so courtly . . .*" Ibid.

EPILOGUE

"*There was some resentment . . .*" Neumeyer, "The Case of the Battling Barristers," 64.
"*This was a law firm . . .*" Ibid.
"*He was wonderful . . .*" Osborne, "Heavy Hitter, Natural Born Killer."
"*excellent, honest, and . . .*" Kim, "Casino Mogul Takes Stand in Trial."
"*I would never have . . .*" Notes in Henry C. Rogers Papers.
"*Greg would walk into . . .*" Paul MacNamara eulogy for Bautzer in Henry C. Rogers Papers.
"*I've been asked . . .*" Irwin, interview by Rogers.
"*You know Mark, your father . . .*" Mark Bautzer, interview by Rogers.
"*He was everyone's idol . . .*" Ruddy, interview by the author.

BIBLIOGRAPHY

BOOKS

Barlett, Donald L., and James B. Steele. *Empire*. New York: W. W. Norton, 1979.
———. *Howard Hughes: His Life and Madness*. New York: W. W. Norton, 2004.
Bart, Peter. *Fade Out: The Calamitous Final Days of MGM*. New York: William Morrow, 1991.
Behlmer, Rudy. *Henry Hathaway*. Lanham, MD: Rowman & Littlefield, 2001.
Bergman, Ingrid, and Alan Burgess. *Ingrid Bergman: My Story*. New York: Delacorte Press, 1980.
Bernstein, Matthew. *Walter Wanger: Hollywood Independent*. Berkeley: University of California Press, 1994.
Bessette, Roland L. *Mario Lanza: Tenor in Exile*. Portland: Amadeus Press, 1999.
Blair, Betsy. *The Memory of All That: Love and Politics in New York, Hollywood, and Paris*. New York: Alfred A. Knopf, 2003.
Bret, David. *Clark Gable: Tormented Star*. New York: Carroll & Graf Publishers, 2007.
———. *Joan Crawford: Hollywood Martyr*. New York: Caroll & Graf Publishers, 2007.
Brown, Peter Harry, and Pat H. Broeske. *Howard Hughes: The Untold Story*. Boston: Dutton Adult, 1996.
Canales, Luis. *Imperial Gina: The Strictly Unauthorized Biography*. Boston: Branden Publishing Co., 1990.
Churchwell, Sarah Bartlett. *The Many Lives of Marilyn Monroe*. New York: Metropolitan Books, 2004.
Considine, Shaun. *Bette & Joan: The Divine Feud*. New York: Dell Publishing, 1989.
Cook, David. *Lost Illusions: American Cinema in the Shadow of Watergate and Viet Nam*. Los Angeles: University of California Press, 2002.
Crane, Cheryl, and Cindy De La Hoz. *Lana: The Memories, the Myths, the Movies*. Philadelphia: Running Press, 2008.
Crane, Cheryl, and Cliff Jahr. *Detour: A Hollywood Story*. New York: Arbor House William Morrow, 1988.

Crawford, Christina. *Mommie Dearest*. New York: William Morrow, 1978.

Curtis, Tony, and Peter Golenbock. *American Prince: A Memoir*. New York: Harmony Books, 2008.

Davies, Marion, and Kenneth·Marx. *The Times We Had*. New York: Ballantine Books, 1990.

Drosnin, Michael. *Citizen Hughes: The Power, the Money and the Madness*. Austin: Holt, Rinehart, and Winston, 1985.

Evans, Robert. *The Kid Stays in the Picture*. New York: Hyperion, 1994.

Falsani, Cathleen. *Sin Boldly: A Field Guide for Grace*. Grand Rapids, MI: Zondervan Press, 2008.

Finstad, Suzanna. *Natasha: The Biography of Natalie Wood*. New York: Harmony Books, 2001.

Fleming, E. J. *Carole Landis: A Tragic Life in Hollywood*. Jefferson, NC: McFarland & Co., 2005.

———. *The Fixers: Eddie Mannix, Howard Strickling and the MGM Publicity Machine*. Jefferson, NC: McFarland & Co., 2005.

Giesler, Jerry, as told to Pete Martin. *The Jerry Giesler Story*. New York: Simon & Schuster, 1960.

Guiles, Fred Lawrence. *Joan Crawford: The Last Word*. New York: Birch Lane Press, 1995.

Guinn, J. M. *A History of California and an Extended History of Its Southern Coast Counties, Also Containing Biographies of Well-Known Citizens of the Past and Present*. Chicago: Historic Record Co., 1907.

Hack, Richard. *Howard Hughes: The Private Diaries, Memos and Letters*. Beverly Hills: New Millennium Press, 2001.

Hamilton, George, and William Stadiem. *Don't Mind If I Do*. New York: Touchstone, 2008.

Higham, Charles. *Howard Hughes: The Secret Life*. New York: G. P. Putnam, 1993.

Higham, Charles, and Roy Moseley. *Princess Merle: The Romantic Life of Merle Oberon*. New York: Coward-McCann, 1983.

Hope, Bob, and Bob Thomas. *The Road to Hollywood: My Forty-Year Love Affair with the Movies*. Garden City, NY: Doubleday, 1977.

Hudson, Rock, and Sara Davidson. *Rock Hudson: His Story*. New York: William Morrow, 1986.

Hyams, Joe. *Bogie: The Biography of Humphrey Bogart*. New York: New American Library, 1966.

Jewell, Richard, and Vernon Harbin. *The RKO Story*. New York: Arlington Press, 1982.

Kashner, Sam, and Nancy Schoenberger. *A Talent for Genius: The Life and Times of Oscar Levant*. New York: Villard, 1994.

Kelley, Kitty. *His Way: The Unauthorized Biography of Frank Sinatra*. New York: Bantam Books, 1986.

Kobal, John. *People Will Talk*. New York: Alfred A. Knopf, 1986.

Kotsilibas-Davis, James, and Myrna Loy. *Myrna Loy: Being and Becoming*. New York: Alfred A. Knopf, 1987.

Lambert, Gavin. *Natalie Wood: A Life*. New York: Alfred A. Knopf, 2004.

Lamour, Dorothy, and Dick McInnes. *My Side of the Road*. Englewood Cliffs, NJ: Prentice-Hall, 1981.

Leaming, Barbara. *Marilyn Monroe*. New York: Crown Publishers, 1998.

Lee, Peggy. *Miss Peggy Lee: An Autobiography*. New York: Donald I. Fine, 1989.

Lenzer, Robert. *The Great Getty: The Life and Loves of J. Paul Getty, the Richest Man in the World*. New York: Crown Books, 1985.

Maheu, Robert, and Richard Hack. *Next to Hughes*, New York: Harper Collins, 1992.

McCann, Graham. *Marilyn Monroe*. New Brunswick, NJ: Rutgers University Press, 1987.

Montville, Leigh. *The Mysterious Montague: A True Tale of Hollywood, Golf, and Armed Robbery*. New York: Doubleday, 2008.

Morris, Sylvia Jukes. *Rage for Fame: The Ascent of Clare Boothe Luce*. New York: Random House, 1997.

Newhart, Bob. *I Shouldn't Even Be Doing This*. New York: Hyperion Press, 2007.

Niklas, Kurt, as told to Larry Hamm. *The Corner Table: From Cabbages to Caviar, Sixty Years in the Celebrity Restaurant Trade*. Beverly Hills, CA: Tuxedo Press, 2000.

O'Neil, Tom. *Movie Awards: The Ultimate, Unofficial Guide to the Oscars, Golden Globes, Critics, Guild, & Indie Honors*. New York: Perigee, 2003.

Quirk, Lawrence J., and William Schoell. *Joan Crawford: The Essential Biography*. Lexington: University Press of Kentucky, 2002.

Richmond, Peter. *Fever: The Life and Music of Miss Peggy Lee*. New York: Henry Holt and Co., 1989.

Rogers, Ginger. *Ginger: My Story*. Boston: G. K. Hall & Co., 1992.

Russo, Gus. *Supermob: How Sidney Korshak and His Criminal Associates Became America's Hidden Power Brokers*. New York: Bloomsbury, 2006.

San Pedro High School. *Black and Gold*. School yearbook. San Pedro, CA, 1926.

Schechter, Scott. *Judy Garland: The Day-by-Day Chronicle of a Legend*. New York: Cooper Square Press, 2002.

Spoto, Donald. *Notorious: The Life of Ingrid Bergman*. New York: Harper Collins, 1997.

Staggs, Sam. *All About "All About Eve": The Complete Behind-the-Scenes Story of the Bitchiest Film Ever Made*. New York: St. Martin's Press, 2000.

Thomas, Bob. *Joan Crawford*. New York: Simon & Schuster, 1978.

Tosches, Nick. *Dino: Living High in the Dirty Business of Dreams*. New York: Dell Publishing, 1992.

Turner, Lana. *Lana: The Lady, the Legend, the Truth*. New York: E. P. Dutton, 1982.

Vanderbilt, Gloria. *It Seemed Important at the Time*. New York: Simon & Schuster, 2004.

Wanger, Walter, and Joe Hyams. *My Life with Cleopatra*. New York: Bantam Books, 1963.

Wayne, Jane Ellen. *Ava's Men: Her Life and Loves*. London: Robson Books, 2004.

———. *The Golden Girls of MGM*. New York: Carroll & Graf, 2002.

Wilkerson, Tichi, and Marcia Borie. *Hollywood Legends: The Golden Years of the Hollywood Reporter*. Los Angeles: Tale Weaver Publishing, 1988.

Wilkerson, W. R., III. *The Man Who Invented Las Vegas*. Beverly Hills: Ciro's Books, 2000.

Wynter, Dana. *Other People Other Places*. Dublin: Caladrius Press, 2005.

ARTICLES

Adamson, Ken. "Ann Savage." *Hollywood Heritage*, 2009.

Amdur, Neil. "U.S. Open Won't Recognize Test Taken by Dr. Richards." *New York Times*, April 13, 1977.

Anderson, Jack. "Hughes Courtships Were Much Like Corporate Business." *Kingman Daily Mirror*, April 16, 1976.

Atlanta Journal. "Writer Quits, but Show Must Go On." March 17, 1985.

Brent, Brandy. Carrousel. *Los Angeles Times*, November 23, 1949.

Buhrman, Robert. "Hello Greg? . . . This Is Howard Hughes." *Los Angeles*, December 1969, 36–39.

Burns, Sally. "Love Comes Last." *Modern Screen* 43, no. 1 (June 1951): 87–89.

Crowther, Bosley. Review of *The Groom Wore Spurs*. *New York Times*, March 14, 1951.

Dallos, Robert E. "Bautzer Will Push MGM, Fox Merger." *Los Angeles Times*, March 30, 1971.

———. "Kerkorian Beats MGM Attempt to Halt Tender." *Los Angeles Times*, August 9, 1969.

———. "Kerkorian Reports 1,325,000 Shares." *Los Angeles Times*, August 12, 1969.

———. "Kerkorian Seeks Columbia Stock." *Los Angeles Times*, November 21, 1978.

———. "Kerkorian Ups Price in New Offer for MGM." *Los Angeles Times*, September 11, 1969.

———. "Kerkorian Violated Securities Laws." *Los Angeles Times*, August 8, 1969.

Diehl, Bill. "Zhivago Scripter Writes His Rites." Hollywood Chatterbox. *St. Paul Pioneer Press*, April 28, 1995.

Fidler, Jimmie. Jimmie Fidler in Hollywood. *Los Angeles Times*, December 21, 1939.

———. Jimmie Fidler in Hollywood. *Los Angeles Times*, May 9, 1940.

———. Jimmie Fidler in Hollywood. *Los Angeles Times*, May 15, 1940.

———. Jimmie Fidler in Hollywood. *Los Angeles Times*, June 4, 1940.

———. Jimmie Fidler in Hollywood. *Los Angeles Times*, June 21, 1940.

———. Jimmie Fidler in Hollywood. *Los Angeles Times*, October 16, 1940.

———. Jimmie Fidler in Hollywood. *Los Angeles Times*, November 25, 1940.

Gardner, Robert. Robert Gardner's Verdicts. *Daily Pilot*, August 30, 2005.

Gindick, Tia. "Mystique." *Los Angeles Times*, April 29, 1979.

Haber, Joyce. "Harvey Rite at Robbin's Gala (Almost)." *Los Angeles Times*, January 4, 1973.

———. "Hughes Alive, Well . . . but Don't Quote Me." *Los Angeles Times*, January 20, 1972.

———. "Joe and Elke and Life in a Doll's House." *Los Angeles Times*, April 7, 1974.

———. "This Brooks Follows His Own Course." *Los Angeles Times*, July 6, 1975.

———. "$20 Million Deal Sealed at Bistro." *Los Angeles Times*, October 29, 1973.

Harris, Radie. "Wynter Victorious." *Photoplay* 50, no. 1 (September 1956): 18–19, 105.

Hollywood Box Office. "Fidelity Will Film Sex Features in 18 Months." August 28, 1948.

Hopper, Hedda. "Astaire Way of Life Aims at Happiness." *Los Angeles Times*, August 17, 1952.

———. "Columnist Discounts Hendrix Tiff." *Los Angeles Times*, September 1, 1949.

———. Entertainment. *Los Angeles Times*, December 6, 1962.

———. Entertainment. *Los Angeles Times*, December 13, 1963.

———. Hedda Hopper. *Los Angeles Times*, September 17, 1954.

———. Hedda Hopper. *Los Angeles Times*, August 20, 1962.

———. Hedda Hopper's Hollywood. *Los Angeles Times*, August 20, 1938.

———. Hedda Hopper's Hollywood. *Los Angeles Times*, June 14, 1939.

———. Hedda Hopper's Hollywood. *Los Angeles Times*, August 15, 1939.

———. Hedda Hopper's Hollywood. *Los Angeles Times*, September 15, 1939.

———. Hedda Hopper's Hollywood. *Los Angeles Times*, June 13, 1941.

———. Hedda Hopper's Hollywood. *Los Angeles Times*, May 15, 1946.

———. Hedda Hopper's Hollywood. *Los Angeles Times*, October 9, 1946.

———. "Jessel Preparing Scripts for Haver." *Los Angeles Times*, September 7, 1949.

———. "Law Student Mari Blanchard Has Case." *Los Angeles Times*, February 7, 1954.

———. Looking at Hollywood. *Los Angeles Times*, February 10, 1947.

———. "Niven Sees Himself as Star of Classics." *Los Angeles Times*, July 12, 1949.

———. "Out-of-Court Settlement for Marion Davies Seen." *Los Angeles Times*, October 16, 1951.

———. "Randall Will Costar." *Los Angeles Times*, June 1, 1957.

———. "Subversive Elements Detected in Pictures." *Los Angeles Times*, May 21, 1951.

Jacobs, Joyce. "Wedding Vows Taken over Spain." *Los Angeles Times*, October 5, 1984.

Kendall, Read. Around and About in Hollywood. *Los Angeles Times*, January 13, 1939.

———. Around and About in Hollywood. *Los Angeles Times*, February 13, 1939.

Kilgallen, Dorothy. "Grant, Selznick Mystery Combination; Taylors Want to Adopt Twins." *Toledo Blade*, July 4, 1947.

Kim, Victoria. "Casino Mogul Takes Stand in Trial." *Los Angeles Times*, August 21, 2008.

King, Francis. From Waikiki, *Los Angeles Times*, May 30, 1937.

Lansky, Karen. "O, Happy Days!: Mid-century Memoirs; Seven Southern Californians Recall Growing Up in the '40s and '50s." *Los Angeles Times*, February 4, 1990.

LeBlanc, Jerry. "Superstar Lawyer: Greg Bautzer." *Hartford Courant*, July 12. 1970.

Life. "Howard Hughes." September 7, 1962.

Loper, Mary Lou. "The Bistro's Secret of Success." *Los Angeles Times*, January 20, 1972.

Los Angeles Times. "Actors' Agent Attempts Death." December 13, 1947.

———. "Arnstein Suit Settled." June 6, 1939.

———. Around and About in Hollywood. November 11, 1937.

———. "Attorney Bautzer Held on Drunk Charge." December 17, 1945.

———. "Attorney for Kerkorian to Run MGM, UA," February 9, 1982.

———. "Bautzer Sidesteps Story He Will Wed Actress." May 4, 1956.

———. Beau Peep Whispers. February 13, 1938.

———. "Carole Landis Asks Divorce." September 18, 1940.

———. "Carole Landis Charges Mate Blocked Career." November 13, 1940.

———. Chatterbox. March 28, 1937

———. Chatterbox. May 30, 1937.

———. Chatterbox. December 5, 1938.

———. "Court Fight Still Looms over Ingrid's Daughter." March 25, 1950.

———. "Court's Ability to Restrain Mexico Divorce to Be Tested." January 8, 1942.

———. "Crain Divorce Case Smolders in Law Offices." June 23, 1956.

———. "Crowd Hears Girl, 17, Accuse Flynn in Court." November 3, 1942.

———. Day in Sacramento. February 6, 1963.

———. "Dr. Lindstrom Given Bergman Property Plan." December 20, 1949.

———. "Flynn Arraigned on New Charge." October 23, 1942.

———. "Ginger Rogers Dodges on French Romance." August 18, 1952.

———. "Gregson Bautzer's Bride Gets Divorce." April 25, 1945.

———. "Group C Boasts All Boys." April 28, 1926.

————. "Hearst and Purity." July 20, 1934.

————. "Hearst-Davies Pact Legality Attacked." August 27, 1951.

————. "Hearst Will Filed for Probate in L.A. Court." August 15, 1951.

————. "Hitler Fraud Suspect Freed." April 9, 1937.

————. "Hollywood Playboy Faces Court Today in Check Case." August 8, 1937.

————. "Hollywood Sees Hoax in Reports of Bergman Baby." December 13, 1949.

————. "Ingrid Bergman Business Manager Quits." September 24, 1949.

————. "Ingrid Bergman Gives Birth to Twin Daughters." June 19, 1952.

————. "Ingrid Bergman Orders Suit for Divorce Filed in Mexico." January 27, 1950.

————. "Ingrid Plans Visit to Pia in July or Early August." June 28, 1952.

————. "Ingrid Will Return for Custody Fight." March 17, 1950.

————. "Ingrid's Daughter Spurns Italy Visit." June 14, 1952.

————. "Irvin Cobb's Ashes Laid to Rest in Kentucky." October 8, 1944.

————. "Jeanne Crain Denies Misconduct Charges." June 29, 1956.

————. "Jeanne Crain Drops Her Demands for Protection." June 26, 1956.

————. "Judge Testifies for Ingrid." June 10, 1952.

————. "Kerkorian Waves Olive Branch: Ready to Meet with MGM." September 3, 1969.

————. "Marion Davies Presents $1,500,000 to UCLA." January 9, 1958.

————. "Miss Lamour's Friend Nearly Misses Boat." May 30, 1941.

————. "Montague Decision Set." July 29, 1937.

————. "Montague Shifts Fight." August 3, 1937.

————. "Mrs. Sinatra's Suit Against Mate Delayed." September 9, 1950.

————. "Nicky Arnstein Explains." May 25, 1939.

————. "Orators Want to Honor State." May 12, 1927.

————. Out of Town Society, August 11, 1901.

————. "Paulette Will Seek Divorce from Meredith." March 29, 1949.

————. "Principal Points Made in Interview." January 10, 1972.

————. "Producer Evans Cuts 20th Ties." August 12, 1966.

————. "San Pedro Postmaster Is Not Believer in Hoodoos." May 14, 1910.

————. "Second Prize Oration." May 15, 1926.

————. "Settlement Seen as Near in Suit Against Hughes." July 11, 1952.

————. "Stromboli Ban Urged by Bishop." February 9, 1950.

————. "Turpitude Ban No Bar to Ingrid." March 18, 1950.

————. "Visit to Ingrid by Pia Barred by Court Action." June 25, 1952.

————. "Where Hughes's Billions Go." April 6, 1976.

————. "Wife Involves 'New Look' in Divorce Action." December 4, 1947.

Luther, Claudia. "Fees of $600,000 Denied by Judge." *Los Angeles Times*, August 19, 1977.

MacNamara, Paul. "Gone with the Winds." *Los Angeles*, July 1988, 26–36.

Marx, Samuel. "Speaks for Ghosts." *Los Angeles Times*, October 14, 1973.

Moran, Monica. "How a White Millionaire Won Diahann." *Silver Screen* 38, no. 3 (March 1968): 23–25, 65–66.

Morrow, Lance. "Goodbye to Our Mary." *Time*, March 14, 1977.

Murphy, Kim. "Suit Citing Forgotten Deed Could Scuttle Sale." *Los Angeles Times*, November 22, 1986.

Neumeyer, Katherine. "The Case of the Battling Barristers." *Los Angeles*, February 1991, 60–68.

Osborne, D. M. "Heavy Hitter, Natural Born Killer." *American Lawyer* 17, no. 10 (December 1995).

Oulahan, Richard, and William Lambert. "The Tyrant's Fall That Rocked the TV World." *Life*, September 10, 1965.

Overend, William. "Greg Bautzer, Attorney to the Stars, Dies." *Los Angeles Times*, October 27, 1987.

Parsons, Louella. "Dorothy Lamour Makes Friends Everywhere—but Not So Garbo." *Washington Post*, August 24, 1941.

Pollock, Dale. "Inchon! Shooting for the Moonies." *Los Angeles Times*, May 16, 1982.

———. "Moon Film: A $1 Million Sweepstakes." *Los Angeles Times*, September 16, 1982.

Rosenfield, Paul. "Aubrey: A Lion in Winter." *Los Angeles Times*, April 27, 1986.

San Pedro Daily News. "Att'y Bautzer to Be Laid to Rest Monday." December 3, 1921.

San Pedro Pilot. "Bautzer Dies from Injuries." December 2, 1921.

———. "E. H. Bautzer Funeral to Be Held Monday." December 3, 1921.

Sederberg, Arelo. "MGM-Kerkorian Talks Set? Report at Odds." *Los Angeles Times*, August 29, 1969.

Shprintz, Janet. "Pellicano, Christensen Found Guilty." *Variety*, August 29, 2008.

Sloane, Leonard. "Lawyer Keeps Late Hours with Clients." *New York Times*, December 14, 1969.

Snow, Richard. "Counsel for the Indefensible." *American Heritage* 38, no. 2 (February–March 1987): 72–75, 103–104.

St. Louis Globe Dispatch. Edward F. Bautzer's obituary. May 28, 1910. Reprinted in *Osage County Historical Society Newsletter*, January 1997, 2.

St. Louis Republic. "Clayton Editor Invites Rival to Mortal Combat." March 27, 1901.

Time. "Hearst's Bombshell." September 3, 1951.

———. "Latin America: Man of Affairs." February 11, 1946.

———. "Lion and the Cobra." November 12, 1973.

———. "Mexico: Lady of Letters." August 12, 1946.

———. "Pia's Answer." June 23, 1952.

———. "Restaurants: Hollywood Institution." July 3, 1944.

———. "Return of Smiling Jim." October 31, 1969.

———. "Tycoon Davies." August 1, 1955.

Toledo Blade. Screen Gossip. July 1, 1947.

Tosches, Nick. "The Man Who Kept the Secrets." *Vanity Fair*, April 6, 1997.

Townsend, Phyllis. "Torch Song." *Photoplay*, July 1952, 40–41, 88.

University of Nevada–Las Vegas Libraries. "Welcome Home, Howard!: Or Whatever Became of the Daring Aviator." http://digital.library.unlv.edu/hughes/.

Van Treuren, Richard G. "An Effective Umbrella." *Naval History*, May/June 1998, 41–44.

———. "Georgia Draw: A Rare Duel Between Air and Sea." *Foundation* 21, no. 2 (Fall 2000): 62–68.

Washington Post. The Ear. November 8, 1981.

Wallace, Irving. "The Loves of Lana Turner." *Liberty*, September 5, 1942, 36–39.

Wood, Robert E. "MGM Will Oppose $35 Million Offer." *Los Angeles Times*, July 24, 1969.

Zack, A. J. "A Conversation with Greg Bautzer." 54th anniversary issue, *Hollywood Reporter*, December 1984, 39–40.

LEGAL OPINIONS

Altman v. Bautzer. 54 Cal. App. 2d 543 (1942).

Bard v. Kent. 19 Cal. 2d 449 (1942).

Blanton v. Curry. 20 Cal. 2d 793 (1942).

Contant v. Wallace. 62 Cal. App. 768 (1923).

Hughes Tool Co. v. Trans World Airlines, Inc. 409 U.S. 363 (1973).

In re Marriage of McKim. 6 Cal. 3d 673 (1972) (Stanley Mosk, dissenting).

Peckham v. Warner Bros. Pictures, Inc. 42 Cal. App. 2d 187 (1940).

Summa Corporation v. Trans World Airlines. 540 A.2d 403 (1988).

Wilkinson v. Fisherman's Etc. Supply Co. 57 Cal. App. 165 (1922).

FBI DOCUMENTS

All FBI documents are from the Charles Higham Papers

Ailshie, Vice Consul William K. "Activities of Katherina Mathilde Kruger (Hilda Kruger)." American Consulate memorandum, Mexico City, April 3, 1941.

Angell, Special Agent H. Frank. FBI memorandum, Los Angeles, February 7, 1941.

———. FBI memorandum, Los Angeles, February 20, 1941.

———. FBI memorandum, Los Angeles, May 27, 1941.

Findlay, Special Agent J. G. FBI memorandum, Los Angeles, June 29, 1940.

Friedermann, Special Agent W. G. FBI memorandum, New York, February 19, 1940.

Hoover, Director J. Edgar. Letter to Adolf A. Berle Jr., Washington, DC, February 12, 1941.

———. Letter to Adolf A. Berle Jr., Washington, DC, March 19, 1942.

Hughes, Consul Morris N. "Relations of Hilda Kruger with Licenciado Ramon Beteta, Under Secretary of the Treasury." American Consulate memorandum, Mexico City, July 1, 1941.

McGregor, Robert G., Jr. Letter to Freddie [Unknown], American Consular Service, June 16, 1941.

Pope, Special Agent J. D. FBI memorandum, New York City, January 30, 1941.

OTHER DOCUMENTS

Bautzer, Greg. Application for transfer to flight training (LTA), April 27, 1942. In US Navy personnel file of Lt. Comdr. Bautzer.

———. Letter to Admiral Charles E. Rosendahl, March 7, 1944. In Vice Admiral Charles E. Rosendahl Papers.

———. Letter to Admiral Charles E. Rosendahl, April 6, 1944. In Vice Admiral Charles E. Rosendahl Papers.

———. Letter to Admiral Charles E. Rosendahl, July 14, 1945. In Vice Admiral Charles E. Rosendahl Papers.

———. Letter to Jean Rosendahl, March 7, 1944. In Vice Admiral Charles E. Rosendahl Papers.

Mannix, E. J. Letter to Greg Bautzer, November 22, 1945. In Vice Admiral Charles E. Rosendahl Papers.

Missouri State Board of Health. Certificate of death for Paul Garfield Bautzer. St. Louis, Missouri, August 8, 1914. Available online at Missouri Digital Heritage, www.sos.mo.gov/images/archives/deathcerts/1914/1914_00027628.PDF.

Office of Chief of Naval Operations. "American Republics—Totalitarian Penetration In—Social Forces." Navy intelligence report, March 9, 1942. In Charles Higham Papers.

Rosendahl, Admiral Charles E. Letter to Greg Bautzer, March 15, 1944. In Vice Admiral Charles E. Rosendahl Papers.

Sickel, Commander H. G., USN, Army and Navy Munitions Board. Memorandum to Chief of the Bureau of Navigation, February 2, 1942. In US Navy personnel file of Lt. Comdr. Bautzer.

US Navy. Personnel file of Lt. Comdr. Bautzer, Gregson Edward, USNR. USN Military Records, National Records Center, St. Louis, MO.

Young, Col. William. Police report, Office of Chief of Police, Metropolitan Police Department, City of St. Louis, May 25, 1910. In personal collection of David Stielow.

SPECIAL COLLECTIONS

Davies, Marion, Papers. Margaret Herrick Library, Academy of Motion Pictures Arts and Sciences, Los Angeles, CA.

Higham, Charles, Papers. Cinematic Arts Collection. Edward L. Doheny Jr. Memorial Library, University of Southern California, Los Angeles, CA.

Rogers, Henry C., Papers. 1966–1992. MSS 3726, box 24. L. Tom Perry Special Collections Library, Harold B. Lee Library, Brigham Young University, Provo, UT.

Rosendahl, Vice Admiral Charles E., Papers. History of Aviation Collection. Special Collections, Eugene McDermott Library, University of Texas at Dallas.

INTERVIEWS

Bautzer, Greg. Interview in "Joan Crawford." *The Hollywood Greats*, BBC, 1978.

Bautzer, Mark. Interview by Henry Rogers, c. 1990. In Henry C. Rogers Papers.

Beckerman, Sidney. Interview by Henry Rogers, c. 1990. In Henry C. Rogers Papers.

Blau, Louis. Interview by Henry Rogers, c. 1990. In Henry C. Rogers Papers.

Cavalier, Dan. Interview by the author, April 27, 2009.

Dahl, Arlene. Interview by the author, May 7, 2011.

Del, Ernest. Interview by the author, September 13, 2011.

Dorso, Dick. Interview by Henry Rogers, c. 1990. In Henry C. Rogers Papers.

Dugan, Johnny. Interview by Henry Rogers, c. 1990. In Henry C. Rogers Papers.

Erpicum, Bernard. Interview by the author, August 10, 2011.

Fahey, John. Interview by the author, October 9, 2009.

Groman, Arthur. Interview by Henry Rogers, c. 1990. In Henry C. Rogers Papers.

Harris, Richard S. Interview by Henry Rogers, c. 1990. In Henry C. Rogers Papers.

Higham, Charles. Interview by the author, June 17, 2011.

Irwin, Woody. Interview by Henry Rogers, c. 1990. In Henry C. Rogers Papers.

Korshak, Sidney. Interview by Henry Rogers, c. 1990. In Henry C. Rogers Papers.

Kroll, Fred. Interview by the author, October 9, 2009.

Levy, Michael I. Interview by the author, May 18, 2011.

Lindström, Pia. Interview by the author, June 8, 2011.

Maass, Herbert. Interview by Henry Rogers, c. 1990. In Henry C. Rogers Papers.

McDougall, Charles. Interview by the author, October 6, 2009.

Miller, Ann. Interview by Henry Rogers, c. 1990. In Henry C. Rogers Papers.

Morgan, Andre. Interview by the author, May 9, 2011.

Newhart, Bob. Interview by the author, May 16, 2011.

Niklas, Kurt. Interview by Henry Rogers, c. 1990. In Henry C. Rogers Papers.

Parker, Jean. Interview by the author, August 15, 2009.

Puck, Wolfgang. Interview by the author, August 9, 2011.

Rosenfelt, Frank. Interview by Henry Rogers, c. 1990. In Henry C. Rogers Papers.

Ruddy, Albert S. Interview by the author, June 8, 2011.

Schwartz, Bernard. Interview by Henry Rogers, c. 1990. In Henry C. Rogers Papers.

Schwartz, Robert. Interview by the author, 2011.

Silbert, Bernard. Interview by Henry Rogers, c. 1990. In Henry C. Rogers Papers.

Stein, Stanton "Larry." Interview by the author, April 29, 2011.

Stuart, Carole. Interview by the author, December 12, 2010.

Sullivan, Lea. Interview by the author, April 3, 2011.

Tucker, Maybe. Interview by Henry Rogers, c. 1990. In Henry C. Rogers Papers.

Wagner, Robert. Interview by the author, July 21, 2011.

Weintraub Ferrer, Lori. Interview by Henry Rogers, c. 1990. In Henry C. Rogers Papers.
———. Interview by the author, May 1, 2012.

Wynter, Dana. Interview by Henry Rogers, c. 1990. In Henry C. Rogers Papers.
———. Interviews by the author, February 18–April 22, 2011.

INDEX

Pleasant Hill Library
Contra Costa County Library
2 Monticello Ave.
Pleasant Hill, Ca. 94523
(925) 646-6434

Customer ID: **********5407

Items that you checked out

Title: A legacy of spies /
ID: 31901067104523
Due: Monday, December 4, 2023
Messages:
Item checked out.

Title: Cimino : The deer hunter, Heaven's gate,
       and the price of a vision /
ID: 31901067994105
Due: Monday, December 4, 2023
Messages:
Item checked out.

Title: Galileo's error : foundations for a new
       science of consciousness /
ID: 31901067189680
Due: Monday, December 4, 2023
Messages:
Item checked out.

Title: The man who seduced Hollywood : the
       life and loves of Greg Bautzer,
       tinseltown's most powerful lawye
ID: 31901055116091
Due: Monday, December 4, 2023
Messages:
Item checked out.

Total items: 4
Account balance: $0.00
Ready for pickup: 0
11/13/2023 2:02 PM

Renew on line or by phone
ccclib.org
1-800-984-4636

Have a great day

12/31